Microsoft Azure Monitoring & Management: The Definitive Guide

Avinash Valiramani

Microsoft Azure Monitoring & Management: The Definitive Guide

Published with the authorization of Microsoft Corporation by: Pearson Education, Inc.

ISBN-13: 978-0-13-757102-4
ISBN-10: 0-13-757102-X

Library of Congress Control Number: 2022947667

1 2022

TRADEMARKS

Microsoft and the trademarks listed at http://www.microsoft.com on the "Trademarks" webpage are trademarks of the Microsoft group of companies. All other marks are property of their respective owners.

WARNING AND DISCLAIMER

SPECIAL SALES

For information about buying this title in bulk quantities, or for special sales opportunities (which may include electronic versions; custom cover designs; and content particular to your business, training goals, marketing focus, or branding interests), please contact our corporate sales department at corpsales@pearsoned.com or (800) 382-3419.

For government sales inquiries, please contact governmentsales@pearsoned.com.

For questions about sales outside the U.S., please contact intlcs@pearson.com.

CREDITS

EDITOR-IN-CHIEF
Brett Bartow

EXECUTIVE EDITOR
Loretta Yates

SPONSORING EDITOR
Charvi Arora

DEVELOPMENT EDITOR
Kate Shoup

MANAGING EDITOR
Sandra Schroeder

SENIOR PROJECT EDITOR
Tracey Croom

COPY EDITOR
Sarah Kearns

INDEXER
Tim Wright

PROOFREADER
Jen Hinchliffe

TECHNICAL EDITOR
Thomas Palathra

EDITORIAL ASSISTANT
Cindy Teeters

COVER DESIGNER
Twist Creative, Seattle

COMPOSITOR
codeMantra

GRAPHICS
codeMantra

COVER ILLUSTRATION
NesaCera/Shutterstock

Pearson's Commitment to Diversity, Equity, and Inclusion

Pearson is dedicated to creating bias-free content that reflects the diversity of all learners. We embrace the many dimensions of diversity, including but not limited to race, ethnicity, gender, socioeconomic status, ability, age, sexual orientation, and religious or political beliefs.

Education is a powerful force for equity and change in our world. It has the potential to deliver opportunities that improve lives and enable economic mobility. As we work with authors to create content for every product and service, we acknowledge our responsibility to demonstrate inclusivity and incorporate diverse scholarship so that everyone can achieve their potential through learning. As the world's leading learning company, we have a duty to help drive change and live up to our purpose to help more people create a better life for themselves and to create a better world.

Our ambition is to purposefully contribute to a world where

- Everyone has an equitable and lifelong opportunity to succeed through learning
- Our educational products and services are inclusive and represent the rich diversity of learners
- Our educational content accurately reflects the histories and experiences of the learners we serve
- Our educational content prompts deeper discussions with learners and motivates them to expand their own learning (and worldview)

While we work hard to present unbiased content, we want to hear from you about any concerns or needs with this Pearson product so that we can investigate and address them.

- Please contact us with concerns about any potential bias at https://www.pearson.com/report-bias.html.

Contents at a Glance

About the author   *xi*

Acknowledgments   *xii*

Introduction to Azure monitoring and management services   *xiii*

Chapter 1	**Azure Backup**	**1**
Chapter 2	**Azure Site Recovery**	**23**
Chapter 3	**Azure Migrate**	**69**
Chapter 4	**Azure Monitor**	**111**
Chapter 5	**Azure Network Watcher**	**151**
Chapter 6	**Azure Portal**	**191**
Chapter 7	**Azure Cloud Shell**	**209**
Chapter 8	**Azure Service Health**	**225**
Chapter 9	**Azure Cost Management**	**245**
	Index	*267*

Contents

About the author   xi

Acknowledgments   xii

Introduction to Azure monitoring and management services   xiii

Chapter 1   Azure Backup   1

Overview 1

Key features. 3

Design and deployment concepts and considerations 4

   Recovery Services vault   4

   Backup Center   5

   Data plane   6

   Management plane   6

   Backup agents   7

   Supported backup types   7

   Backup policy   8

   Backup compression   8

   Backup monitoring   9

   Alerts   9

   Security   9

   Azure Backup walkthrough   10

Best practices 21

Chapter 2   Azure Site Recovery   23

Overview 23

Azure–to–Azure disaster recovery 25

   Replication policy   25

   Data security   26

   Multi-VM consistency   26

   Target environment configuration   26

   Failover and failback   27

Test and planned failovers   27

Network security   28

Azure–to–Azure disaster recovery walkthrough   28

Hyper-V–to–Azure disaster recovery 40

Replication components   41

Replication policy 41

Data security   44

Failover and failback   44

Test, planned, and unplanned failovers   44

Network requirements   45

Hyper-V–to–Azure disaster recovery walkthrough   45

Recovery plans 61

Best practices 67

Chapter 3   **Azure Migrate**   **69**

Overview 69

Key features 70

Assessment tools   70

Migration tools   71

Deployment concepts and considerations 72

Azure Migrate Discovery and Assessment Tool   72

Azure Migrate Server Migration Tool   74

Networking   76

Scaling   77

Azure Migrate walkthrough   78

Best practices 110

Chapter 4   **Azure Monitor**   **111**

Overview 111

Key benefits 111

Concepts and considerations 112

Data types   113

Data collection   115

Data segregation **116**

Data retention **116**

Data redundancy **116**

Data security **117**

Data visualization **117**

Data export **122**

Alerts **122**

Azure Monitor walkthrough **123**

Best practices **149**

Chapter 5 **Azure Network Watcher** **151**

Overview **151**

Key features. **153**

Connection Monitor **153**

Topology Monitor **161**

IP Flow Verify **163**

NSG Diagnostic **166**

Next Hop **169**

Effective Security Rules **171**

VPN Troubleshoot **173**

Packet Capture **176**

Connection Troubleshoot **179**

NSG Flow Logs **183**

Diagnostic Logs **187**

Chapter 6 **Azure Portal** **191**

Overview **191**

Key features. **193**

Customization and usability concepts and considerations **194**

Azure Portal settings **194**

Custom dashboards **197**

Azure Marketplace **200**

Help and support **202**

Best practices **207**

Chapter 7   **Azure Cloud Shell**   **209**

Overview 209

Key features. 209

Usage concepts and considerations 210

    Azure file share   **210**

    Azure drive   **213**

    Cloud Shell Editor   **213**

    Embed Cloud Shell   **213**

    Cloud Shell deployment in a vNET   **213**

    Azure Cloud Shell walkthrough   **214**

Best practices 222

Chapter 8   **Azure Service Health**   **225**

Overview 225

Azure Status 226

Service Health. 227

    Service Health walkthrough   **228**

Resource Health. 235

    Health status indicators   **236**

    Create a Resource Health alert walkthrough   **237**

    Check a resource's health walkthrough   **241**

Best practices 243

Chapter 9   **Azure Cost Management**   **245**

Overview 245

Key features. 245

Design and deployment concepts and considerations 246

    Cost planning   **246**

    Budgets   **247**

    Cost Analysis   **250**

    Advisor recommendations   **258**

    Index   *267*

About the author

Avinash Valiramani is an IT Infrastructure and Cloud Architect with more than 16 years of expertise in areas of Microsoft Technologies such as Microsoft Azure, Microsoft 365, Windows Server, Active Directory, Microsoft Exchange, SCCM, Intune, and Hyper-V. He is a certified Architect on Azure Infrastructure, Azure Artificial Intelligence, Azure Security, and Microsoft365. He has been working primarily with large to mid-size enterprises globally in designing their Cloud Architecture, planning migration strategies and executing complex implementations. Avinash is publishing four books as part of the Microsoft Azure Best Practices series, including this current one, collating real-world experiences to deliver a comprehensive and concise experience for new and budding technologists. Avinash also holds certifications in Amazon AWS, Barracuda, Citrix, VMware, and many other IT/Security industry certifications to complement his Microsoft expertise. He has authored a course on Azure Virtual Desktop for O'Reilly Media and is planning many others in the coming months. You can follow Avinash on Twitter at @avaliramani and he will soon be posting frequent blogs on www.avinashvaliramani.com and www.cloudconsulting.services.

Acknowledgements

At the outset, my biggest thanks and gratitude to Loretta Yates for trusting me with this huge responsibility. The books in this series would not have been possible without your confidence in me and I will be forever grateful for that.

I would like to acknowledge Celine for all her support to me throughout the journey of these last two books. Celine, sincerely a Big Thank You for pushing and guiding me, whenever I needed it. These books would not have been possible without your constant support.

To my family, I am forever grateful for all your love and support.

To my extended family, thank you for tolerating my absence for over a year and a half while I closed myself off to focus on these books.

A special thank you to Kate Shoup for editing and reviewing this third book in this series. Your guidance and attention to detail throughout these series of books has been immensely valuable. Kate, it has been a wonderful experience working on these books with you and I could not have hoped for a better editor for this collaboration.

Thanks to Thomas Palathra, Sarah Kearns, and Tracey Croom for adding the final touches to bring this across the finish line. This book is the fruit of all our labour, I am extremely happy, and grateful we worked together on it.

Lastly, thanks to Charvi Arora and the entire Microsoft Press/Pearson team for their constant support and guidance on this project.

Three down, one more to go!

Introduction to Azure monitoring and management services

Welcome to *Azure Monitoring and Management: The Definitive Guide.* This is the third book in the series on Azure Infrastructure, and provides in-depth information about the various Azure services that support monitoring and management capabilities and shares best practices based on real-life experiences with the product in different environments.

This book focuses primarily on those Azure monitoring and management services generally available during 2021 and early 2022, encompassing developmental work done on these services over the years. A few monitoring and management features and functionalities were under preview at the time of this writing and could change before they are generally available; hence, we have decided to cover the most notable ones in subsequent iterations of this book as they go live globally.

Overview

Over the years, Microsoft has introduced various services related to the Azure monitoring and management stack to simplify, automate, and optimize workload deployments; make management easier; and improve monitoring of Azure compute, networking, and storage services. Microsoft has released regular updates to these services, introducing additional features and functionality, enhancing the service's support matrix, and making it easier to deploy and manage with each iteration.

Following is a brief timeline of the announcement of each of these services in public preview or general availability.

- **Azure Backup**   Oct 2014
- **Azure Site Recovery**   Oct 2014
- **Azure Migrate**   July 2019
- **Azure Monitor**   Mar 2017
- **Azure Network Monitor**   Jan 2018
- **Azure Portal**   Dec 2015
- **Azure Cloud Shell (Bash)**   Nov 2017
- **Azure Cost Management**   Sept 2017

Each service provides customers with various options to address their infrastructure management, redundancy, resiliency, and recovery requirements.

This book dives into each of these services to highlight important considerations in deploying and managing them and to share associated best practices. You will initially focus on the features provided by each service and on service requirements; thereafter, you will explore in-depth concepts of each service and the components that make up that service. This will allow you to better understand how each service can deliver value in your Azure deployment. After this, you will focus on deployment considerations and strategies, with step-by-step walkthroughs that illustrate deployment and management methods followed by best practices.

Cloud service categories

As in earlier books in this series, let us start by first discussing the different types of cloud service categories. Currently, cloud services are broken down into four main categories: infrastructure as a service (IaaS), platform as a service (PaaS), function as a service (FaaS), and software as a service (SaaS). SaaS is not relevant to the content covered in this Microsoft Azure book series; hence we will focus on better understanding the first three categories:

- **Infrastructure as a service (IaaS)**   Using virtual machines (VMs) with storage and networking is generally referred to as infrastructure as a service (IaaS). This is a traditional approach to using cloud services in line with on-premises workloads. Most on-premises environments use virtualization technologies such as Hyper-V to virtualize Windows and Linux workloads. Migrating to IaaS from such an environment is much easier than migrating to PaaS or FaaS. Over time, as an organization's understanding of various other types of cloud services grows, it can migrate to PaaS or FaaS.

- **Platform as a service (PaaS)**   One of the biggest benefits of using a cloud service is the capability to offload the management of back-end infrastructure to a service provider. This model is called platform as a service (PaaS). Examples of back-end infrastructure include different layers of the application, such as the compute layer, storage layer, networking layer, security layer, and monitoring layer. Organizations can use PaaS to free up their IT staff to focus on higher-level tasks and core organizational needs instead of on routine infrastructure monitoring, upgrade, and maintenance activities. Azure App Service and Azure Container Service are examples of Azure PaaS offerings.

- **Function as a service (FaaS)** Function as a service (FaaS) offerings go one step beyond PaaS to enable organizations to focus only on their application code, leaving the entire back-end infrastructure deployment and management to the cloud service provider. This provides developers with a great way to deploy their code without worrying about the back-end infrastructure deployment, scaling, and management. It also enables the use of microservices architectures for applications. An example of an Azure FaaS offering is Azure Functions.

From the Azure monitoring and management stack, the services largely fall under the PaaS category. For example:

- Azure Backup is a PaaS service that allows you to configure and manage backups in Azure and on-premises environments to protect both IaaS and PaaS workloads.

- Azure Site Recovery is a PaaS service that allows you to configure and manage disaster recovery for your workloads hosted in on-premises environments, such as Hyper-V and VMWare VMs, physical servers, and VMs hosted in Azure.

Each of these cloud-service categories has various features and limitations. Limitations might relate to the application, technological know-how, costs for redevelopment, among others. As a result, most organizations use some combination of different types of these cloud services to maximize their cloud investments.

Each service provides a different level of control and ease of management. For example:

- IaaS provides maximum control and flexibility in migration and use.

- FaaS provides maximum automation for workload deployment, management, and use.

- PaaS provides a mix of both at varying levels, depending on the PaaS service used.

Each service also offers varying levels of scalability. For example:

- IaaS requires the use of additional services to achieve true scalability and load balancing—for example, using Azure Load Balancer, a PaaS service, to balance requests across multiple Azure IaaS VMs.

- PaaS and FaaS services are generally designed with built-in scalability and load-balancing features.

Cost-wise, each service provides varying levels of efficiency. For example:

- FaaS offerings charge for compute services based only on the usage hours for compute services, making it extremely cost-effective.

- IaaS products charge for compute services regardless of usage once the compute service (for example, a VM) is online.

- PaaS offerings are a mixed bag depending on how the services are configured. Some PaaS products charge for compute resources regardless of usage, while others, if configured correctly, charge based on usage alone. For example, Azure Site Recovery is charged based on different factors:

  - There is a monthly site recovery license fee per protected physical or virtual server, based on average monthly usage.

  - The back-end storage used to store the replica data is billed based on storage usage per month and for any disk costs incurred during disaster recovery drills. In addition, storage transactions are billed based on monthly usage.

  - Bandwidth is charged for when replicating Azure VMs to another Azure region.

  - Recovery points created based on the replication policy will result in snapshots of the replica storage; these are charged for as well.

  - If you perform disaster recovery drills, there are additional charges for compute, networking, and storage resources based on actual consumption during each drill.

Service selection factors and strategies

There are certain factors to consider when selecting the Azure monitoring and management service for a given environment, based on application architecture, connectivity requirements, application security requirements, application delivery requirements, and other business needs. Let us start by understanding some of these key factors and the Azure monitoring and management services that best address them:

- **Securely manage Azure environment** The management stack provides multiple services that you can leverage to securely manage your Azure environment. These include the Azure Portal and Azure Cloud Shell services. While most admins heavily use the Azure Portal for most deployment, monitoring, and management activities, it is highly recommended that you develop Azure Cloud Shell skills, as it will allow you to perform repetitive actions in a much faster and more automated manner.

- **Build redundancy for recovery of infrastructure** The Azure Backup and Azure Site Recovery services provide features to help you build redundancy for your environment. Based on your organizational requirements, you might deploy either one or both of these services. For example, Azure Backup is useful for long-term recovery point storage to allow you to restore data that might be days, weeks, months, or years old, whereas Azure Site Recovery is more suitable for short-term recovery points that can help you quickly recover Azure workloads in another Azure region with minimal downtime, but only if you restore from recovery points that are 48 to 72 hours old. Azure Backup can be considerably slower to use for data restoration compared to Azure Site Recovery, as you may need to deploy some infrastructure before you are able to recover the required data.

- **Migrate on-premises resources** The Azure Migrate service is best suited to migrate on-premises hosted physical or virtual servers or other cloud-hosted IaaS VMs. Azure Site Recovery service allows you to synchronize your on-premises servers to Azure and migrate them over, but the Azure Migrate service is built to better assess and manage such migration activities.

- **Optimizing Azure spends** The Azure Cost Management service can help you better understand your Azure spends and areas for optimization and cost reduction. The service provides you with automated recommendations based on analysis of data collected by the service on the usage and sizing of each service. In addition, you can use the data provided by the service to perform manual assessments and optimizations based on your experience and understanding of your environment and hosted workloads.

- **Monitoring Azure services** The Azure Monitor, Azure Network Monitor, and Azure Service Health services can help you to monitor the health of the overall Azure environment, Azure region, and services provided in a particular region or specific Azure networking components such as VPN. As we dive deeper into each service throughout this book, you will have more clarity on when each service can be leveraged in your environment.

As you can see, different factors can help you determine the monitoring or management service to use. As your understanding of these services improves during the course of reading this book, as you start to deploy and manage your Azure environment, and as your business needs evolve over time, you will be able to make better and wiser decisions on which service to leverage to meet those business demands.

Who is this book for?

Microsoft Azure Monitoring & Management: The Definitive Guide is for anyone interested in Azure infrastructure solutions—IT and cloud administrators, network professionals, security professionals, developers, and engineers. It is designed to be useful for the entire spectrum of Azure users. Whether you have basic experience using Azure or other on-premises or cloud virtualization technologies or you are an expert, you will still derive value from this book. This book provides introductory, intermediate, and advanced coverage of each monitoring and management service.

The book especially targets those who are working in medium-to-large enterprise organizations and have at least basic experience in administering, deploying, and managing Azure infrastructure or other virtualization technologies such as Microsoft Hyper-V, and are looking to enhance their understanding of how to build resiliency and redundancy in their on-premises and cloud environments and leverage the wide range of infrastructure services provided by Microsoft Azure.

How is this book organized?

This book is organized into nine chapters:

- Chapter 1: Azure Backup
- Chapter 2: Azure Site Recovery
- Chapter 3: Azure Migrate
- Chapter 4: Azure Monitor
- Chapter 5: Azure Network Watcher
- Chapter 6: Azure Portal
- Chapter 7: Azure Cloud Shell
- Chapter 8: Azure Service Health
- Chapter 9: Azure Cost Management

Each chapter focuses on a specific Azure monitoring and management service, covering its inner workings in depth, with walkthroughs to guide you in building and testing the service and real-world best practices to help you maximize your Azure investments.

The approach adopted for the book is a unique mix of didactic, narrative, and experiential instruction.

- The didactic component covers the core introductions to the services.

- The narrative leverages what you already understand and acts as a bridge to introduce concepts.

- The experiential instruction takes into account real-world experiences and challenges in small and large environments and the factors to consider while designing and implementing workloads. Step-by-step walkthroughs on how to configure each Azure monitoring and management service and its related features and options enable you to take advantage of all the benefits each service has to offer.

System requirements

To get the most out of this book, you must meet the following system requirements:

- **An Azure subscription**   Microsoft provides a 30-day USD200 trial sub-scription that can be used to explore most services covered in this book. Some services, such as dedicated hosts, cannot be created using the trial subscription, however. To test and validate these services, you will need a paid subscription. If you plan to deploy any of these restricted services, you will need to procure a paid subscription.

- **Windows 10/11**   This should include the latest updates from Microsoft Update Service.

- **Azure PowerShell**   For more information, see *docs.microsoft.com/en-us/powershell/azure/install-az-ps*.

- **Azure CLI**   For more information, see *docs.microsoft.com/en-us/cli/azure/install-azure-cli*.

- **Display monitor**   This must be capable of 1024 x 768 resolution.

- **Pointing device**   You need a Microsoft mouse or compatible pointing device.

About the companion content

The companion content for this book can be downloaded from the following pages:

MicrosoftPressStore.com/AzureMonitoringTDG/downloads or *github.com/ avinashvaliramani/AzureMonitoringMgmtTDG*

The companion content includes PowerShell and CLI code for each walkthrough in the book (where applicable).

Errata, updates, & book support

We've made every effort to ensure the accuracy of this book and its companion content. You can access updates to this book—in the form of a list of submitted errata and their related corrections—at:

MicrosoftPressStore.com/AzureMonitoringTDG/errata

If you discover an error that is not already listed, please submit it to us at the same page.

For additional book support and information, please visit *MicrosoftPressStore. com/Support*.

Please note that product support for Microsoft software and hardware is not offered through the previous addresses. For help with Microsoft software or hardware, go to *support.microsoft.com*.

Stay in touch

Let's keep the conversation going! We're on Twitter: *twitter.com/MicrosoftPress*.

Chapter 1

Azure Backup

Overview

Microsoft provides a comprehensive backup service solution in Azure called Azure Backup. You can use Azure Backup to back up on-premises, cloud-based, and Azure-based workloads for short-term and long-term retention in a secure yet cost-effective manner. Azure Backup has evolved over the years, adding a number of key features that have drastically improved its usability, reliability, and redundancy. As a result, it is a de-facto backup solution for most organizations that use Azure or are migrating to it.

Azure Backup provides different backup agents or solutions that you can use to back up your workloads, either in your on-premises environment or in Azure environments. These include the following:

- **Microsoft Azure Recovery Services (MARS)**   You can deploy the MARS agent in Azure or in on-premises Windows virtual machines (VMs) for files or for folder-level or system-state backups.

- **Microsoft System Center Data Protection Manager (DPM)**   Microsoft DPM has existed as a backup solution for years to manage on-premises physical or virtual Hyper-V or VMWare-based backups. It supports integration with Azure Backup for cloud-based data transfer and retention, providing a central console for managing those backups. DPM requires additional licensing apart from the costs associated with the Azure Backup service.

- **Microsoft Azure Backup Server (MABS)**   MABS is a modified version of DPM that was redeveloped and integrated with Azure Backup. It is included in the cost of the Azure Backup service. MABS helps address scenarios in which an on-premises backup server is required to back up and maintain a local copy of backups for short-term retention and Azure Storage is used for long-term retention. It supports backups of additional application workloads such as Microsoft Exchange, Microsoft SharePoint, and so on. You can even use it to back up Azure VMs to address specific backup scenarios with custom backup frequency and retention requirements.

- **Azure Backup extension**   The Azure Backup extension helps in scenarios where you want to back up an entire Azure VM (Windows/Linux) instead of individual files or folders or the system state alone.

As you can see, Azure Backup provides different toolsets to address different scenarios and environment requirements. Therefore, it is important to select the right option for your environment or workload based on its backup requirements.

In addition to Azure IaaS, on-premises VMs, and physical on-premises servers, Azure Backup also supports the backup of various Azure services, as detailed here (see Figure 1-1):

- **Azure Managed Disks** Azure Backup supports the backup and retention of Azure Managed Disks directly to a backup or Recovery Services vault.

- **Azure file shares** Azure Backup integrates with Azure files and enables you to configure backups as part of the service for short-term and long-term retention of file share data.

- **SQL Server running in Azure VMs** Azure Backup supports SQL database-aware backups using the MARS agent or MABS solution, ensuring that restoration is possible in a consistent manner.

- **SAP HANA databases running in Azure VMs** Azure Backup supports SAP HANA database-aware backups using the MARS agent or MABS solution, ensuring that restoration is possible in a consistent manner.

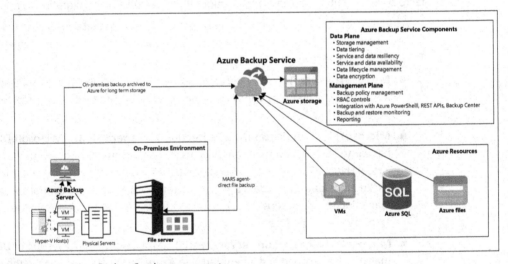

FIGURE 1-1 Azure Backup Service components.

> **NOTE** This support capability is constantly enhanced, so the preceding list might not include all the services covered by the time you read this book. Be sure to review any updated guidance specific to the workload you are trying to back up.

Key features

Azure Backup provides many key features. A few of the most important ones are detailed here:

- **Cost-effective cloud-based solution**   Azure Backup provides an extremely cost-effective backup solution that addresses the needs of most small and large organizations. The service charges for backup storage are based on consumption, meaning that you need not procure or pay for storage before using it. You can add or remove workloads from the backup scope. Service charges will update monthly based on actual usage.

- **Integrated service in Azure**   Azure Backup is integrated into Azure, making it intuitive and easy to use. You can quickly begin backing up your workloads without procuring additional licensing or deploying additional servers for backup management.

- **Scalable by design**   Azure Backup is scalable by design, supporting the backup of a single VM or thousands of VMs, without requiring you to provision hardware or infrastructure in advance.

- **Highly available storage**   Azure Backup uses Azure Storage to store backups. As such, it employs the redundancy options available in Azure Storage, such as LRS, GRS, and ZRS storage, for data redundancy across regions.

- **Support for various Azure services**   Azure Backup provides support for various Azure services and is constantly updated to support more services. The current list of services supported includes Azure VMs, Azure file shares, Azure Blob storage, and Azure managed disks.

- **Different backup tools for different scenarios**   Azure Backup provides different backup tools such as the MARS agent, Azure Backup Server, DPM, and Azure Backup extension to address the needs of different organizations and scenarios.

- **Support for short- and long-term retention**   Azure Backup supports both short-term and long-term backup retention and enables you to apply different backup policies to different workloads. In this way, you can retain backups per the requirements of each unique workload.

- **Secure by default**   Azure Backup uses TLS encryption to transfer backups to the backup or Recovery Services vault, making it secure by default. Backups are stored in Azure Storage, which is encrypted. Azure Backup also supports the backup of servers with encryption set up using BitLocker and/or Azure-Managed or Customer-Managed encryption keys with Azure Key Vault.

- **No online data transfer costs**   Azure Backup does not charge for any online data transfer to or from the service. Only offline transfers, if performed for initial backup uploads, are charged for on a one-time basis.

- **Centralized monitoring and management**   With Azure Backup, you can monitor and manage backups in a central console in the Azure Portal, making it easy to set up alerts from a single location. Azure Backup also supports integration with Azure Monitor to address advanced reporting scenarios.

- **Support for various management tools**   Azure Backup supports management using the Azure Portal, Azure PowerShell, Azure command-line interface (CLI), ARM Templates, and REST APIs.

> **NOTE**   The remainder of this chapter focuses primarily on backup scenarios involving the MARS agent, as that is the most widely used backup option in the Azure Backup service.

Design and deployment concepts and considerations

Microsoft has evolved Azure Backup over time, applying its expertise in on-premises backups using Microsoft System Center Data Protection Manager (DPM) and providing more integrations for backing up various solutions such as Windows Server, Microsoft SQL, Microsoft SharePoint, Microsoft Exchange, Windows file servers, Azure VMs, Azure Storage, and an ever-growing list of supported solutions.

The Azure Backup service is built up of different components that provide a holistic, secure, scalable, and integrated backup service. As such, it should be your *de facto* backup service in Azure. Let's go through each of these components to give you a better understanding of which backup components will likely work best in your environment, how to deploy them, and how best to secure and manage them.

Recovery Services vault

A Recovery Services vault is the central storage entity in Azure that manages the backup configuration, backup jobs, and associated backup data for Azure IaaS VMs, Azure file share, SQL, and SAP HANA database backups and other workloads supported by the service. The vault also serves as a central location to monitor and manage backups configured using Azure Backup Server, DPM, Windows Server, and more.

The main features of the vault include the following:

- **Centralized management and monitoring**   The Recovery Services vault provides a single central management console to set up, manage, and monitor backups configured using the MARS agent. This makes it easy to keep an eye on backup status and set up alerts in case of backup or restore failures.
- **Enhanced security of backed-up data**   The Recovery Services vault allows you to set up a security PIN that prevents unauthorized configuration changes and data deletion. Whenever someone attempts such an action in the service, the vault enforces the PIN requirement; if the wrong PIN is entered, the action will be denied. For on-premises backups, the vault enforces a 16-character passphrase that is set up at the time of backup creation and is used to encrypt the data when stored in Azure.

- **Role-based access control (RBAC) using Azure AD**   The Recovery Services vault supports RBAC leveraging Azure AD to control and limit access to the service only to authorized administrators based on their role or operational requirements.

- **Data resiliency and recovery**   The vault supports integration with LRS, ZRS, and GRS Azure Storage accounts to provide data resiliency across zones within an Azure region or across Azure regions. The vault also supports data restoration across paired Azure regions, thereby helping in scenarios where data must be brought online in a secondary region, or audit or compliance checks must be adhered to.

- **Protection against malicious attacks**   The vault protects against malicious attacks by allowing the restoration of clean data before the date of the attack based on your retention policies. If you have enabled soft delete data retention, then the vault ensures that any malicious deletion of the vault data can be recovered for a period of 14 days after the deletion.

- **Scalable by design**   Azure currently supports 1,000 VMs using the MARS agent, 2,000 backup data sources or items, and 200 backup policies per Recovery Services vault. At present, each subscription supports 500 Recovery Services vaults, making it a highly scalable service that can address the backup requirements for most large organizations.

Backup Center

Backup Center provides a unified management experience for enterprises to govern, monitor, operate, and analyze backups at scale. As such, it is consistent with Azure's native management experiences. Backup Center offers the following:

- **Single pane of glass to manage backups**   Backup Center is designed to function well across a large and distributed Azure environment. You can use the Backup Center to efficiently manage backups spanning multiple workload types, vaults, subscriptions, regions, and Azure Lighthouse tenants.

- **Data source-centric management**   Backup Center provides views and filters centered on the data sources you're backing up—for example, VMs and databases. This allows a resource owner or a backup admin to monitor and operate backups of items without focusing on which vault an item is backed up to. A key feature of this design is the ability to filter views by data source-specific properties, such as data-source subscription, data-source resource group, and data-source tags. For example, if your organization assigns different tags to VMs belonging to different departments, you could use Backup Center to filter backup information based on the tags of the underlying VMs being backed up without needing to focus on the tag of the vault.

- **Connected experiences**   Backup Center provides native integrations to existing Azure services that enable management at scale. For example, the Backup Center uses Azure Policy to help you govern your backups. It also leverages Azure workbooks and Azure Monitor Logs to provide you with detailed reports on backups. So, you don't need to learn any new principles to use the varied features that the Backup Center offers. You can also discover community resources from the Backup Center.

Data plane

Azure Backup is broken down into two main components: the data plane and the management plane. Each plane provides specific functions and complements the other to ensure the service works as intended.

The functions performed by the data plane include the following:

- **Data protection** The data plane ensures that the data-protection policies set up in the vault configuration are adhered to. It ensures that any data that is accidentally or maliciously deleted is available for recovery for 14 days. This is provided at no additional cost to all customers, as long as they enable the configuration.

- **Data encryption at rest** The data plane ensures that all backup data at rest is encrypted based on the encryption configuration set up in the service. It performs data decryption as needed in the event of a data-restore operation.

- **Data lifecycle management** The data plane manages the entire lifecycle of the backup data, ensuring that it adheres to the retention policies set up in the vault configuration.

- **Storage-management automation** The data plane manages the automatic provisioning, resizing, and scaling of the storage accounts used for the backup data.

Management plane

The management plane performs an additional set of complementary functions that support the overall management and access security of the vault. These include the following:

- **Backup policy management** The management plane provides the capability to centrally configure and manage backup and retention policies.

- **Enforcement of RBAC controls** The management plane provides the capability to configure RBAC permissions to control and limit access to the vault to authorized admins based on their role requirements. It monitors, authorizes, and logs all access requests, making it easier to track unauthorized requests.

- **Support for management tools** The management plane provides the capability to manage the Recovery Services vault using the Azure Portal, Azure PowerShell, Azure CLI, REST APIs, and Backup Center.

- **Reporting and management** All reporting, alerting, and management functionality is configurable thanks to capabilities provided within the management plane. It supports integration with Log Analytics for centralized backup monitoring across multiple vaults.

- **Faster restores using snapshots** The management plane handles snapshot backups for Azure VM and Azure files, which allow for faster data restores than from a storage vault. This can help you reduce the RTO in your environment during any data-restore operations.

Backup agents

Azure Backup service components provide two main types of backup agents:

- **MARS agent**   This supports system-state, file-level, and folder-level backups of Azure IaaS VMs and on-premises Windows Servers. It integrates with DPM and MABS servers to store local disk backups from those components in Azure for long-term retention.

- **Azure VM extension**   This is installed only on Azure IaaS VMs to carry out entire VM-level backups.

Supported backup types

Azure Backup supports various types of backups, which are selected based on the workload being backed up. Each type of backup provides different capabilities for backup and restoration. In general, most backup policies include a combination of these backup types to provide faster backups and limit data loss:

- **Full backups**   These are backups of target data sources that include entire VMs, databases, or file/folder structures. You should always start any new backup with a full backup to provide Azure Backup with a full copy of the data source, which it will need before it can perform any incremental, differential, or transaction log backups. Azure Backup currently allows only one full backup per day.

- **Differential backups**   Differential backups contain data from the last full backup. These types of backups are supported for SQL and SAP HANA databases running in Azure VMs. Differential backups are not the most efficient, as they take repeated backups of data modified since the last full backup, regardless of any changes to the data taking place on that day. It is important to use this backup type carefully. It can help speed up restores in certain scenarios, such as database backups, but also can result in additional use of backup storage. Azure Backup allows only one differential backup per day, and not on the same day as a full backup.

- **Incremental backups**   These backups contain data from the last full or incremental backup. Incremental backups are supported by SAP HANA databases running in Azure VMs. They are more efficient than differential backups, as they only back up changes since the last backup. This reduces any redundant backups of unchanged blocks. Incremental backups cannot be scheduled along with differential backups. Only one of the two can be set up to run on a regular basis. Incremental backups can be performed only once per day, and not on the same day as a full backup.

- **Transaction log backups**   These backups are supported by both SQL and SAP HANA databases running in Azure VMs. They are incremental log backups of the databases running on the target VMs. They can be scheduled to run once every 15 minutes at most. You can use transaction log backups along with full and incremental backups for a comprehensive database-backup strategy.

Backup policy

A backup policy defines a backup's schedule and retention configuration. You can apply different backup policies to different workloads, based on each workload's schedule and retention requirements. For example, you might create a backup policy that backs up a critical application server at 9 p.m. each day, with a retention of 365 days. In contrast, you might create a backup policy that backs up a non-critical application server every Sunday at 9 p.m., with a retention of four weeks.

You can have a maximum of 200 policies per vault and 100 items targeted per policy. If multiple applications or servers have the same retention and scheduling requirements, it is best to use the same backup policy to avoid hitting the subscription limit. If you reach the limit of 100 items for that policy, create a duplicate policy for the remaining items.

Backup scheduling

When you schedule backups, you must define the time and frequency at which backups should occur. This could be daily, weekly, monthly, yearly, or a combination of schedules:

- Daily backups occur daily at the time specified.
- Weekly backups require you to select the day of the week and the time when the backup should take place.
- Monthly backups require you to define the day of the month and the time when the backup should take place.
- Yearly backups require you to define the day of the year and the time when the backup should take place.

It is highly recommended that you schedule production backups during off-peak hours to limit its impact. Also, stagger backup jobs across the backup window so there aren't too many backup jobs taking place at the same time. Otherwise, the backup jobs could cause a slowdown across your entire environment, and cause the backups to take longer, too.

Backup retention

Backup retention defines how long the backup should be stored in the Recovery Services vault. Any retention period limited to days defines a short-term retention window. Any retention period limited to weeks, months, or years defines a long-term retention window. Be sure to set up retention for each application based on that application's audit, compliance, and recovery requirements.

You can also run backups on demand. For example, before an upgrade activity, you might decide to create a backup so you can roll back to that point in time if required. On-demand backups do not adhere to the retention policies configured or applied to that workload.

Backup compression

Azure Backup supports the compression of on-premises backup data at the source before it is transferred to the Recovery Services vault. This compression is a feature of the MARS agent set up for file or folder backups in the on-premises servers or the Azure Backup Server solution. Backups of Azure VMs using the backup extension do not support compression.

Backup monitoring

Azure Backup has a built-in monitoring engine that keeps track of all backup agents, scheduled backup jobs, job results, restore jobs, and other related administrative activities. You can use this built-in engine to monitor each Recovery Services vault. However, to monitor this information across multiple vaults, it is better to use other options, such as the following:

- **Backup Explorer** Backup Explorer is a pre-defined workbook provided by Microsoft as part of the Azure Monitor service. It provides a singular view of all backups and restore jobs, including job history across all backup vaults to which the admin has access. It can quickly help identify workloads that are currently not set up for backups.
- **Azure Monitor with Log Analytics** You can configure Azure Backup to store all logs in a Log Analytics workspace. Azure Monitor can create visualizations and alerts for job monitoring across multiple vaults.

Alerts

Azure Backup provides a built-in alerting engine that sends email-based alerts to defined users or distribution groups based on identified triggers. Examples of triggers might be backup failures, restore failures, backup data or protection deletion, and so on. The built-in engine provides sufficient capabilities to set up alerts for standard alerting scenarios. However, if custom alerts are required to address the scenarios not covered by the built-in engine, you can use Azure Monitor to set up alerts using Log Analytics for log ingestion.

Security

Azure Backup is secured on multiple levels, starting with backup data security during transit and at rest and extending to service access controls.

With regard to data in transit, Azure ensures that all data transferred from the MARS agent to Azure Backup and storage occurs over HTTPS. Additionally, any data transfer between Azure Backup and storage uses HTTPS, ensuring data security during transit.

Azure encrypts all data stored in the Azure storage (in other words, data at rest) using platform-managed keys or customer-managed keys stored in the Azure Key Vault service. This helps ensure that data is not readable if stolen from the back end. Azure Backup also supports the backup of Azure data encrypted disks using BitLocker encryption with Azure Key Vault integration.

Azure Backup service uses Azure role-based access control (RBAC) for granular access control of the Recovery Services vault. You can use pre-defined security roles available in RBAC to assign access to admins based on their roles and duties. These roles include the following:

- **Backup contributors** Members can create and delete vaults; enable new backups; create, delete, and manage backup policies; stop and delete backup protection; and perform all operators activities.
- **Operators** Members can trigger backup and restore jobs.
- **Readers** Members can read the backup configuration only.

You can also create custom roles with permissions per your environment and assign them to admins for granular control. Apart from the backup service itself, the back-end storage accounts that hold all the backup data are another point of concern. Azure ensures that another user or service, apart from Azure Backup service, cannot access these storage accounts during operations such as backups or restores.

Azure Backup walkthrough

The following sections walk you through the process of creating a Recovery Services vault and setting up Azure Backup to back up your Azure VMs using the Azure Portal, Azure PowerShell, and the Azure CLI. If you are following along, be sure to select resources and resource names based on your environment, including unique Recovery Services vault names for each of your deployments. Also be sure to delete any unwanted resources after you have completed testing to reduce charges levied by Microsoft for these resources.

USING THE AZURE PORTAL

To create a Recovery Services vault and set up an Azure VM backup using the Azure Portal, follow these steps:

1. Log in to the Azure Portal, type **recovery service vaults** in the search box and select it from the list that appears. (See Figure 1-2.)

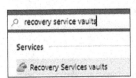

FIGURE 1-2 Search for recovery service vaults.

2. Click **Create** or **Create Recovery Services Vault** to start the Create Recovery Services Vault wizard. (See Figure 1-3.)

FIGURE 1-3 Click Create Recovery Services Vault.

3. In the **Basics** tab of the Create Recovery Services Vault wizard (see Figure 1-4), enter the following information, and click **Next**:

   ■ **Subscription**   Select the subscription that will host the vault.

   ■ **Resource Group**   Select the resource group you want to use to host the Recovery Services vault. Alternatively, to create a new resource group, click the **Create New** link and follow the prompts.

   ■ **Vault Name**   Type a name for the vault. If the name you type is already in use, the wizard will prompt you to select another name.

   ■ **Region**   Select the Azure region in which you want to host the vault.

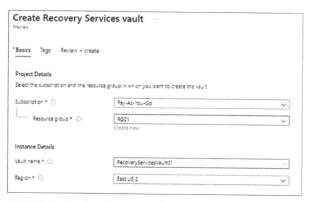

FIGURE 1-4   The Basics tab of the Create Recovery Services Vault wizard.

4. In the **Tags** tab, enter any tags you would like to associate with the vault, or leave the fields blank (see Figure 1-5) and click **Next**.

FIGURE 1-5   The Tags tab of the Create Recovery Services Vault wizard.

5. In the **Review + Create** tab (see Figure 1-6), review your settings and click **Create**.

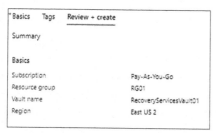

FIGURE 1-6   The Review + Create tab of the Create Recovery Services Vault wizard.

6. After the Recovery Services vault is deployed, click the **Go to Resource** button to access its configuration options. (See Figure 1-7.)

FIGURE 1-7   Go to the vault's configuration page.

7. In the Recovery Services vault's configuration page, click the **Backup** button to start the Backup Goal wizard. (See Figure 1-8.)

FIGURE 1-8   Start the Backup Goal wizard.

8. In the Backup Goal wizard, click the alert message (**The Storage Replication Is Set to Geo-Redundant...**) shown at the top. (See Figure 1-9.)

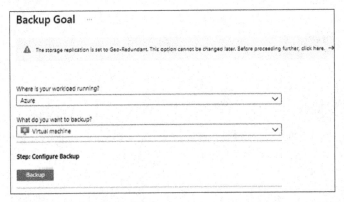

FIGURE 1-9   Backup Goal wizard.

9. A **Backup Configuration** pane opens on the right. (See Figure 1-10.) Set the following options and click **Save**:

- **Storage Replication Type**   For this example, leave this set to **Geo-Redundant**.
- **Cross Region Restore**   Set this to **Enable** if required.

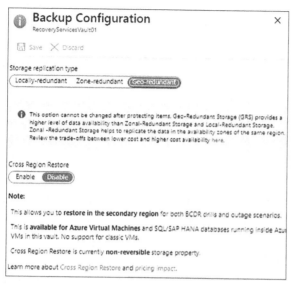

FIGURE 1-10   The Backup Configuration options.

10. Back in the Backup Goal wizard (see Figure 1-11), set the following options. Then click the **Backup** button to start the Configure Backup wizard:

- **Where Is Your Workload Running?**   Leave this set to the default option, **Azure**. Alternatively, if you want to switch to an on-premises machine or some other option, open the drop-down list and select it.
- **What Do You Want to Back Up?**   Leave this set to the default option, Virtual Machine. Alternatively, open the drop-down list and a different option.

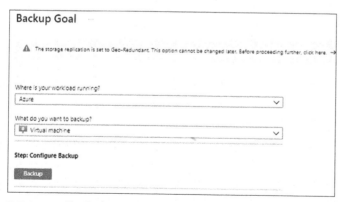

FIGURE 1-11   The Backup Goal wizard (again).

11. In the Configure Backup wizard (see Figure 1-12), under **Backup Policy**, click the **Create a New Policy** link.

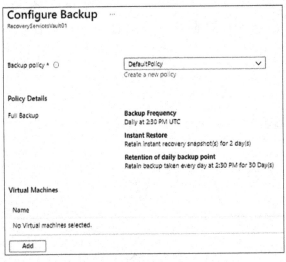

FIGURE 1-12   Configure Backup.

12. In the **Create Policy** window (see Figure 1-13), enter the following information and click **Create**:

- **Policy Name**   Enter a unique policy name.

- **Backup Schedule**   Specify how frequently you want the backup to occur (daily, weekly, monthly, or yearly), at what time the backup should occur, and in what time zone the backup should occur.

- **Instant Restore**   Specify how many days an instant recovery snapshot should be retained. Instant restore will result in local short-term backup retention for quicker restores. It supports a maximum value of 5 days.

- **Retention Range**   Specify the number of days, weeks, months, and years of backups to retain and the day to target for each.

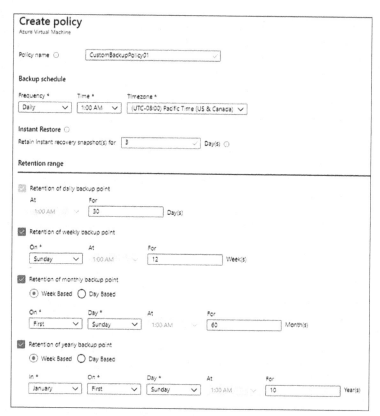

FIGURE 1-13 Create Policy options.

13. Back in the Configure Backup wizard (refer to Figure 1-12), under **Virtual Machines**, click the **Add** button to open the **Select Virtual Machines** window. (See Figure 1-14.)

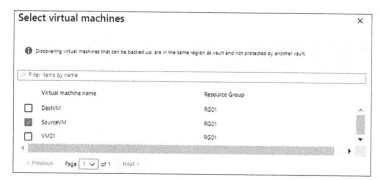

FIGURE 1-14 The Select Virtual Machines window in the Configure Backup wizard.

14. Select the VMs you want to back up and click **Add**.

15. Back in the Configure Backup wizard, verify that the settings are correct.

16. Optionally, select the **OS Disk Only** check box if you want to limit the backup to include only the OS disk of the VM. (See Figure 1-15.)

17. Click **Enable Backup**.

FIGURE 1-15 Review your settings in the Configure Backup wizard and enable the backup.

18. After the backup is deployed to the Recovery Services vault, click the **Go to Resource** button to access the vault's configuration options. (See Figure 1-16.)

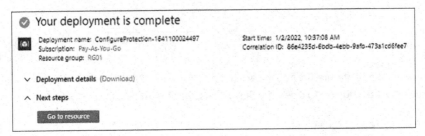

FIGURE 1-16 Go to the backup's configuration page.

19. In the Recovery Services vault's configuration page, under **Protected Items**, click **Backup Items**. (See Figure 1-17.)

FIGURE 1-17   The Backup Items option in the Recovery Services vault configuration page.

20. In the right pane, under **Primary Region**, select **Azure Virtual Machine**. (See Figure 1-18.)

FIGURE 1-18   Recovery Services vault – Primary Region.

A summary of backups you've created is displayed. (See Figure 1-19.)

FIGURE 1-19   List of configured backups.

21. Click the backup you just created to see more details about it. (See Figure 1-20.)

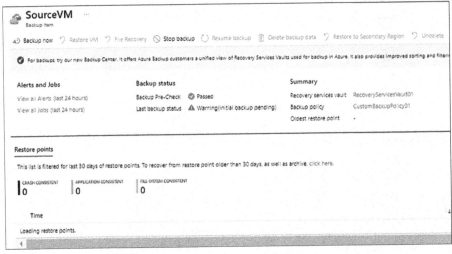

FIGURE 1-20 Detailed information about the backup you configured.

22. Do one of the following:

- Click **Backup Now** to initiate a backup manually.
- Wait for the backup to be triggered automatically, according to the schedule you set.

23. If you elected to initiate the backup manually, select the date until which the backup should be retained (see Figure 1-21) and click **OK** to start the backup.

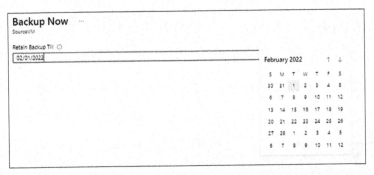

FIGURE 1-21 Start a manual backup.

24. After the manual backup begins, click **Notifications**. Then select the backup job currently running (see Figure 1-22) to see a detailed view of the backup's progress (see Figure 1-23).

FIGURE 1-22 The Notifications page.

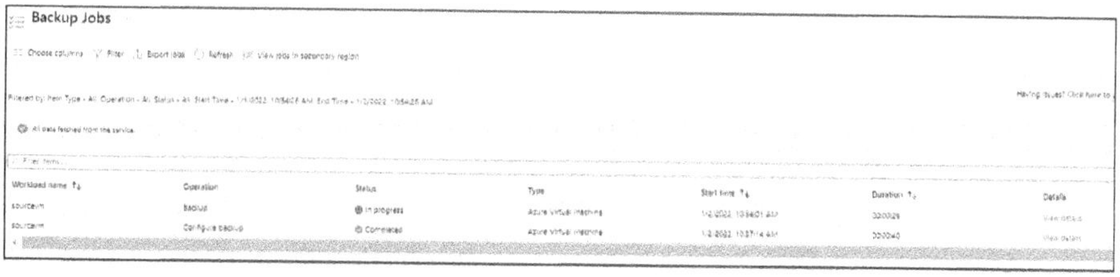

FIGURE 1-23 Monitoring the backup job.

USING AZURE POWERSHELL

You can create a Recovery Services vault, set up a backup policy, and enable backups for an Azure VM using the New-AzRecoveryServicesVault, New-AzRecoveryServicesBackup-ProtectionPolicy, and Enable-AzRecoveryServicesBackupProtection Azure PowerShell commands. The following code shows you how. Use this snippet to create the same Recovery Services vault and VM backup as you did in the Azure Portal; when you do, be sure to either delete the previous Recovery Services vault or give this new vault a different name:

```
#Register the vault service
Register-AzResourceProvider -ProviderNamespace "Microsoft.RecoveryServices"

#Define variables
$vaultname = "RecoveryServicesVault01"
$rg = "RG01"
$location = "EastUS2"
$VM = "SourceVM"
#Create Recovery Services vault
New-AzRecoveryServicesVault -ResourceGroupName $RG -Name $vaultname -Location $location

#Set the storage redundancy and cross region restore config
Get-AzRecoveryServicesVault -Name $vaultname | Set-AzRecoveryServicesVaultContext
Get-AzRecoveryServicesVault -Name $vaultname | Set-AzRecoveryServicesBackupProperty
-BackupStorageRedundancy GeoRedundant -EnableCrossRegionRestore
```

```
#Create Backup policy
$SchedulePolicy = Get-AzRecoveryServicesBackupSchedulePolicyObject -WorkloadType "AzureVM"
$Date = Get-Date
$SchedulePolicy.ScheduleRunTimes.Add($Date.ToUniversalTime())
$Retention = Get-AzRecoveryServicesBackupRetentionPolicyObject -WorkloadType "AzureVM"
$Retention.DailySchedule.DurationCountInDays = 30
$policy = New-AzRecoveryServicesBackupProtectionPolicy -Name CustomBackupPolicy01
-RetentionPolicy $Retention -SchedulePolicy $SchedulePolicy -VaultId $vaultname.ID
-WorkloadType AzureVM

#Enable Azure VM Backup
Enable-AzRecoveryServicesBackupProtection -ResourceGroupName $RG -Name $VM -Policy $policy

#Trigger Backup Now
$bkpcontainer = Get-AzRecoveryServicesBackupContainer -ContainerType "AzureVM"
-FriendlyName $VM
$bkpitem = Get-AzRecoveryServicesBackupItem -Container $bkpcontainer -WorkloadType
"AzureVM"
Backup-AzRecoveryServicesBackupItem -Item $item

#Monitor backup status
Get-AzRecoveryservicesBackupJob
```

USING AZURE CLI

You can create a Recovery Services vault, set up a backup policy, and enable backups for an Azure VM using the az backup vault create and az backup protection enable-for-vm Azure CLI commands. The following code shows you how. Use this snippet to create the same vault as you did in the Azure Portal and Azure PowerShell; when you do, be sure to either delete the previous vault or give this new vault a different name.

> **NOTE** Creating a custom policy using the Azure CLI requires knowledge of writing and editing JSON templates. Therefore, it would be best to use the Azure Portal or Azure PowerShell to create new policies and associate them using CLI. In this example, we will use the default policy instead of a custom policy to overcome this.

```
#Define variables
vaultname = "RecoveryServicesVault01"
rg = "RG01"
location = "East US 2"
vm = "SourceVM"
#Create the Recovery Services vault
az backup vault create --resource-group $rg \
    --name $vaultname \
    --location $location
```

```
#Set vault storage replication type and cross region restore config
az backup vault backup-properties set --name $vaultname  \
    --resource-group $rg \
    --backup-storage-redundancy "GeoRedundant" \
    --cross-region-restore-flag "True"

#Enable backup for SourceVM
az backup protection enable-for-vm --resource-group $rg --vault-name $vaultname --vm $vm
--policy-name DefaultPolicy

#Start the Backup Now
az backup protection backup-now --resource-group $rg --vault-name $vaultname
--container-name $vm --item-name $vm --backup-management-type AzureIaaSVM
--retain-until 02-02-2021

#Monitor backup progress
az backup job list --resource-group $rg --vault-name $vaultname --output table
```

Best practices

Following are some general best practices for using Azure Backup:

- **Set the correct Azure Backup storage replication type**   Azure Backup supports storage that uses either the LRS, ZRS, or GRS replication type. Each provides a progressively higher level of redundancy, but also increases the cost incurred. By default, the service creates a GRS storage for backups. However, if that level of redundancy is not required, or if you want to control the costs incurred by the storage, change this replication type before you create any backups. Once backups are initiated, this configuration cannot be changed.

- **Limit internet connectivity for backups**   Azure Backup for VMs is performed directly over the Azure network, so there is no need to open access to any internet URLs for it. However, SQL and SAP HANA databases running on Azure VMs require connectivity using either the internet or Private Link to Azure Backup. If Azure Private Link is not a viable option, ensure that internet access for backups is limited to the network URLs required for Azure Backup. Azure publishes a list of these URLs publicly and updates them periodically as changes take place.

- **Use Private Endpoint and Private Link for SQL and SAP HANA backups**   Although SQL and SAP HANA databases running on Azure VMs can be backed up over the internet, it is best to set up a Private Endpoint for Azure Backup to connect to using Private Link to ensure these backups take place over a private internal connection. This will prevent any chance of a man-in-the-middle attack.

- **Use Backup Center for better management**   Backup Center is a free Azure service to centrally manage all backups spread across all Recovery Services vaults. Use this service to get a single view of all backups taking place in your environment.

- **Use Azure Policy for automated backup scheduling**   In large organizations with hundreds or thousands of VMs, keeping track of and ensuring all new VMs are set up for backups per the organization's requirements can be a daunting task. Use Azure Policy to define and apply a backup policy for any new VMs that are set up in a particular subscription, region, or resource group. This enables you to define the vault and backup policy that should be assigned automatically.

- **Use Log Analytics for centralized monitoring and reporting**   Integrate all Recovery Services vaults with the Log Analytics service so that all metrics for each vault, including all backups, are automatically captured for the purposes of generating detailed reports and long-term tracking.

- **Use Azure Policy for automated diagnostic logging**   You can use Azure Policy to configure all Recovery Services vaults with a policy to set up the Log Analytics configuration automatically. This eliminates the management overhead involved with performing this activity manually for new vaults.

- **Use the archive tier to reduce costs**   Azure Backup supports the use of the archive storage tier for long-term retention backups of Azure VMs and SQL servers running in Azure VMs. This enables you to push monthly and yearly backup data to the archive tier if it must be retained for more than six months. This can help you bring down the cost of your backup storage significantly.

- **Set up security defaults to protect against malicious attacks**   Security defaults define the PIN and soft delete retention policies to ensure that unauthorized changes to the service and any malicious or accidental delete operations can be prevented or easily reversed. Be sure to set both up as soon as you create a new vault.

Chapter 2

Azure Site Recovery

Overview

Microsoft introduced the Azure Site Recovery (ASR) service in public preview in June 2014. ASR initially focused on Hyper-V–to–Hyper-V and on-premises Hyper-V–to–Azure recovery scenarios. Over time, the service evolved to include additional capabilities, such as support for various operating systems, Azure IaaS VMs, and complex workloads that you could replicate in coordination with each other so you could bring them online in Azure with a similar recovery point. The simplicity, stability, and cost effectiveness provided by ASR has made it a very popular service used by organizations for their business continuity and disaster recovery (BCDR) strategy.

The key features of this service include the following:

- **Simplified interface to set up, monitor, and manage BCDR**   ASR provides an intuitive interface that makes it possible to easily set up, monitor, and manage the service.

- **Support for most commonly used operating systems**   ASR supports the replication of most operating systems, and the support list is expanding on a regular basis. This makes it possible to use ACR as a one-stop BCDR solution for most organizations.

- **Support to define replication schedules to meet the RTO and RPO objectives for most organizations**   ASR supports replication as low as 30 seconds for Hyper-V VMs and continuous replication for Azure VMs. VMware support is currently under preview but is expected to allow continuous replication.

- **Support for any workload**   ASR supports the replication of any workload as long as it is hosted on a supported operating system. This makes it a viable solution to address most organizations' needs.

- **On-premises Hyper-V–to–Hyper-V replication, monitoring, and recovery orchestration across multiple DR sites**   ASR supports replication monitoring and failover coordination for on-premises Hyper-V–to–Hyper-V servers across multiple interconnected sites. Hyper-V replication is used for data replication, but ASR helps automate all the recovery steps from the cloud.

- **Azure–to–Azure IaaS VM replication, monitoring, and recovery orchestration across Azure regions** ASR added support for Azure VM replication and failover across Azure regions in 2017. This allowed organizations to set up a BCDR strategy for their critical cloud workloads across multiple Azure regions.

- **On-premises Hyper-V–and physical servers–to–Azure replication, monitoring, and recovery orchestration** ASR supports the entire recovery management for workloads hosted in on-premises Hyper-V and physical servers to Azure VMs. Azure Storage hosts the replicated data. VMs are created only after a failover is initiated, reducing the costs associated with a secondary datacenter.

- **App-consistent snapshots to recover applications more efficiently** ASR supports using app-consistent snapshots for replication to ensure that applications are replicated using disk data, all data in memory, and all transactions in process.

- **Simplified and cost-effective pricing** ASR charges a fixed fee per server for the replication software; Azure Storage costs for replicated data are charged only after the VMs are failed over in Azure. This makes it extremely cost-effective when the DR site in Azure is not actively used to host VMs, as the majority of costs are related to running the VM. All this makes it possible for most organizations to afford a BCDR solution for their environment.

- **Testing DR without interruption to production** ASR supports the activation of the replicated data in isolated networks in Azure. This enables you to test VMs to make sure your application, database, and other workloads are working as needed before you need to actually use them in a DR scenario. This also enables scenarios in which application upgrades can be tested in the Azure cloud before implementing them in your on-premises environment.

- **Integration with SQL Server AlwaysOn** ASR supports integration with SQL Server AlwaysOn to allow for seamless recovery of both interconnected application and database workloads.

- **Integration with Azure Automation** Azure Automation enables you to set up scripts and automated actions to provision other Azure services or run pre- and post-failover scripts as part of your automated recovery procedure.

- **Multi-VM consistency using replication groups** ASR supports setting up multi-VM replication groups so that multiple VMs are replicated together, and app-consistent and crash-consistent recovery points are created to facilitate failover. This enables you to address scenarios that require multiple VMs to be maintained at the same consistency.

ASR supports various recovery scenarios that can be used by organizations in different ways, depending on their individual needs. The following sections cover the two most important scenarios that ASR supports: Azure–to–Azure disaster recovery and on-premises Hyper-V–to–Azure disaster recovery. Read these sections to obtain a better understanding of how both these scenarios can be set up, managed, and monitored using ASR.

Azure–to–Azure disaster recovery

ASR enables you to set up the replication of an Azure IaaS VM to another Azure region. After you enable replication, ASR installs the Site Recovery agent extension on the Azure VM that is used to register the VM to the ASR service. Once this is done, existing disk data and changes to the disk are transferred to the target storage account or managed disk based on your selection. Data is transferred using Microsoft's private network rather than the public internet, regardless of the Azure region selected, ensuring your data is transferred in a secure manner. Replication is continuous and crash-consistent, and app-consistent recovery points are created based on the replication policy that you set up for a VM.

Replication policy

The replication policy created and associated by default during the DR setup process defines the following:

- **Recovery-point retention**   This defines how far back in time ASR allows for recovery. The service retains recovery points based on retention timelines you define. At this time, the maximum supported recovery-point retention duration is 15 days for managed disks and 3 days for unmanaged disks; the default is 24 hours.

> **NOTE**   The higher the recovery-point retention period, the more data that is retained for that VM, and therefore the more you are charged for the storage used by the service.

- **Crash-consistent recovery points**   These are snapshots of the state of the VM disk taken and sent to the target region. These recovery points do not capture the data in memory and can therefore result in applications being brought online in an inconsistent state when recovered. Although most applications these days support crash-consistent recovery points, it is best to use app-consistent recovery points for recovery, if possible. By default, these are created every 5 minutes.

- **App-consistent recovery points**   These are snapshots of the on-disk data along with all processes, data, and transactions running in memory. These are captured using the Volume Shadow Copy Service on Windows Servers. App-consistent snapshots take longer than crash-consistent snapshots and can add load to the server depending on the available resources and frequency defined. You should test to make sure these snapshots are not causing significant overhead or resize your VM workload to accommodate the additional load. The minimum frequency supported for this snapshot is 1 hour; the default setting is 4 hours.

You can define a replication policy based on your application, workload, or recovery point objective (RPO) requirements and set up your replication configuration to use that policy when setting up replication.

Data security

ASR does not intercept, scan, or analyze data transferred between source and target regions. This makes the entire process transparent to the service and eliminates the risk of the replicated data being used for malicious purposes. Data is encrypted in transit as well as encrypted while at rest when stored in the target region.

Multi-VM consistency

Multiple interdependent VMs can be set up in a replication group during replication setup so they are replicated to the target region with shared crash-consistent and app-consistent recovery points. This might be necessary when multiple application, interface, and database servers require that level of data consistency across each to ensure a supported failover. All VMs in a replication group must be failed over at the same time and cannot be failed over individually.

A replication group can contain a maximum of 16 VMs. VMs can be added to a replication group only when they are being set up for replication. To add a VM that is already replicating to a replication group, you must re-create the replication for that VM. Multi-VM consistency is quite resource intensive. It is therefore recommended that you enable it only in scenarios in which it is important for VMs to have such shared snapshots.

> **NOTE** All VMs that are part of a multi-VM consistency replication group must communicate with each other over port 20004. Make sure any firewalls or network security groups set up between the VMs are configured to allow this traffic.

Target environment configuration

You can define different configuration items for the target environment, even after setting up replication. However, there are a few configuration items that can be defined only during the initial setup. Following is a brief list of some of the key items that are supported at this time:

- **Target VM SKU**   You can define this during replication setup, leave it set to automatic, or modify it after replication setup. When set to automatic, ASR will select a VM SKU that is the same or similar based on resource availability in the target region.

- **Target resource group**   You can define the target resource group during replication setup or leave it set to automatic, in which case the service will create a new resource group or modify an existing one after replication setup.

- **Target virtual network**   You can define the target virtual network during replication setup or leave it set to automatic, in which case the service will create a new one or modify an existing one after replication setup.

- **Target subnet**   The service automatically assigns the VM to a subnet based on the source VM subnet setup. You can modify the target subnet after replication setup.

- **Target name**   The service automatically assigns a target name based on the source VM name. You can modify the target name after replication setup.

- **Target disk type**   You can define the target disk type during replication setup. The service automatically selects the disk type based on the source disk setup, but you can change it if required during replication setup.

- **Target subscription**   The service automatically selects the subscription based on the source VM subscription, but if there is another subscription associated with the same Azure AD tenant, you can select it instead during replication setup.

- **Target proximity group**   The service automatically sets the target proximity group to None, but you can change this during replication setup.

- **Target VM availability configuration**   The service automatically sets the target VM availability configuration based on the source VM, but you can change this at replication setup.

Failover and failback

In the event of a disaster in the primary region, you can failover the Azure VM to the target region using the ASR service. You will be asked to select the recovery point to use for the restoration. The target VM will then be created based on the settings you've defined and the replicated data.

The target VM is created in an unprotected state. Once the primary region is back online, you can set up failback replication for the VM. At this time, the site recovery service checks whether the source disk is still available. If one exists, it will check it for consistency and determine the missing changes to replicate over. If no disk exists, it will start the replication of the entire disk.

You can perform a failback in the same manner as the failover and perform it whenever you have the appropriate downtime.

Test and planned failovers

ASR supports test and planned failover options. Each option is useful in different scenarios.

In a test failover, ASR creates a VM in a test network defined by you, with the replicated data. It is recommended that you set up an isolated test network without connectivity to the primary network to avoid accidental writes from test applications to the primary database or other unexpected issues. The test VM does not commit write operations to the replication data. This enables you to make changes to the test VM—for example, application or database upgrades—without affecting the primary server or the replication in any way. You can perform test failovers to validate your VM and its workload failover as needed in the secondary region to perform application or database upgrade testing or for compliance auditory reasons. When you are finished testing, you can simply clean up the test environment; the test VM and associated disks will be deleted from the secondary Azure region, while the original replication continues unimpeded.

During a planned failover, ASR brings the VM online in the secondary region and allows changes to the VM to be committed to disk. While the changes are not replicated to the primary region, replication from the primary site is stopped. Use this option in scenarios where your primary VM is down or you are migrating to the secondary region.

Network security

You can control outbound replication traffic using network security groups (NSGs) in the source Azure region. ASR requires that any NSG rules set up enable outbound replication traffic. You can use service tags that Microsoft provides to define such outbound traffic rules. This ensures that any IP changes in the Microsoft services are automatically applied to your environment, as the service tags are updated by Microsoft when such changes occur, supporting uninterrupted replication for your workloads.

Azure–to–Azure disaster recovery walkthrough

The following section walks you through the process of setting up and testing Azure–to–Azure replication for a VM using the Azure Portal.

> **IMPORTANT** If you are following along, you'll want to select resources and unique resource names based on your environment for each of your deployments.

> **IMPORTANT** If you are following along, delete any unwanted resources after you have completed testing to reduce charges being levied by Microsoft for these resources.

Using Azure Portal

SETUP AZURE REPLICATION

To set up Azure–to–Azure VM replication using the Azure Portal, follow these steps:

1. Log in to the Azure Portal, browse to the VM you want to replicate, and click it to select it.

2. In the left pane of the selected VM's configuration blade (see Figure 2-1), click **Disaster Recovery** to start the Azure Site Recovery wizard.

SourceVM
Virtual machine

Search (Ctrl+/)

Overview

Activity log

Access control (IAM)

Tags

Diagnose and solve problems

Settings

Networking

Connect

Windows Admin Center (preview)

Disks

Size

Security

Advisor recommendations

Extensions + applications

Continuous delivery

Availability + scaling

Configuration

Identity

Properties

Locks

Operations

Bastion

Auto-shutdown

Backup

Disaster recovery

FIGURE 2-1 Options in the SourceVM configuration blade.

3. In the **Basics** tab of the Azure Site Recovery wizard, open the **Target Region** drop-down list and choose the region in which you would like to replicate the VM. (See Figure 2-2.) Then click **Next: Advanced Settings**.

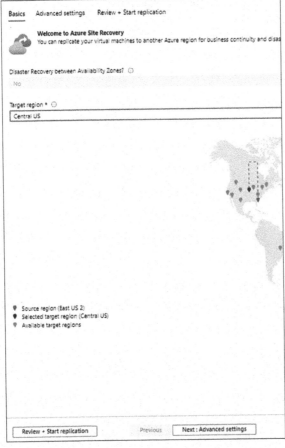

FIGURE 2-2 Basics tab.

4. In the **Advanced Settings** tab (see Figure 2-3), enter the following information and click **Next: Review + Start Replication**:

- **Subscription** Select the subscription in which you want to create the replica VM.
- **VM Resource Group** Select the resource group in which to create the replica VM. Alternatively, the wizard will create one automatically.
- **Virtual Network** Select the virtual network to use for the replica VM. Alternatively, the wizard will create one automatically.
- **Availability** Specify whether the replica VM should be set up with availability enabled or leave it set to the default (Single Instance).
- **Proximity Placement Group** Specify whether the replica VM should be placed in a proximity placement group.
- **Cache Storage Account** Select an existing Azure storage account to use as the replication cache. Alternatively, the wizard will create one automatically.

- **Vault Subscription** Select the subscription in which to set up the Recovery Services vault.

- **Recovery Services Vault** Select an existing Recovery Services vault. Alternatively, the wizard will create one automatically.

- **Vault Resource Group** Select an existing resource group in the target location. Alternatively, the wizard will create one automatically.

- **Replication Policy** Select an existing replication policy from the drop-down list. Alternatively, the wizard will create one automatically.

- **Update Settings** Specify whether ASR should manage all update settings or if you will do so manually.

- **Automation Account** Select an existing automation account to use for the site recovery configuration. Alternatively, the wizard will create one automatically.

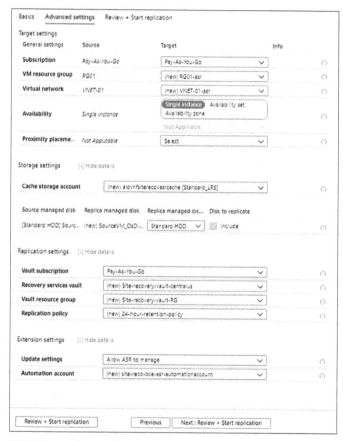

FIGURE 2-3 Advanced Setting tab.

5. On the **Review + Start Replication** tab, check your settings and click **Start Replication**. (See Figure 2-4.)

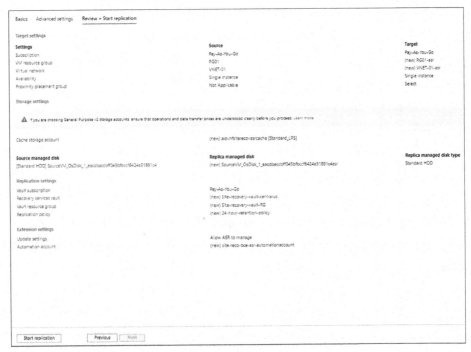

FIGURE 2-4 Review + Start Replication tab.

ASR creates the resources you requested, starting a number of jobs one after another to create all the different components.

6. Monitor the jobs to ensure they all complete successfully. (See Figure 2-5.)

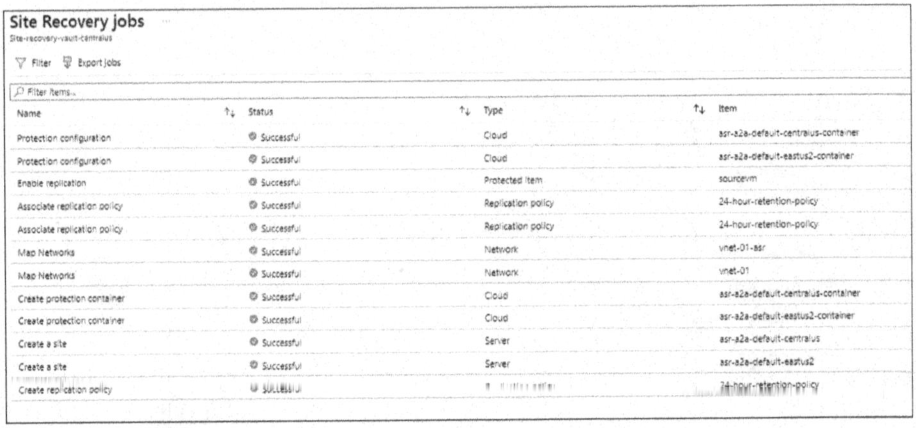

FIGURE 2-5 Site Recovery Jobs page.

> **NOTE** In the event of any errors or failures, you will need to select the error message to view more details to identify the root cause and resolve the issue. You will then have to reinitiate the entire process.

MONITOR REPLICATION

When all the jobs are complete, in the Site Recovery service, under Replicated Items, you will see the SourceVM you just replicated.

7. Click **SourceVM** under **Replicated Items**.

   A SourceVM **Overview** page displays the status of the replication, or sync. Notice in Figure 2-6 that **Replication Health** is **Healthy**, but **Status** is **0% Synchronized**.

FIGURE 2-6   The SourceVM Overview page with Replication Health and Status data.

8. Refresh and monitor this page until synchronization is complete.

   When synchronization is complete, Status will change to Protected. (See Figure 2-7.) At this point, you can make changes to the replica VM configuration.

FIGURE 2-7   The SourceVM overview page with the updated Replication Health and Status data.

CUSTOMIZE REPLICA CONFIGURATIONS

9. In the left pane of the SourceVM's Replicated Items configuration blade, click **Compute**.

10. On the **Compute Properties** page (see Figure 2-8), enter the following information and click **Save**:

    - **Name**   Type the VM name in the **Name** row of the **Target Settings** column.
    - **Resource Group**   Enter the resource group in the **Resource Group** row of the **Target Settings** column.
    - **Size**   Enter the size in the **Size** row of the **Target Settings** column.

FIGURE 2-8 Compute settings.

11. In the left pane of the SourceVM's Replicated Items configuration blade, click **Network**.

12. Click **Edit** to make changes to the following settings, if desired. (See Figure 2-9.) Then click **Save**:

    - **Target Network**
    - **Test Failover Network**
    - **Accelerated Networking**
    - **Subnet**
    - **Network Security Group**
    - **Private IP Address**
    - **Public IP**

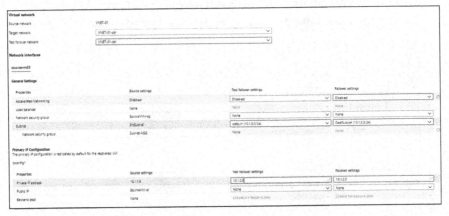

FIGURE 2-9 Network settings.

13. In the left pane of the SourceVM's Replicated Items configuration blade, click **Disks** to monitor pending changes to the source VM to assess how the sync is progressing. (See Figure 2-10.)

FIGURE 2-10 Disks replication status.

Next, you'll perform a test failover to test the replica VM.

14. Back in the **Overview** page in the SourceVM's Replicated Items configuration blade, click the **Test Failover** button. (See Figure 2-11.) A Test Failover page opens.

FIGURE 2-11 Click the Test Failover button.

15. In the **Test Failover** page (see Figure 2-12), set the following options as shown and click **OK**:

   ■ **From** This automatically lists the Azure region where your source VM is running.

   ■ **To** This automatically lists the Azure region where your replica VM is set to be created.

   ■ **Choose a Recovery Point** Choose the recovery point to restore to and create the replica VM. You will generally want to select **Latest Processes (Low RTO)** for the least data loss possible.

   ■ **Azure Virtual Network** This automatically lists the Azure virtual network where your replica VM is set to be created.

Test failover
SourceVM

Failover direction
From ○
East US 2

To ○
Central US

Recovery Point
Choose a recovery point ○
Latest processed (low RTO) (1 out of 1 disks) (1/16/2022, 11:55:29 AM)   ⌄

Azure virtual network * ○
VNET-01-asr   ⌄

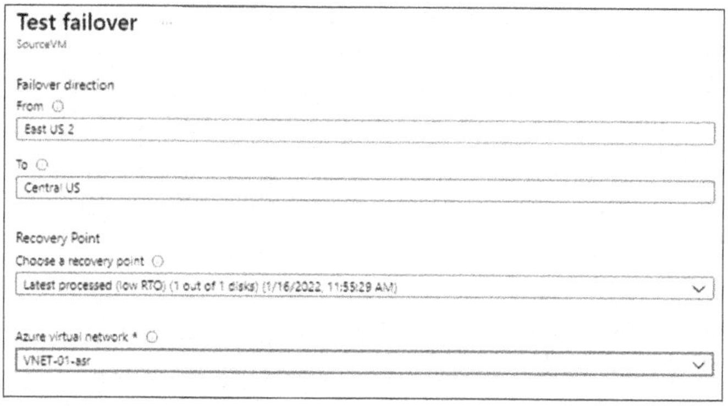

FIGURE 2-12 Test Failover page.

ASR stores the recovery point in the target region and creates a new VM with a name similar to the source VM. For example, if the source VM were named DC01, the new VM would be named DC01-test. Figure 2-13 shows the result.

NOTE You can log in to the VM using Azure Bastion (if provisioned in the target region) or by assigning a public IP to the VM.

FIGURE 2-13   SourceVM-test Overview page.

16. Log in to the new VM and verify that all the data, apps, and services reflect correctly.

Now that you have finished testing, you're ready to clean up the test environment.

CLEANUP TEST FAILOVER

17. Back in the **Overview** page in the SourceVM's Replicated Items configuration blade (see Figure 2-14), click the **Cleanup Test Failover** button.

FIGURE 2-14   Click the Clean Test Failover button.

18. In the **Test Failover Cleanup** dialog box (see Figure 2-15), type any notes from the test that you would like to record in the **Notes** box. These could include the test participants, test outcomes, issues encountered, or changes to incorporate in future tests or after testing the replication configuration.

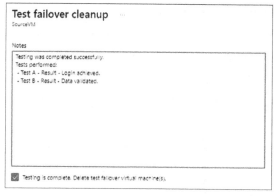

FIGURE 2-15 The Test Failover Cleanup dialog box.

19. Select the **Testing Is Complete. Delete Test Failover Virtual Machine(s)** check box and click **OK** to initiate the cleanup job.

20. From the **Test Failover Cleanup** page (see Figure 2-16), monitor the cleanup job to ensure it completes successfully.

FIGURE 2-16 Test Failover Cleanup page, showing the progress of the cleanup job.

If all your tests have completed successfully, you're ready to perform a full failover of the VM to the Azure region to which you are replicating.

PERFORM FAILOVER

21. Back in the **Overview** page in the SourceVM's Replicated Items configuration blade (see Figure 2-17), click the **Failover** button.

FIGURE 2-17 Click the Failover button.

22. In the **Failover** dialog box (see Figure 2-18), verify your settings, select the **Shut Down Machine Before Beginning Failover** check box if desired, and click **OK** to launch the ASR failover job.

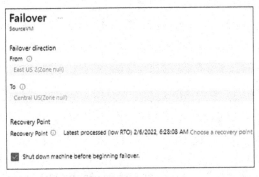

FIGURE 2-18 Failover dialog box.

23. On the **Failover** page (see Figure 2-19), monitor the progress of the replication job to ensure all the steps complete successfully. If any errors occur, they will appear highlighted on the page, and you will need to analyze and fix them before re-running the failover job.

FIGURE 2-19 Failover job summary page.

24. When the failover is complete, browse to the failed-over VM in the target region, log in to the VM, and validate that your application, database, or required services are online and working as intended.

Now it's time to commit the VM. When you commit the VM, you will no longer be able to change the recovery point. Committing the VM will allow you to set up re-protect to enable the sync of the failed-over VM back to the source location, if required.

25. Back in the **Overview** page in the SourceVM replica's configuration blade (see Figure 2-20), click the **Commit** button. Then, when prompted, click the **Confirm** button.

FIGURE 2-20   Click the Commit button.

Now you can set up re-protection for the failed-over VM with the source VM. This provides redundancy for the failed-over VM in case of a disaster in the new site.

26. To set up re-protection, in the **Overview** page in the SourceVM's Replicated Items configuration blade, click the **Re-protect** button.

27. In the **Re-protect** page (see Figure 2-21), validate or customize the settings as needed and click **OK** to start the re-protection job.

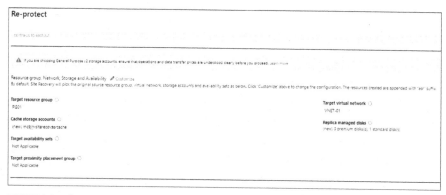

FIGURE 2-21   Re-protect page.

28. Monitor the progress of the re-protection job to confirm that all the steps finish successfully. (See Figure 2-22.)

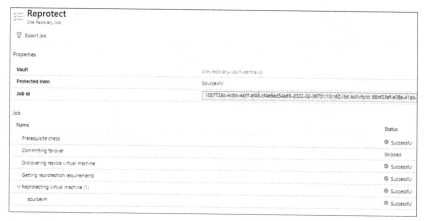

FIGURE 2-22   Reprotect page for the Site Recovery job.

29. When the re-protection job is complete, return to the **Overview** page in the SourceVM's configuration blade to monitor the replication status. (See Figure 2-23.) When Status is at 100% or Healthy, you can test failover or failover the VM if you want to switch back to your primary site.

FIGURE 2-23 Overview page of the SourceVM replica showing the replication status.

Hyper-V–to–Azure disaster recovery

Companies that use Hyper-V with or without System Center Virtual Machine Manager (SCVMM) can benefit from using ASR to set up a disaster recovery for their on-premises environment in Azure. Considering the costs associated with ASR and its comprehensive integration with Hyper-V and SCVMM, it is an ideal solution for organizations of any size.

In the past, setting up a disaster-recovery (DR) site meant hosting infrastructure in another datacenter and managing all the associated networking components, upgrades, and updates for each infrastructure layer on an ongoing basis. Due to the initial setup and ongoing maintenance costs of such a design, most small and mid-size businesses shied away from setting up a DR site, and instead relied on offsite backups for their recovery strategy. Today, however, thanks to cost benefits and ease of management and maintenance, all organizations can benefit from ASR.

ASR supports Hyper-V hosts starting from Windows Server 2012 R2 (with the latest updates) to the latest Windows Server release. Similarly, for VMM, the minimum supported version is Virtual Machine Manager 2012 R2 to the latest release.

For Hyper-V VMs, you can replicate all VMs that are supported for hosting in Azure. It is therefore important that you check for the most recent guidance from Microsoft published online regarding the latest support matrix for Hyper-V hosts, VMM servers, and Hyper-V VMs. This guidance changes from time to time as different operating systems reach end of life or end of support.

> **NOTE** ASR integrates with Microsoft applications such as SharePoint, Exchange, Dynamics, SQL Server, and Active Directory, and works closely with leading vendors, including Oracle, SAP, IBM, and Red Hat.

Replication components

ASR uses different components, depending on your Hyper-V environment:

- **Hyper-V with VMM/Hyper-V cluster with VMM**   In this scenario (see Figure 2-24), you deploy the ASR Provider agent on the VMM server and the Recovery Services agent on each Hyper-V host. The Hyper-V VMs do not require anything to be installed on them.

- **Hyper-V without VMM/Hyper-V cluster without VMM**   In this scenario, you deploy the ASR Provider agent and Recovery Services agent on each Hyper-V host. The Hyper-V VMs do not require anything to be installed on them. (See Figure 2-25.)

Each scenario requires you to provision a Recovery Services vault, a storage account, and a virtual network in the same Azure region to reference during replication setup. Replication can be set as frequently as every 30 seconds (except in scenarios where premium storage is used for replication) or as infrequently as every 5 minutes, enabling you to achieve extremely low recovery point objectives and low data loss.

> **NOTE**   Although LRS and GRS storage account types are supported, it is recommended to use GRS, if costs permit, so your replicated data is maintained in multiple Azure regions. This way, a failover can be initiated in a secondary region if the primary Azure region is also down when an on-premises outage occurs.

> **NOTE**   Initial replication from on-premises must be performed over the network. Offline replication for the initial data or any subsequent data transfers is not supported.

Replication policy

Similar to Azure–to–Azure replication, you must create a replication policy and associate it with your replication configuration during the DR setup process. This involves setting the following options:

- **Copy Frequency**   This defines how often delta sync occurs after the initial replication is completed. Options range from 30 seconds to 5 minutes.

- **Recovery Point Retention**   This defines how far back in time ASR allows for recovery, as the service retains recovery points based on retention timelines that you define. The maximum supported recovery-point retention at this time is 24 hours.

- **App-Consistent Recovery Points**   These are snapshots of the on-disk data along with all processes, data, and transactions running in memory. They are captured using the Volume Shadow Copy Service on Windows Servers. App-consistent snapshots take longer than crash-consistent snapshots and can add load to the server depending on the available resources and frequency defined. You should test to make sure these snapshots are not causing significant overhead or resize your VM workload to accommodate the additional load. The minimum frequency supported for this snapshot is 1 hour.

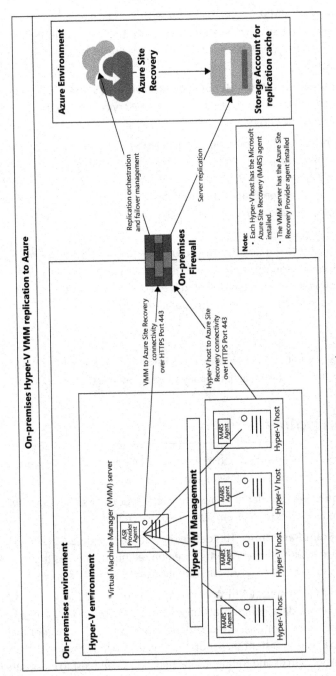

FIGURE 2-24 Hyper-V with VMM/Hyper-V cluster with VMM topology.

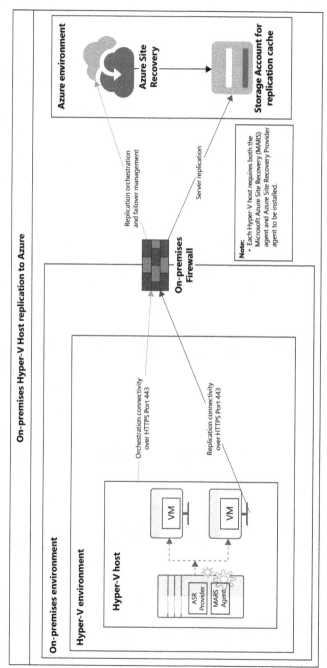

FIGURE 2-25 Hyper-V without VMM/Hyper-V cluster without VMM topology.

You can also define whether the replication should initialize immediately once the configuration is completed or schedule it to be initiated at a later time in the day.

Data security

Similar to the Azure–to–Azure DR scenario, ASR does not intercept, scan, or analyze data transferred between your on-premises and Azure target regions. This makes the entire process transparent to the service and eliminates the risk of the replicated data being used for malicious purposes. ASR only obtains metadata information to monitor replication health and coordinate failover activities. Data is encrypted in transit as well as encrypted while at rest when stored in the target region.

Failover and failback

In case of a disaster in the on-premises Hyper-V environment, you can failover the Azure VM to the target region using the ASR service. You will be asked to select the recovery point to use for the restoration. The target VM will then be created based on settings you've defined and the replicated data.

The target VM is created in an unprotected state. Once the on-premises datacenter is back online, you can set up failback replication for the VM from Azure to the on-premises Hyper-V host. At this time, you can choose to either perform a delta sync, during which ASR will check the source disk for consistency and determine the missing changes to replicate over, or, if that is not possible, to choose the full download option so the entire disk is replicated from Azure back on-premises. (In most cases when the Azure VM has been running for quite a few days, you will have to perform the full download option to set up failback.) Once replicated, you can perform a failback in the same manner as the failover whenever you have the appropriate amount of downtime available.

Test, planned, and unplanned failovers

Similar to Azure–to–Azure disaster recovery, ASR supports test and planned failover options even for Hyper-V VMs replicating to Azure. In addition, it supports unplanned failover in case the primary site has gone offline without giving you the ability to perform a graceful failover to Azure.

In a test failover, ASR creates a VM in a test network defined by you, with the replicated data for that Hyper-V VM. It is recommended that you set up an isolated test network without connectivity to the primary network to avoid accidental writes from test applications to the primary database or other unexpected issues. The test VM does not commit write operations to the replication data. This enables you to make changes to the test VM—for example, application or database upgrades—without affecting the primary server or the replication in any way. You can perform test failovers to validate your VM and its workload failover as needed in Azure to perform application or database upgrade testing or for compliance auditory reasons. This can also help in scenarios in which you are running low on resources on-premises and need a temporary test environment to quickly validate application changes. When you are finished testing, you can simply clean up the test environment; the test VM and associated disks will be deleted from Azure, while the original replication on-premises continues unimpeded.

During a planned failover, ASR performs a final delta sync from on-premises Hyper-V to ensure all changes are replicated to Azure. Thereafter, a VM is built based on the target configuration and brought online in the defined Azure region. The VM allows changes to be committed to disk. Although the changes are not replicated to the primary region, replication from the primary site is stopped, and the primary VM is shut down before the failover is initiated. Use this option in scenarios when you are migrating from on-premises to Azure.

If your on-premises environment is already offline, you will have to perform an unplanned failover. In such a scenario, ASR is unable to replicate any final changes from the on-premises VM. It will allow you to choose from one of the already replicated recovery points, however.

Network requirements

ASR primarily uses the public internet to replicate data directly to Azure Storage public endpoints. Replication occurs over SSL, ensuring data is protected during transit. Replication over a point-to-site (P2S) or site-to-site (S2S) VPN is not supported at this time. You must ensure your Hyper-V hosts have access to the Azure Storage endpoints over the internet for data transfers to take place.

Although P2S and S2S connectivity is not supported, ASR does support replication over ExpressRoute connections from on-premises to the Azure datacenter in which you are hosting your DR site. You must set up the Azure Storage used for storing replication logs to use ExpressRoute with Microsoft peering for this to work.

Hyper-V–to–Azure disaster recovery walkthrough

The following section walks you through the process of setting up and testing Hyper-V (without VMM)–to–Azure replication for a VM using the Azure Portal.

PREREQUISITES   To build the base environment required to perform the steps in this walkthrough, you need a basic understanding of installing and configuring Hyper-V hosts, and of creating, configuring, and managing Hyper-V VMs.

IMPORTANT   Before you begin, review all the prerequisites and ensure your Hyper-V hosts and VMs are updated and compatible for replication to Azure.

IMPORTANT   If you are following along, you'll want to select resources and unique resource names based on your environment for each of your deployments.

IMPORTANT If you are following along, delete any unwanted resources after you have completed testing to reduce charges being levied by Microsoft for these resources.

Using the Azure Portal

Setting up Hyper-V–to–Azure replication using the Azure Portal involves creating a Recovery Services vault, preparing the infrastructure, preparing your Hyper-V servers, configuring Hyper-V replication, setting up replication, customizing the configuration, performing test and planned failovers, and completing the migration. Follow these steps:

CREATE RECOVERY SERVICES VAULT

1. Start by creating the Recovery Services vault. To do so, log in to the Azure Portal, type **recovery service vaults** in the search box, and select it from the list that appears. (See Figure 2-26.)

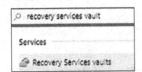

FIGURE 2-26 Search for the Recovery Services vault service.

2. Click **Create** or **Create Recovery Services Vault** to start the Create Recovery Services Vault wizard. (See Figure 2-27.)

FIGURE 2-27 Click Create Recovery Services Vault.

3. In the **Basics** tab of the Create Recovery Services Vault wizard (see Figure 2-28), enter the information, and click **Next**:

   ▪ **Subscription**   Select the subscription that will host the vault.

   ▪ **Resource Group**   Select the resource group you want to use to host the Recovery Services vault. Alternatively, to create a new resource group, click the **Create New** link and follow the prompts.

- **Vault Name**   Type a name for the vault. If the name you type is already in use, the wizard will prompt you to select another name.

- **Region**   Select the Azure region in which you want to host the vault.

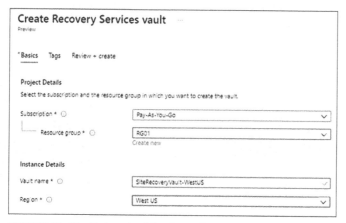

FIGURE 2-28   The Basics tab of the Create Recovery Services Vault wizard.

4. In the **Tags** tab, enter any tags you would like to associate with the vault or leave the fields blank (see Figure 2-29) and click **Next**.

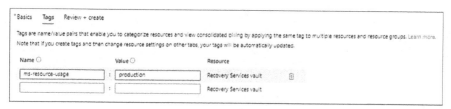

FIGURE 2-29   The Tags tab of the Create Recovery Services Vault wizard.

5. In the **Review + Create** tab (see Figure 2-30), review your settings and click **Create**.

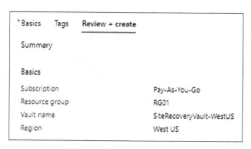

FIGURE 2-30   The Review + Create tab of the Create Recovery Services Vault wizard.

INTEGRATE HYPER-V ENVIRONMENT FOR REPLICATION

6. After the Recovery Services vault is deployed, click the **Go to Resource** button to access its configuration options.

7. In the Recovery Services vault's configuration page, click the **Enable Site Recovery** button to begin creating the necessary ASR infrastructure. (See Figure 2-31.)

FIGURE 2-31   Site Recovery Vault-West US overview page.

8. On the **Protect Your Infrastructure for Disaster Recovery** page (see Figure 2-32), under **Hyper-V Machines to Azure**, click the **Prepare Infrastructure** link to launch the Prepare Infrastructure wizard.

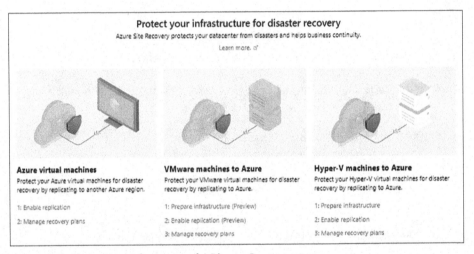

FIGURE 2-32   Protect Your Infrastructure for Disaster Recovery page.

9. In the **Deployment Planning** tab of the Prepare Infrastructure wizard (see Figure 2-33), open the **Deployment Planning Completed?** drop-down list and choose **I Will Do It Later**. Then click **Next**.

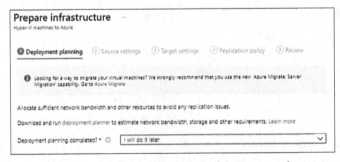

FIGURE 2-33   The Deployment Planning tab of the Prepare Infrastructure wizard.

10. In the **Source Settings** tab, next to **Are You Using System Center VMM to Manage Hyper-V Hosts?**, select the **No** option button.

11. Next to **Hyper-V Site**, click the **Add Hyper-V Site** link. (See Figure 2-34.)

FIGURE 2-34 The Source Settings tab of the Prepare Infrastructure wizard.

12. In the **Create Hyper-V Site** pop-up (see Figure 2-35), under **Name**, enter a unique name for the site. Then click **Create**.

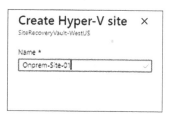

FIGURE 2-35 Create Hyper-V Site pop-up.

13. Back in the **Source Settings** tab of the Prepare Infrastructure wizard, open the **Hyper-V Site** drop-down list and choose the site you just created. (See Figure 2-36.)

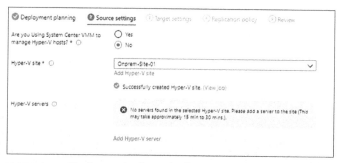

FIGURE 2-36 The Source Settings tab of the Prepare Infrastructure wizard with the Hyper-V site listed.

14. Next to **Hyper-V Servers**, click the **Add Hyper-V Server** link to start the Add Server wizard.

15. In the Add Server wizard (see Figure 2-37), do the following:

- Click the **Download** link in step 3 to download the Microsoft ASR Provider agent for Hyper-V.

- Click the **Download** link in step 4 to download the vault registration key. Save this key in a safe location on your hard drive, as you will need it later for the host registration.

FIGURE 2-37 Add Server wizard.

16. Copy the installer and vault registration key to each of the Hyper-V hosts and run the installer on each.

    Now you're ready to prepare your Hyper-V servers.

17. Run the installer to launch the Azure Site Recovery Provider Setup (Hyper-V Server) wizard. (You'll do this for each Hyper-V host.)

18. On the **Microsoft Update** page (see Figure 2-38), select the **On** option button to automatically check for Microsoft updates, and click **Next**.

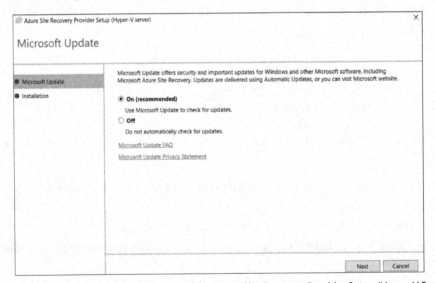

FIGURE 2-38 Microsoft Update page of the Azure Site Recovery Provider Setup (Hyper-V Server) wizard.

19. On the **Installation** page (see Figure 2-39), click the **Browse** button and select the location where you want to install the Provider agent. Then click **Install**.

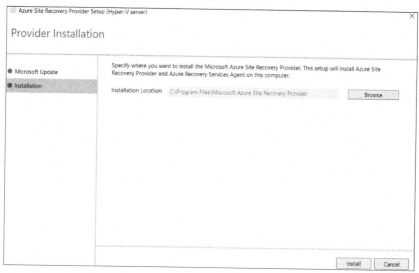

FIGURE 2-39 Provider Installation page of the Azure Site Recovery Provider Setup (Hyper-V Server) wizard.

20. Confirm that the agent is installed successfully. (See Figure 2-40.) Then click **Register** to start the Microsoft Azure Site Recovery Registration wizard.

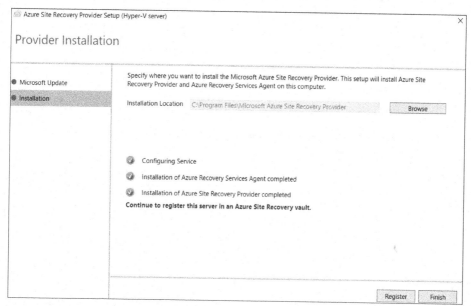

FIGURE 2-40 Confirm that the agent is installed successfully and click Register.

21. In the **Vault Settings** page of the Microsoft Azure Site Recovery Registration wizard (see Figure 2-41), click **Browse**, locate and select the vault registration key you copied in step 16, and click **Next**.

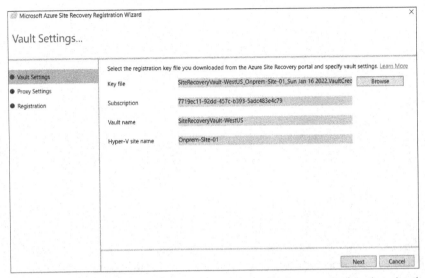

FIGURE 2-41 Vault Settings page of the Microsoft Azure Site Recovery Registration wizard.

22. On the **Proxy Settings** page (see Figure 2-42), select the **Connect Directly to Azure Site Recovery Without a Proxy Server** option button (as shown here) or the **Connect to Azure Site Recovery Using a Proxy Server** option button, depending on how internet connectivity is managed in your environment, and click **Next**.

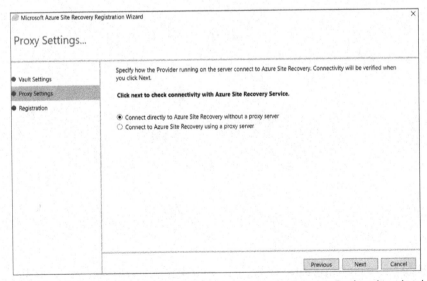

FIGURE 2-42 Proxy Settings page of the Microsoft Azure Site Recovery Registration wizard.

23. On the **Registration** page, monitor the progress of the registration process. When it is complete, click **Finish**. (See Figure 2-43.)

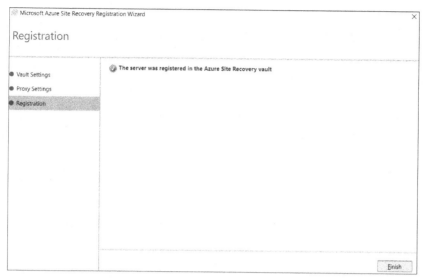

FIGURE 2-43 Proxy Settings page of the Microsoft Azure Site Recovery Registration wizard.

24. Back in the **Source Settings** tab of the Prepare Infrastructure wizard, confirm that the host you registered appears in the list of Hyper-V servers (see Figure 2-44), and click **Next**.

> **NOTE** It can take 15 to 30 minutes for the registered host to appear in the Source Settings page of the Prepare Infrastructure wizard.

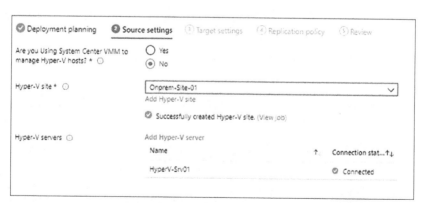

FIGURE 2-44 The Source Settings tab of the Prepare Infrastructure wizard with the Hyper-V server listed.

25. In the **Target Settings** tab, open the **Subscription** drop-down list and select the subscription in which you want to create the replication.

26. Leave **Post-Failover Deployment Model** set to **Resource Manager** (the default).

If you have provisioned the necessary storage accounts and networks in the target region, you'll see them listed in the Target Settings tab. (See Figure 2-45.) If not, you'll see error messages prompting you to provision them. (See Figure 2-46.)

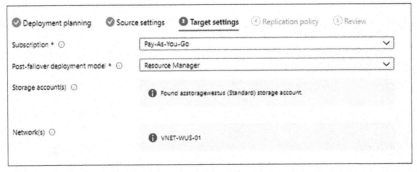

FIGURE 2-45 Target Settings tab in the Prepare Infrastructure wizard with storage accounts and networks correctly provisioned.

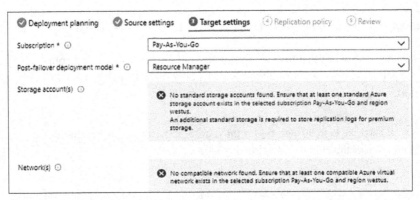

FIGURE 2-46 Target Settings tab in the Prepare Infrastructure wizard without storage accounts and networks correctly provisioned.

27. In the **Replication Policy** tab (see Figure 2-47), under the Replication Policy drop-down list, click the **Create New Policy and Associate** link.

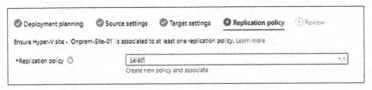

FIGURE 2-47 Replication Policy tab of the Prepare Infrastructure wizard.

28. In the **Create and Associate Policy** dialog box (see Figure 2-48), enter the following information and click **Create**:

- **Name**   Enter a unique name for the policy.

- **Source Type**   Select **Hyper-V**.
- **Target Type**   Select **Azure**.
- **Copy Frequency**   Select a value between 5 and 15 minutes.
- **Recovery-Point Retention in Hours**   Enter the recovery-point retention period.
- **App-Consistent Snapshot Frequency in Hours**   Enter the app-consistent snapshot frequency.
- **Initial Replication Start Time**   Select **Immediately**. Alternatively, choose a specific time to start the replication.

FIGURE 2-48   Create and Associate Policy dialog box.

29. Back in the **Replication Policy** tab of the Prepare Infrastructure wizard, confirm that the replication policy was successfully created and associated (see Figure 2-49) and click **Next**.

FIGURE 2-49   Replication Policy tab in the Prepare Infrastructure wizard with the replication policy successfully created and associated.

30. In the **Review** tab (see Figure 2-50), review your settings and click **Finish**.

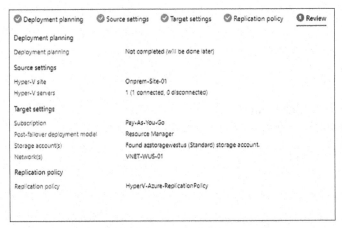

FIGURE 2-50 Review tab in the Prepare Infrastructure wizard.

Now you can set up replication.

SETUP REPLICATION

31. Switch to the Site Recovery service and, under **Hyper-V Machines to Azure**, click **Enable Replication** to start the Enable Replication wizard.

32. In the **Source Environment** tab of the Enable Replication wizard, open the **Source Location** drop-down list and select the Hyper-V site configuration you created earlier. (See Figure 2-51.) Then click **Next**.

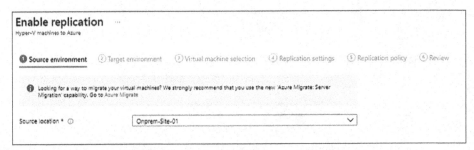

FIGURE 2-51 Source Environment tab of the Enable Replication wizard.

33. In the **Target Environment** tab (see Figure 2-52), enter the following information and click **Next**:

- **Subscription** Select the subscription you want to set as the target environment.
- **Post-Failover Resource Group** Select the resource group you want to use.
- **Post-Failover Deployment Model** Select **Resource Manager**.
- **Storage Account** Select the storage account to use.
- **Network** Select **Configure Now for Selected Machines**.

- **Virtual Network**   Select the virtual network to use.

- **Subnet**   Select the subnet to use.

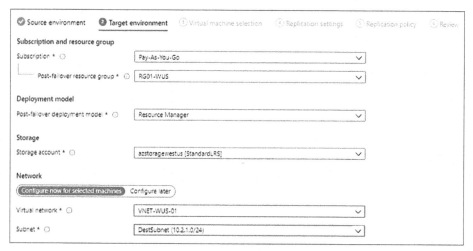

FIGURE 2-52   Target Environment tab of the Enable Replication wizard.

34. In the **Virtual Machine Selection** tab (see Figure 2-53), select the VMs for which you want to enable replication and click **Next**.

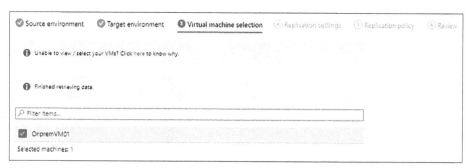

FIGURE 2-53   Virtual Machine Selection tab of the Enable Replication wizard.

35. In the **Replication Settings** tab (see Figure 2-54), for each VM selected in the previous step, select the OS type, OS disk, and disks to replicate, and click **Next**.

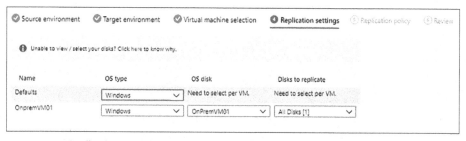

FIGURE 2-54   Replication Settings tab of the Enable Replication wizard.

36. In the **Replication Policy** tab (see Figure 2-55), select the replication policy you created earlier and click **Next**.

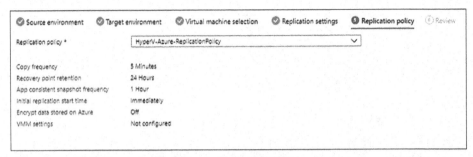

FIGURE 2-55 Replication Policy tab of the Enable Replication wizard.

37. In the **Review** tab (see Figure 2-56), check your settings and click **Enable Replication**.

FIGURE 2-56 Review tab of the Enable Replication wizard.

38. On the **Enable Replication** page (see Figure 2-57), monitor the progress of the job to ensure that all the steps complete successfully. If any errors occur, they will appear highlighted on the page, and you will need to analyze and fix them before re-running the enable replication process.

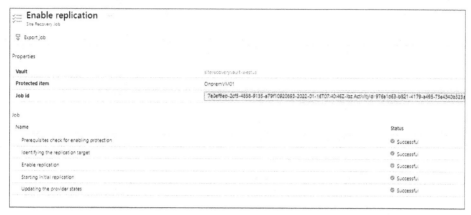

FIGURE 2-57 Enable Replication page.

39. When replication is enabled, switch to the **Overview** page for the replicated VM in the Recovery Services vault (see Figure 2-58). Notice that **Replication Health** shows **Healthy**, and **Status** shows the amount of replication that has been completed thus far. When **Status** reaches **100%** or **Protected**, you can proceed to the next steps.

FIGURE 2-58 Overview page of the replicated VM's configuration blade.

40. In the left pane of the replicated VM's configuration blade, click the **Compute and Network** option to access all compute and network settings for the replicating VM. (See Figure 2-59.) You can edit any or most of the settings shown on this page based on your requirements.

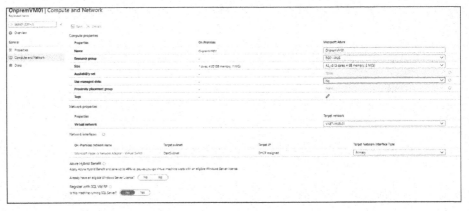

FIGURE 2-59 Compute and Network options.

41. Repeat steps 17–40 for all replicated VMs.

TEST FAILOVER

42. Repeat steps 14–16 in the "Test Failover" section of the Azure–to–Azure disaster recovery walkthrough to perform a test failover to validate that the replicated machines will work correctly in Azure after a failover.

CLEANUP TEST FAILOVER

43. Repeat steps 17–20 in the "Cleanup Test Failover" section of the Azure–to–Azure disaster recovery walkthrough to perform a cleanup after successful failover testing.

PERFORM FAILOVER

44. After you complete a successful test failover, repeat steps 20–24 in the "Perform Failover" section of the Azure–to–Azure disaster recovery walkthrough to fail over the VM(s) to Azure.

45. Log in to the VM to confirm that your workload is working correctly.

46. Switch to the **Overview** page for the replicated VM in the Recovery Services vault (see Figure 2-60) and click **Complete Migration**.

FIGURE 2-60 Overview page of the replicated VM's configuration blade.

47. In the **Complete Migration** page, read the message about what completing migration entails and click **OK**.

48. Monitor the migration job to ensure that all the steps completed successfully. (See Figure 2-61.)

FIGURE 2-61   Complete Migration page.

Recovery plans

Recovery plans help you to define groups of interconnected and interdependent VMs to failover together in an orchestrated manner. You can also separate interdependent VMs that require other services to be online, before they are brought online into different groups, and sequence them accordingly.

At this time, ASR supports the creation of a maximum of seven groups, and a maximum of 100 protected VMs can be managed in a single recovery plan. If you have more VMs, you will have to define multiple recovery plans. You also need to plan and identify the right group to associate a VM within a recovery plan based on its dependency on services running in other VMs. For example, you want to bring database VMs online before bringing application VMs online so that application services do not error out when trying to connect to the database. Similarly, you want to bring Active Directory and DNS services online before bringing database servers online because SQL services running using AD service accounts would fail in the absence of an active DC in the network.

Recovery plans help you both in failover to Azure and failback from Azure. In addition, you can use scripts to perform additional activities before and after a group is brought online. This can include creation of other Azure resources such as Firewall, NAT gateways, application gateways, and so on, or triggering runbooks that carry out a set of activities.

The same VM can be part of multiple recovery plans. Based on the order in which a recovery plan is triggered, if a VM in one recovery plan is already online, the subsequent plan will ignore it during its sequence.

The benefits of using a recovery plan are as follows:

- It supports the structured activation of VMs in Azure.

- Interdependent or connected services can be brought online gracefully.

- Other dependent services, such as Firewall, WAF, NSG, Public IP, and so on, can be built in parallel and need not be pre-provisioned, reducing costs.
- It supports task automation, reducing overall recovery time.
- It can be used to test failover to ensure that the VMs function as needed after failover without any manual intervention.

Recovery plan walkthrough

The following section walks you through the process of creating a recovery plan for five VMs replicated to Azure using the Azure Portal. Make sure that you set up replication for multiple VMs first to be able to create the recovery plan with multiple groups.

USING THE AZURE PORTAL

To create a recovery plan using the Azure Portal, follow these steps:

1. Locate and select the Recovery Services vault you created earlier for VM replication.
2. In the left pane of the Recovery Services vault's configuration blade, under **Manage**, click **Recovery Plans (Site Recovery)**. (See Figure 2-62.)

FIGURE 2-62 Click the Recovery Plans (Site Recovery) option.

3. In the right pane, click **Recovery Plan**. (See Figure 2-63.)

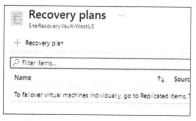

FIGURE 2-63 Create a recovery plan.

4. In the Create Recovery Plan dialog box (see Figure 2-64), enter the following information:

- **Name** Enter a unique name for the recovery plan.
- **Source** Select the source Hyper-V site.
- **Target** Select **Microsoft Azure**.
- **Allow Items with Deployment Model** Leave this set to **Resource Manager** (the default).

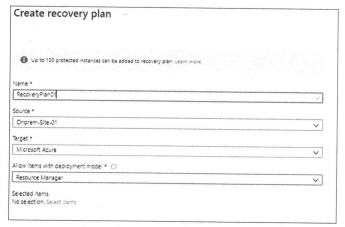

FIGURE 2-64 Create Recovery Plan dialog box.

5. Under **Selected Items**, click the **Select Items** link. Then, in the **Select Items** pane, select the VMs to include in the recovery plan. (See Figure 2-65.)

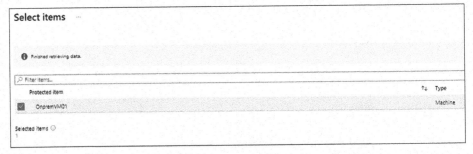

FIGURE 2-65 Select the VMs to include in the recovery plan.

6. After you select all the required VMs, click the **Create** button to create the recovery plan. (See Figure 2-66.)

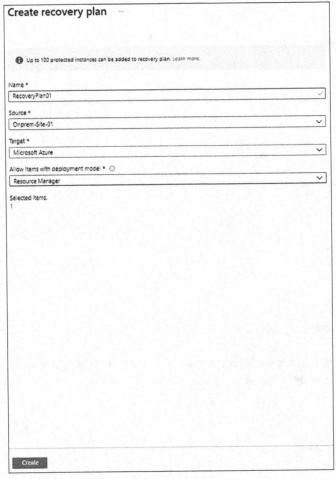

FIGURE 2-66 Create the recovery plan.

7. After the plan is created, go to its **Overview** tab. (See Figure 2-67.)

FIGURE 2-67 Overview tab of Recoveryplan01.

8. Click the **Customize** button.

9. Use any of the following options to customize the recovery plan. (See Figure 2-68.)

   ■ **Group** Create new groups in the plan to group VMs together for activation during the failover process.

   ■ **Save** Save changes made to the plan.

   ■ **Discard** Discard changes made to the plan.

   ■ **Change Group** Change the order of the VMs in a single group or across groups.

> **TIP** You can also add custom steps to perform at the start or end of a group activation.

FIGURE 2-68 Customize the recovery plan.

10. Back in the recovery plan's **Overview** tab, click **Test Failover** or **Failover**.

11. In the **Test Failover** or **Failover** dialog box (see Figure 2-69), specify the direction of the failover, the recovery point, and whether the source VMs should be shut down. Then click **Test Failover** or **Failover**.

FIGURE 2-69 The Failover dialog box.

12. When the test failover or failover job is initiated, monitor it until it completes success-fully. (See Figure 2-70.)

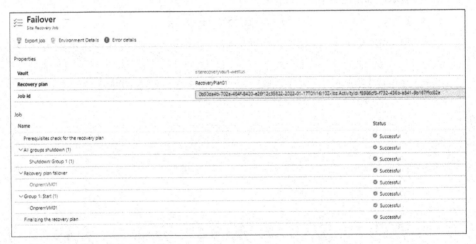

FIGURE 2-70 Failover job status page.

13. When the test failover or failover is complete, log in to the VM and verify that your application, database, or workload is working correctly.

14. In the VM's **Overview** page (see Figure 2-71), click the **Commit** button to ensure no further changes are made to your workload.

FIGURE 2-71 Overview tab of the VM configuration.

15. When prompted, click **OK** to confirm that you want to commit the VM and start the commit job.

16. Monitor the job progress to make sure all the job steps complete successfully. (See Figure 2-72.)

FIGURE 2-72 Commit job page.

Best practices

Following are some general best practices for building and maintaining your ASR environment:

- **Use service tags to reduce complexity in network security rules** Service tags are a great way to manage traffic rules associated with Azure services. Use service tags whenever possible to reduce the management overhead of tracking and maintaining service changes that could potentially affect communications with the ASR service.

- **Use RBAC ASR roles** Azure provides three RBAC roles specifically for ASR to enable you to granularly control access to the service. Use these roles to restrict access to admins based on their administrative activities in your environment. These roles include the following:

- **Site Recovery Contributor** This role provides all access to ASR components and operations. Recommended for DR administrators in charge of maintaining and managing your DR environment.

- **Site Recovery Operator** This role limits access to initiating failover and failback operations. Recommended for administrators in charge of DR failover and failback in the absence of the DR administrators.

- **Site Recovery Reader** This role limits access to viewing ASR configuration and management operations. Recommended for administrators in charge of monitoring the DR environment but not performing any further administrative actions.

- **Use test failover functionality** The test failover option in ASR is a great way to test application updates and upgrades and validate that your DR is working as expected before the need to trigger an actual DR operation arises. Use this functionality at least once to ensure your DR plan works as intended.

- **Perform regular DR drills** It is highly recommended that you perform regular DR drills so that administrators and business teams are aware of all the procedures to activate when the need arises. Clearly document the different roles and activities in your DR plan to avoid confusion.

- **Use Accelerated Networking in Azure–to–Azure scenarios** Accelerated Networking is a feature available for Azure VMs that enables single root I/O virtualization (SR-IOV) to the Azure VM. This improves the network performance of the VM by bypassing the host from the network data path. If Accelerated Networking can benefit your VM in Azure, set up the configuration even for the target VM in the secondary Azure region as part of the ASR configuration.

- **Exclude unwanted disks from replication configuration** ASR enables you to exclude unwanted disks from the replication configuration. This can reduce storage usage on the Azure end and speed up replication as bandwidth usage is optimized. Examples of such disks include the SQL Server tempdb disk and the paging file disk on a Windows VM.

- **Monitor app-consistent backups for performance** Use app-consistent backups for your application as far as possible but ensure that you monitor your on-premises environment for the impact associated with the frequency of the snapshots. If you notice a detrimental impact, you may need to increase resources to your on-premises workloads or reduce the snapshot frequency.

- **Build recovery plans for each unique application** It is a good practice to build a recovery plan for each unique application if multiple servers need to be placed online for that application. This helps you bring individual applications online for testing as and when needed. This also helps you in including any scripts and steps exclusively required for each application within its respective recovery plan, making it easier to track and manage this on a regular basis.

Chapter 3

Azure Migrate

Overview

Microsoft introduced Azure Migrate in November of 2017 to consolidate a set of Azure services to discover, assess, and migrate on-premises workloads to the Azure Cloud. Initially, the service was limited to assessing and migrating VMware virtual machines (VMs) to Azure. Over time, however, Microsoft added new features to the service to allow you to migrate a number of different workloads, including the following:

- VMs
- Web applications
- Databases
- Large amounts of data not associated with VMs, databases, or web apps
- Virtual Desktop Infrastructure (VDI) running in on-premises or co-located datacenters or other cloud services such as Amazon Web Services (AWS) or Google Cloud Platform (GCP)

Azure Migrate service centralizes tools provided by Microsoft and integrated third-party solutions used for the discovery, assessment, and migration of workloads. Currently, third-party solutions include RackWare, Carbonite, and Cloudamize, among many others. Each solution provides different capabilities that are specialized in different workloads based on your individual needs. More importantly, Azure Migrate provides an integrated set of discovery, assessment, and migration tools from Microsoft itself that work seamlessly together for the migration of a majority of workloads. It is therefore important to identify which solution will work best in your environment before choosing which one to use.

> **NOTE** This chapter focuses on the tools provided by Microsoft as part of the Azure Migrate service.

Key features

The key features of the Azure Migrate service are as follows:

- **Centralized migration service**   Azure Migrate consolidates all the different tools provided by Microsoft to discover, assess, and migrate workloads to Azure. This enables you to easily track, monitor, and manage all your migrations.

- **Support for different workloads**   Azure Migrate provides the capability to assess and migrate workloads such as VMs, databases, web apps, data storage, and VDI.

- **Support for different source platforms**   Azure Migrate provides the assessment and migration capabilities of specific workloads hosted on different infrastructure platforms such as Hyper-V, VMware, and physical servers.

- **Support for different cloud platforms**   Azure Migrate provides the assessment and migration capabilities of specific workloads hosted on different cloud platforms such as Amazon Web Services (AWS) and Google Cloud Platform (GCP).

- **Extensibility**   You can extend Azure Migrate functionality using offerings from third-party solution providers, also known as independent software vendors (ISVs). In other words, you can use tools that you are more comfortable with or have prior investments in to achieve your migration objectives.

- **Migration to different services**   Azure Migrate enables you to migrate your workloads to different Azure services such as Azure VMs, Azure SQL Database, Azure SQL Managed Instance, Azure App Service, Azure Virtual Desktop, and Azure Storage. So, you can optimize your migration and use cloud-native solutions to maximize your cloud investments.

The following sections discuss some of the various tools provided by Microsoft to assess and migrate your workloads.

Assessment tools

Assessment tools include the following:

- **Azure Migrate Discovery and Assessment Tool**   This tool enables you to discover and assess on-premises physical servers and Hyper-V- or VMware-based VMs. It requires the deployment of a lightweight appliance on a VM or physical server in the on-premises environment to perform an agent-based or agentless assessment that sends continuous server metadata and performance data to Azure. It then generates readiness reports to provide you with clarity on:

  - Whether the on-premises workload meets the prerequisites for migration to Azure.
  - The estimated size and VM SKU the workload could use post-migration.
  - Associated dependencies with other servers that would need to be incorporated into the migration plan.
  - The estimated costs for running the workloads in Azure post-migration.

- **Data Migration Assistant**   You can use this tool to assess on-premises SQL Server workloads for migration to Azure SQL Database, Azure SQL Managed Instance, or SQL Server hosted on Azure VMs. It can help identify potential migration roadblocks, migration approaches, and strategies based on the assessment to ensure the migration is as efficient as possible.
- **Web App Migration Assistant**   This free tool enables you to assess on-premises websites and web apps for migration to Azure App Service. It provides tools to easily and automatically assess on-premises .NET, Java, and Linux web apps.

Migration tools

Migration tools include the following:

- **Azure Migrate Server Migration Tool**   This tool enables you to migrate on-premises physical servers and Hyper-V- or VMware-based VMs to Azure VMs. It also supports the migration of VMs hosted in other cloud services such as AWS and GCP. You can perform data synchronization in different ways for each of the different source's platforms:
  - **Hyper-V**   You can use provider agents installed on the Hyper-V host migration without requiring the deployment of agents on the VMs.
  - **Physical servers**   Physical servers include servers hosted in AWS, GCP, and standalone ESX hosts, along with servers in a traditional physical server infrastructure. Migration of physical servers requires the use of a replication appliance, which you deploy in the on-premises environment to sync the initial data and data changes to the Azure cloud.
  - **VMware**   You can perform VMware migration using either an agentless or agent-based approach. The agentless approach uses the discovery and assessment appliance, whereas the agent-based approach requires the deployment of a replication appliance in the onpremises environment. VMware migration requires a vCenter appliance to be in place for integration; otherwise, for standalone ESX hosts, the migration must be performed using the same approach as physical servers, using a replication appliance.
  - **Azure Database Migration Service**   This tool enables you to automatically migrate various databases to Azure services, including Azure SQL Database, Azure SQL Managed Instance, SQL Servers running on Azure VMs, Azure Database for MySQL, Azure Database for PostgreSQL, and others with minimal downtime.
  - **Web App Migration Assistant**   In addition to providing assessment capabilities, this tool offers migration capabilities to move your on-premises .NET, Java, or Linux web apps to Azure App Service.
  - **Azure Data Box**   This tool includes different products, such as Data Box, Data Box Disk, Data Box Gateway, and Data Box Heavy to migrate large amounts of data to Azure Storage.

Deployment concepts and considerations

Now that you have a sense of the various features and integrated tools provided by Microsoft within the Azure Migrate service, let's discuss the Azure Migrate Discovery and Assessment Tool and the Azure Migrate Server Migration Tool.

Azure Migrate Discovery and Assessment Tool

One of the most important steps in any migration is to perform a discovery and assessment of your on-premises environment to gain better insight into your workloads and how effectively they will support migration to Azure. Based on the platform(s) on which your on-premises servers are hosted, and on the Azure service that you intend to migrate them to, you will need to use various tools for this discovery and assessment.

To perform discovery and assessment of on-premises Windows or Linux virtual machines hosted on Hyper-V, VMware, or physical servers, you deploy the Azure Migrate appliance that is part of the Azure Migrate Discovery and Assessment Tool. You can deploy the appliance using an Open Virtualization Appliance (OVA) template, Hyper-V VHD, or a PowerShell script, depending on the source platform. The appliance can perform discovery using the vCenter server or Hyper-V hosts set up during appliance configuration, and you can select the VMs that you would like to assess post-discovery. In the case of physical servers, you will need to define the administrative credentials and their IP address/hostnames for the appliance to query and connect to those servers to perform an assessment. VMs hosted in other solutions such as AWS or GCP will need to be set up for discovery and assessment similar to physical servers.

In each scenario, there is a set of Windows and Linux OS versions that are supported by the appliance for discovery and assessment. You will need to refer to Microsoft's publicly available guidance on the latest supported release when you perform your build. This guidance changes based on the end of support or end of life of various Windows and Linux OS releases.

Hypervisor OS version support is also updated on a regular basis based on the OEM's support guidelines. For example, at present, the appliance supports the use of Hyper-V hosts running on Windows Server 2019, Windows Server 2016, and Windows Server 2012 R2. Any version older than this—for example, Windows Server 2012 or Windows Server 2008 R2—is not supported.

> **TIP** Check the supported hypervisor versions at the time of your build. If your current hypervisor is not patched or up to date, you will need to ensure that the prerequisites are met before attempting to use the appliance in your environment.

The appliance performs discovery of the following:

- The metadata of the discovered servers with server details, including current OS and patch levels, CPU size, RAM, disk, network interfaces, and a host of other information based on the underlying hypervisor

- Installed software, ASP .NET web apps, SQL Server instances, and databases
- Dependencies among different on-premises servers that are in the scope of the discovery (identified through agentless dependency analysis)

For assessments that are more accurate, you can set up the appliance to gather performance data from the servers for a set period. This helps it to accurately identify the right size for the Azure VM and disk SKU for these servers. Based on the time period for which you perform the assessment, the appliance collects data points to gain deeper insights and assign a confidence rating to help you understand how suitable its size recommendations are for production use. This confidence rating will be low if the appliance hasn't been able to collect performance data for a sufficient period of time (or at all).

> **NOTE** If you do not perform performance-based assessments, the appliance will use the size information gathered during the metadata discovery of the servers to ascertain an appropriate size.

Data collected by the appliance—including the metadata of the discovered servers and the performance data—is transferred to Azure over HTTPS and stored in Azure Cosmos DB and Azure Storage with encryption, meaning it is encrypted both during transit and at rest.

Each appliance can support thousands of VMs—a limit that continues to scale upward as Microsoft releases newer versions. You can also deploy multiple appliances in an environment if a single appliance does not meet your needs. See the latest guidance available online to determine the number of servers and hosts supported by the appliance, as the limits differ between Hyper-V, VMware, and physical infrastructure environments, and could change depending on the appliance version that you deploy.

Dependency analysis

Now that you have a better understanding of discovery, let's briefly understand dependency analysis and how it can help in your migrations. *Dependency analysis* identifies dependencies among discovered servers so you can better understand the impact of migrating those servers on other related servers in your environment. This enables you to do the following:

- Take into account potential roadblocks and outages when planning and performing workload migrations.

- Analyze and plan for groups of servers that need to be migrated together to ensure they continue to work correctly post-migration.

- Identify dependencies of which you were unaware so you can remove them before the migration if they are no longer required.

- Communicate with all stakeholders, including the ones responsible for dependent workloads, so they can come together for more cohesive planning and migration.

Azure Migrate supports two types of dependency analysis: agentless and agent-based. Agentless dependency analysis is supported only for VMware-based environments that use vCenter servers and is currently in preview at the time of this writing. For its part, agent-based dependency analysis currently covers a broader set of hypervisors and infrastructure. With the agent-based approach:

- You must deploy the Microsoft Monitoring agent (MMA) and the dependency agent on every on-premises server for which you would like to perform dependency analysis.

- Agents gather information about TCP processes and inbound/outbound connections for each process, including the source and destination server name, process, application name, ports, number of connections, latency, and data-transfer information.

- Data is uploaded to Azure Cosmos DB and Azure Storage for analysis using Azure Log Analytics. Azure then uses Service Map to analyze the data, discover application components on Windows and Linux servers, and identify communication routes between servers and services to create a visualization map.

NOTE If you have servers that do not have internet connectivity, you will need to download and install an additional component called Log Analytics Gateway to capture the local data and upload it to Microsoft Azure. The gateway acts as an interface between your on-premises servers and Azure.

Azure Migrate Server Migration Tool

After you have successfully completed the discovery and assessment phase, you must begin migrating your workloads. First, though, you must develop a migration plan to cover all aspects of the migration. These include the following:

- Pre-migration strategy and activities
- Migration strategy
- Roles and responsibilities
- Post-migration Azure management strategies

Taking a planned approach will help you to ensure that you achieve success on all objectives of the migration project.

At a minimum, your migration plan should encompass the following areas. Depending on the size and complexity of your environment and organization, you may have to plan for other areas not covered here:

- **Server readiness** Ensure that all servers are ready for migration to Azure per the assessment report generated using the Azure Migrate Discovery and Assessment Tool. Any servers not listed as ready for migration must be prepared before the migration plan is finalized.

- **End-of-support hardware** It is a good practice to prioritize end-of-support hardware for migration so you do not need to invest in hardware on-premises to support those servers until the migration can be completed.

- **End-of-support software** It is a good practice to prioritize end-of-support software with extended support in Azure for migration. This can help you obtain extended security updates and support for the server OS. It can also help with legacy applications that cannot currently be hosted on newer OS.

- **Server size** While it is easy to scale server size up and down in Azure, you should use the performance-based assessment option to gain deeper insights into your servers so you can size them more appropriately during their initial move.

- **Licensing analysis** Take advantage of any licensing benefits on offer that can help you reduce your Azure spending. For example, applying Azure Hybrid Use Benefit can reduce the cost of running Windows VMs in Azure. Other OEMs such as Red Hat and SUSE may offer similar benefits, depending on your licensing contract.

- **Dependency assessment** Perform a dependency assessment in your environment to obtain a clearer idea of the interconnectivity of servers and services and to ensure outages are minimized during your migration.

- **Cost planning** Costs associated with the Azure environment (based on the assessment reports) must be in line with your budget. Expect deviations, however, as certain services and components are charged based on usage, which the assessment report will not consider. These include networking, monitoring, and management components such as VPN gateways, firewalls, application gateways, bandwidth usage, VM backups, monitoring, and so on.

- **Testing** The Azure Migrate Server Migration Tool enables you to sync and test your servers in Azure by bringing them online in an isolated test environment. In this way, you can confirm that all your applications and services are working as needed in Azure, without affecting your current workloads.

- **Admin training** Incorporate admin training into your migration strategy so your IT team is well prepared to manage the servers and associated Azure infrastructure post-migration.

The Azure Migrate Server Migration Tool is the primary tool for migrating on-premises servers to Azure VMs. The tool provides two migration options: agentless and agent-based.

Agentless migration is supported only for VMware (with vCenter integration) and Hyper-V-based migrations. For Hyper-V migrations, a replication provider is installed on the Hyper-V hosts to manage the agentless replication process. Using the agentless migration option is not recommended in scenarios where your servers are running in an IOPS-constrained environment. This is because agentless migration uses hypervisor-based snapshots to regularly identify and copy delta changes to Azure, which can degrade performance in environments where IOPS are already constrained.

Agent-based migration is appropriate for any type of migration, including VMware and Hyper-V-based VMs, physical servers, AWS and GCP VMs, XenServer-based VMs, and so on. This approach does not use the hypervisor technologies for replication, and hence can be used to synchronize any workload as long as the prerequisites for the agent are met. The Azure Migrate Discovery and Assessment Tool used to gauge server readiness for Azure will analyze these prerequisites.

In an agentless migration approach, the Azure Migrate Discovery and Assessment appliance handles the agentless replication of data to Azure. In an agent-based migration approach, a replication appliance must be deployed on-premises, and an agent deployed on every server that you will be replicating using this appliance.

The replication appliance has multiple components that work together to handle different tasks:

- Communicate with the on-premises servers, gather replication-related data, and send it to Azure Storage.
- Act as a replication gateway for the data transfer to Azure.
- Perform data caching in case connectivity to Azure goes down.
- Perform data compression and encryption before transfer to Azure.
- Perform push installations of the mobility service agent software on the required servers so that data replication can be set up.

You can deploy the appliance either by using an OVA template or by downloading and installing the replication software on a physical server or VM. Be sure to confirm that the appliance prerequisites are in place before starting with any deployment.

Microsoft regularly updates the appliance and provides the updated installer in the Azure Migrate hub. You can automate updates to your appliance or perform them manually. Be sure that if you opt to update your appliance manually, you put in place a process to do this on an ongoing basis. Microsoft recommends always using the latest version of the replication software.

Networking

Azure Migrate supports replication using the public internet in all scenarios. Data is sent over an encrypted HTTPS channel to the Azure Storage endpoint that you configure. The replication appliance, assessment appliance, and Hyper-V hosts all require port 443 connectivity to various Azure URLs to be able to send outbound replication data to Azure. Check the updated list of these URLs provided by Microsoft to ensure that your servers have the necessary network access.

> **NOTE** Data synchronization over private connections using a combination of Azure Private Link over ExpressRoute or VPN gateways has been introduced in preview in certain regions at the time of this writing. This might change by the time you decide to test or use the Azure Migrate service for your environment.

Scaling

In larger environments, discovery, assessment, and replication can be scaled up depending on the source platform and the replication approach you have chosen for your environment, as detailed here.

Discovery and assessment

In a Hyper-V environment, each Azure Migrate appliance used for discovery and assessment can connect to 300 Hyper-V hosts, and can discover and assess as many as 5,000 VMs. If more capacity is required, you can deploy additional Azure Migrate appliances based on the overall environment requirements.

In a VMware environment, each Azure Migrate appliance used for discovery and assessment can only connect to a single vCenter server and can discover and assess as many as 10,000 VMs. If more capacity is required, you can deploy additional Azure Migrate appliances based on the overall environment requirements.

In a physical server environment (including AWS, GCP, and other hypervisors), each Azure Migrate appliance used for discovery and assessment can discover and assess as many as 1,000 servers. If more capacity is required, you can deploy additional Azure Migrate appliances based on the overall environment requirements.

Replication and migration

You achieve agentless replication in a Hyper-V environment by deploying the Hyper-V replication provider service on the Hyper-V host. In scaling scenarios, there should generally not be an issue, as VMs will be replicated using the provider service installed on individual Hyper-V hosts. As more hosts with additional VMs are added, the installation of the provider agent on the host automatically scales up capacity. If a Hyper-V host is unable to handle the replication load for a subset of VMs, those VMs would need to be moved to alternate Hyper-V hosts for replication.

In agent-based Hyper-V replications, the VMs are treated as physical servers and require the deployment of a primary replication appliance. In a scaling scenario, you can add scale-out appliances to work with the primary configuration and replication server. Each appliance supports as many as 200 VMs for replication at a time; this limit is increasing with newer versions of the appliance.

Agentless VMware replication (with a single vCenter server) uses the migration appliance deployed for environment assessment. The primary migration appliance supports as many as 300 VMs at a time. In scaling scenarios, you can add scale-out migration appliances connected to the primary Azure Migrate appliance that you deployed in the environment. This approach can be used to migrate as many as 500 VMs concurrently based on current limitations.

Agent-based VMware replications require the deployment of a primary replication appliance. This appliance supports between 50 and 100 VMs at a time. In scaling scenarios, you can add scale-out replication appliances connected to the primary replication appliance. This approach can help you synchronize between 50 and 100 additional VMs per scale-out server.

Agent-based physical server migrations (including AWS, GCP, and other hypervisors) require the deployment of a primary replication appliance. This appliance supports between 50 and 100 VMs at a time. In scaling scenarios, you can add scale-out replication appliances connected to the primary replication appliance. This approach can help you synchronize between 50 and 100 additional VMs per scale-out server.

Azure Migrate walkthrough

The following section walks you through the process of setting up Azure Migrate, integrating it with a Hyper-V, and migrating a VM to Azure using the Azure Portal.

PREREQUISITES To build the base environment required to perform the steps in this walkthrough, you need a basic understanding of installing and configuring Hyper-V hosts, and of creating, configuring, and managing Hyper-V VMs.

IMPORTANT Before you begin, review all the prerequisites and ensure your Hyper-V hosts and VMs are updated and compatible for replication to Azure.

IMPORTANT If you are following along, you'll want to select resources and unique resource names based on your environment for each of your deployments.

IMPORTANT If you are following along, delete any unwanted resources after you have completed testing to reduce charges being levied by Microsoft for these resources.

Using Azure Portal

CREATE AZURE MIGRATION APPLIANCE

To set up Azure Migrate and migrate a VM using the Azure Portal, follow these steps:

1. Log in to the Azure Portal, type **azure migrate** in the search box, and select it from the list that appears. (See Figure 3-1.)

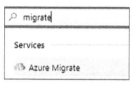

FIGURE 3-1 Search for the Azure Migrate service.

2. Under **Servers, Databases and Web Apps**, click the **Discover, Access and Migrate** button. (See Figure 3-2.)

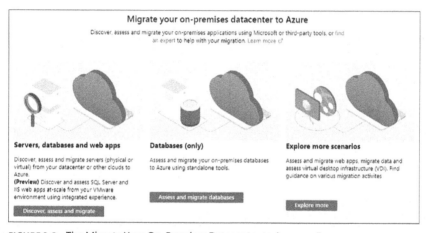

FIGURE 3-2 The Migrate Your On-Premises Datacenter to Azure page.

3. Click the **Create Project** button. (See Figure 3-3.)

FIGURE 3-3 The Create Project button.

4. In the **Create Project** page, enter the following information (see Figure 3-4) and click **Create**:

- **Subscription**   Select the subscription you want to use to create the project.

- **Resource Group**   Select the resource group you want to use to create the project. Alternatively, click the **Create New** link and follow the prompts.

- **Project**   Type a unique name for the project.

- **Geography**   Select the country in which to create the project. Although you can select any country, it is recommended that you choose the country where you intend to host your workloads.

- **Connectivity Method**   Choose **Public Endpoint** or **Private Endpoint** (as shown here).

NOTE   If you choose Private Endpoint, you will be presented with additional options.

FIGURE 3-4   Create Project page.

After the project is created, you will be prompted to set up the discovery process.

5. In the **Azure Migrate: Discovery and Assessment** page, click the **Discover** link. (See Figure 3-5.)

6. On the Discover page (see Figure 3-6), select the following options:

- **Discover Using Appliance**   Click this to select it.

- **Are Your Servers Virtualized**   Choose **Yes, with Hyper-V** from the drop-down list

- **Name Your Appliance**   Enter a unique name for your appliance.

7. Click the **Generate Key** button.

This generates a key file, which you will need later to register the appliance with this Azure Migrate project. Save this key in a safe location.

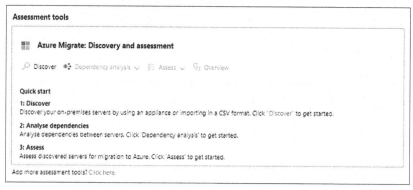

FIGURE 3-5 Azure Migrate: Discovery and Assessment page.

FIGURE 3-6 Discover wizard in the Azure Migrate Discovery and assessment service option.

8. Under **Download Azure Migrate Appliance**, select the **VHD File** option button and click **Download**.

9. When the download is complete, move or copy the downloaded VHD file to your Hyper-V host where you intend to deploy the appliance.

10. Open Hyper-V Manager and connect to the Hyper-V host to which you want to import.

11. Right-click the Hyper-V host in the pane on the left and choose **Import Virtual Machine**. (See Figure 3-7.)

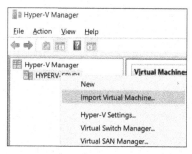

FIGURE 3-7 Importing the VM in Hyper-V Manager.

12. On the **Before You Begin** page of the Import Virtual Machine wizard (see Figure 3-8), click **Next**.

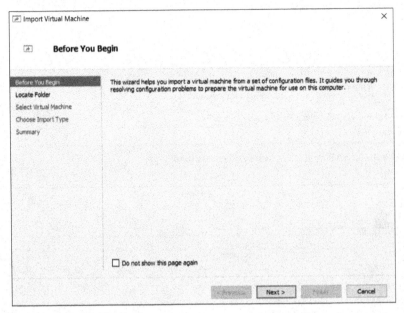

FIGURE 3-8   Before You Begin page.

13. In the **Locate** Folder page (see Figure 3-9), click **Browse**, and select the folder in which you saved the VHD file you downloaded earlier. Then click **Next**.

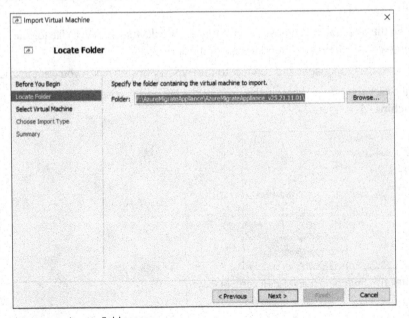

FIGURE 3-9   Locate Folder page.

14. On the **Select Virtual Machine** page (see Figure 3-10), verify that the VM has a name similar to *AzureMigrateAppliance_vXX.XX.XX.XX* and click **Next**.

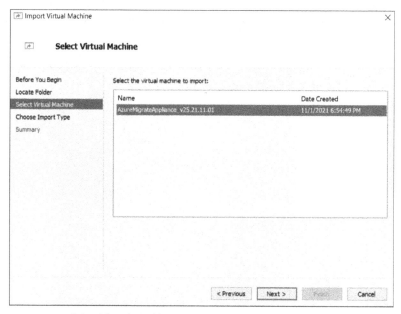

FIGURE 3-10   Select Virtual Machine page.

15. On the **Choose Import Type** page (see Figure 3-11), select **Register the VM In-Place (Use the Existing Unique ID)** or **Copy the VM (Create a New Unique ID)** and click **Next**.

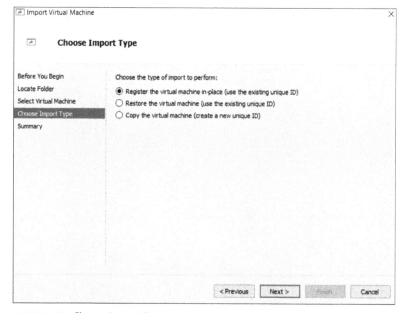

FIGURE 3-11   Choose Import Type page.

16. On the **Connect Network** page (see Figure 3-12), select the virtual switch that will set up the VM in a network that provides internet connectivity once the appliance is online and click **Next**.

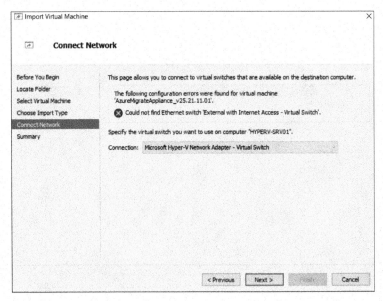

FIGURE 3-12   Connect Network page.

17. On the **Summary** page (see Figure 3-13), check your settings and click **Finish** to import the VM.

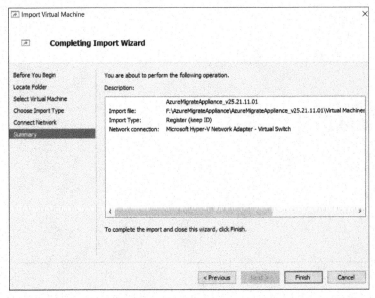

FIGURE 3-13   Summary page.

18. After the VM has been created, connect to it in the Hyper-V console.

19. On the **License Terms** page (see Figure 3-14), read the license terms and click **Accept**.

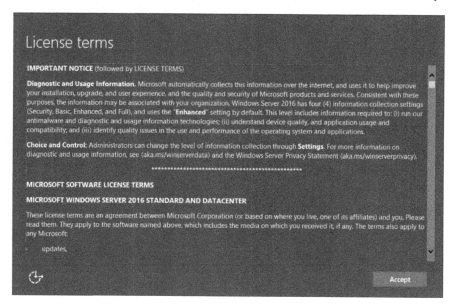

FIGURE 3-14 License Terms page.

20. On the **Customize Settings** page (see Figure 3-15), in the **Password** and **Reenter Password** boxes, enter a secure password for the built-in administrator account. Then click **Finish**.

FIGURE 3-15 Customize Settings page.

21. Use the password you just set up to log in to the VM.

The Microsoft Edge browser opens automatically and connects to the local web server on port 44368 to launch the Appliance Configuration Manager (see Figure 3-16). The manager checks to make sure certain prerequisites have been met. For example, it verifies connectivity to Microsoft Azure, ensures that the appliance is set with the correct date and time, and checks whether there are any updates available to install. If it detects any errors, you will need to rectify them and click the **Rerun Prerequisites** button before you can proceed.

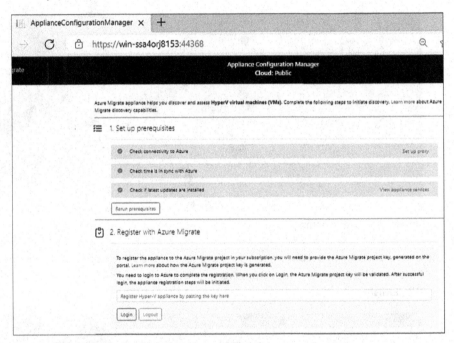

FIGURE 3-16   Appliance Configuration Manager wizard.

22. Under **Register with Azure Migrate** (see Figure 3-17), copy the key you generated earlier, paste it into the box, and click the **Login** button.

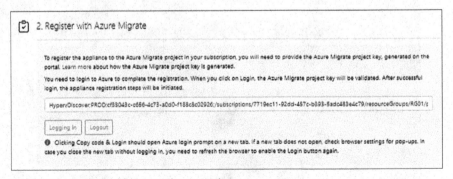

FIGURE 3-17   Register with Azure Migrate section.

23. In the **Continue with Azure Login** pop-up box (see Figure 3-18), click the **Copy Code & Login** button.

FIGURE 3-18 Continue with Azure Login pop-up box.

24. A new tab opens in Microsoft Edge that prompts you to enter the code you copied earlier (see Figure 3-19). Paste in the code and click **Next**.

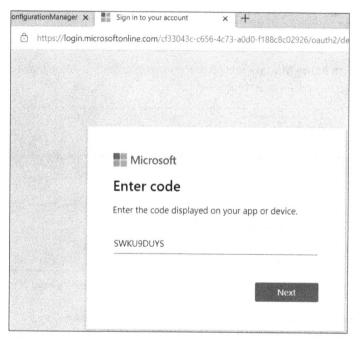

FIGURE 3-19 Microsoft Edge window.

25. On the **Sign-In** page (see Figure 3-20), sign in with a privileged account that has rights to your Azure subscription to connect using Azure PowerShell and register the appliance. Then click **Next**. Then, when sign-in is complete, close the browser window.

FIGURE 3-20 Microsoft Azure PowerShell Sign-In page.

26. The **Register with Azure Migrate** section of the Appliance Configuration Manager shows that the appliance has been registered successfully. (See Figure 3-21.)

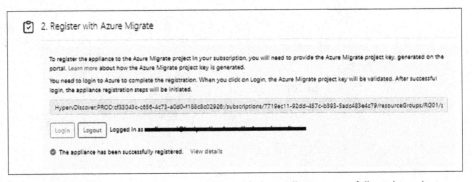

FIGURE 3-21 Register with Azure Migrate section, with the appliance successfully registered.

27. In the **Manage Credentials and Discovery Sources** section of the Appliance Configuration Manager, under **Step 1**, click the **Add Credentials** button.

28. Enter the local administrative credential information for the first Hyper-V host to which the appliance should connect and discover VMs for migration to Azure:

   - Friendly name
   - Username (for each admin account)
   - Password (for each admin account)

29. Repeat the previous two steps as needed until you've entered the local administrative credential information for necessary Hyper-V hosts.

TIP If the Hyper-V hosts are registered in Active Directory, you can add a single domain account that has admin rights on all the Hyper-V hosts.

30. Under **Step 2**, click the **Add Discovery Source** button.

31. Enter the following information about the first Hyper-V host to which the appliance should connect for VM discovery (see Figure 3-22):

- Source type
- Mapped credentials
- IP address/FQDN of the Hyper-V host
- Port number for the management service

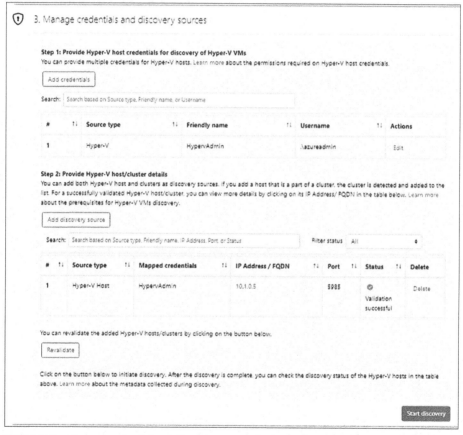

FIGURE 3-22 Manage credential and discovery sources in the appliance configuration manager wizard.

32. Repeat the previous two steps until you've added all the Hyper-V hosts.

33. Click the **Start Discovery** button.

> **NOTE** Depending on the number of Hyper-V hosts you set up for discovery, the discovery process can take anywhere from 15 to 20 minutes to a few hours. When the discovery process is complete, you'll see the success message shown in Figure 3-23.

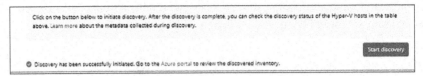

Click on the button below to initiate discovery. After the discovery is complete, you can check the discovery status of the Hyper-V hosts in the table above. Learn more about the metadata collected during discovery.

Start discovery

Discovery has been successfully initiated. Go to the Azure portal to review the discovered inventory.

FIGURE 3-23   Discovery process result message.

34. When the discovery process is complete, you're ready to assess the readiness of the discovered servers for migration to Azure.

SETUP ASSESSMENT

35. Switch back to the **Overview** tab for the Azure Migrate project you created earlier.

36. Locate the **Discover** tab in the **Assessment Tools** section, under **Azure Migrate: Discovery and Assessment**. The **Discovered Servers** section of this tab shows how many VMs were discovered. (See Figure 3-24.)

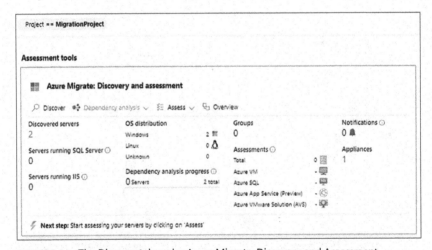

FIGURE 3-24   The Discover tab under Azure Migrate: Discovery and Assessment.

37. Under **Discovered Servers**, click the numeral that represents the number of servers found in discovery.

38. On the **Discovered Servers** page (see Figure 3-25), click **Create Group**.

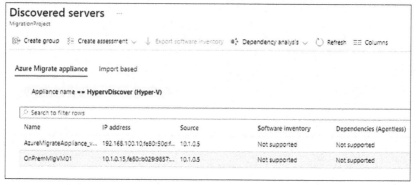

FIGURE 3-25   Discovered servers.

39. On the **Create Group** page (see Figure 3-26), enter the following information, select the VMs you want to include in your assessment, and click **Create**:

- **Discover Source**   Select the servers discovered by the Azure Migrate appliance.
- **Group Name**   Enter a unique name for the group.
- **Group Purpose**   Select **I Want to Use This Group to Create Azure VM Assessments** from the drop-down list.
- **Appliance Name**   Select the appliance you created earlier from the drop-down list.

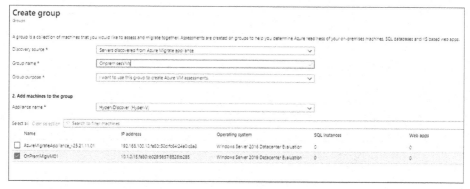

FIGURE 3-26   Create Group page.

40. After the group has been created, click the **Assess** button on the group's page. (See Figure 3-27.)

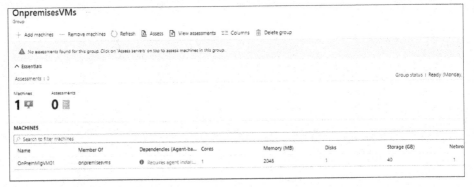

FIGURE 3-27   OnpremisesVMs group page.

41. On the **Create Assessment** page (see Figure 3-28), enter a unique name for the assess-
    ment, choose **Azure VM** from the **Assessment Type** drop-down list, and click **Create**.

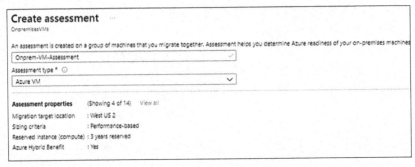

FIGURE 3-28   Create Assessment page.

VIEW ASSESSMENTS RESULTS

42. The results of the assessment appear on the **Assessments** page (see Figure 3-29). The
    initial analysis will likely have a low confidence rating. If you wait for a more thorough
    assessment, you will likely receive a higher confidence rating and a more accurate
    assessment of the VM's compute, memory, and storage requirements.

FIGURE 3-29   View Assessments page.

43. To view the specifics of the assessment, click the entry for the assessment in the
    Assessments page.

The assessment report opens. The **Overview** tab of the assessment report (see Figure 3-30) shows an initial assessment of the VM's readiness for migration to Azure, and monthly cost estimates for the different VM components, including compute and storage (broken up by storage type).

TIP You can recalculate the assessment when a few days or weeks have passed since the initial assessment to obtain a more accurate report.

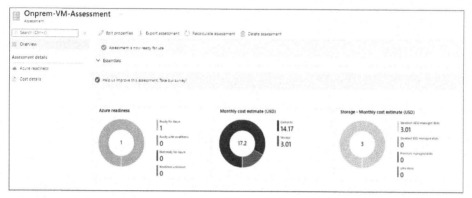

FIGURE 3-30 OnPrem-VM-Assessment page.

44. Click the assessment report's **Azure Readiness** tab to view details about the VMs that are part of the assessment, including the following information (see Figure 3-31):

- The Azure VM readiness state of each VM
- The recommended Azure VM size
- The suggested tool to use to migrate the VM to Azure
- The current OS running on the VM
- The VM boot type
- The number of disks attached to the VM on-premises

FIGURE 3-31 Azure Readiness tab.

45. Click the assessment report's **Cost Details** tab to view monthly cost estimates for each of the VMs that are part of the assessment, including the following information (see Figure 3-32):

- The recommended Azure VM size (this is the same as shown on the Azure Readiness tab)

- The different Azure managed disks that each VM will require

- A monthly compute cost estimate (USD) for each VM

- A monthly storage cost estimate (USD) for each VM

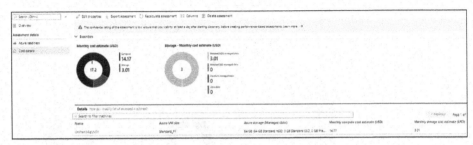

FIGURE 3-32 Cost Details tab.

With the discovery and assessment complete, you're ready to replicate the VMs to Azure.

SETUP REPLICATION APPLIANCE

46. In the **Overview** tab for the Azure Migrate project, in the **Migration Tools** section, under **Azure Migrate: Server Migration**, click **Discover**. (See Figure 3-33.)

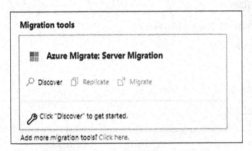

FIGURE 3-33 Azure Migrate: Server Migration.

47. On the **Discover** page (see Figure 3-34), enter the following information and click **Create Resources**:

- **Are Your Machines Virtualized?** Select **Yes, with Hyper-V**.

- **Target Region** Select the region you want to use as your target region.

- **Confirm That the Target Region for Migration Is "West US 2"** Select this check box to confirm that the target region you selected is correct.

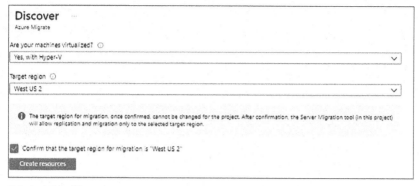

FIGURE 3-34 Discover page.

48. Azure Migrate creates the required back-end resources. (This might take a few minutes.) After the resources are created, you'll see the options shown in Figure 3-35.

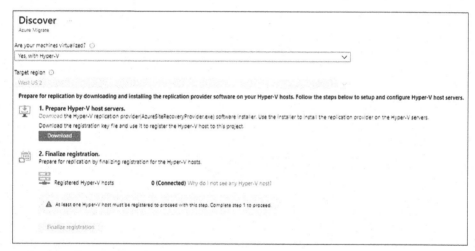

FIGURE 3-35 Download appliance.

49. Under **Prepare Hyper-V Host Servers**, click the **Download** link to download the Hyper-V replication provider software installer.

50. Still under **Prepare Hyper-V Host Servers**, click the **Download** button to obtain a copy of the registration key. Store this key in a safe location.

51. Switch to the Hyper-V host that you want to integrate with the Azure Migrate service and run the installer you just downloaded.

> **NOTE** You will perform the following steps on each of the Hyper-V hosts that you want to integrate with the Azure Migrate service for VM migrations.

The Azure Site Recovery Provider Setup (Hyper-V Server) wizard starts.

52. On the **Microsoft Update** tab (see Figure 3-36), leave the **On** option button selected (use Microsoft Update to check for available updates during the install process) and click **Next**.

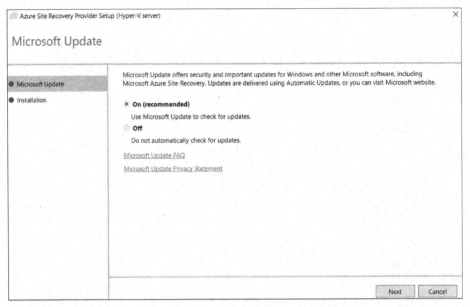

FIGURE 3-36 Microsoft Update.

53. On the **Provider Installation** tab (see Figure 3-37), click **Browse** to locate and select the folder in which you want to install the software. Then click **Install**.

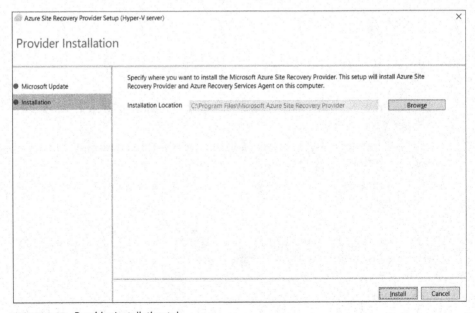

FIGURE 3-37 Provider Installation tab.

54. When the installation is complete, click **Register**. (See Figure 3-38.)

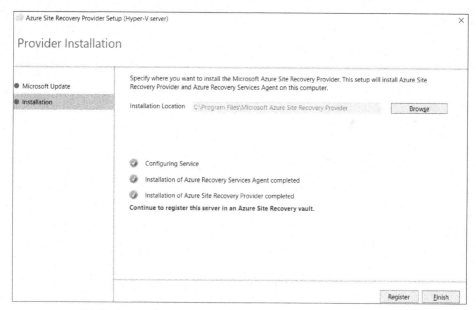

FIGURE 3-38   Click the Register button.

The Microsoft Azure Site Recovery Registration wizard starts.

55. On the **Vault Settings** tab (see Figure 3-39), click **Browse**, locate and select the registration key you downloaded in step 50, and click **Next**.

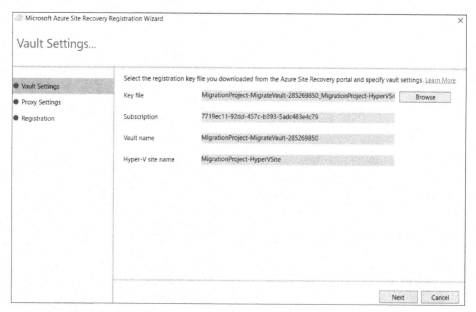

FIGURE 3-39   Vault Settings tab.

56. On the **Proxy Settings** tab (see Figure 3-40), select either the **Connect Directly to Azure Site Recovery Without a Proxy Server** or the **Connect to Azure Site Recovery Using a Proxy Server** option button, depending on your needs, and click **Next**.

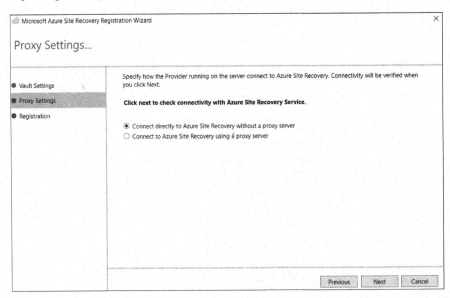

FIGURE 3-40 Proxy Settings tab.

The Microsoft Azure Site Recovery Registration wizard automatically registers the Hyper-V host. The **Registration** tab shows the progress of the operation. (See Figure 3-41.)

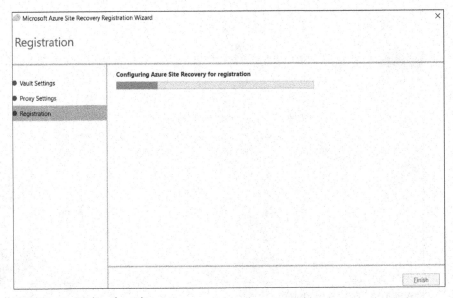

FIGURE 3-41 Registration tab.

57. When registration is complete, click **Finish**. (See Figure 3-42.)

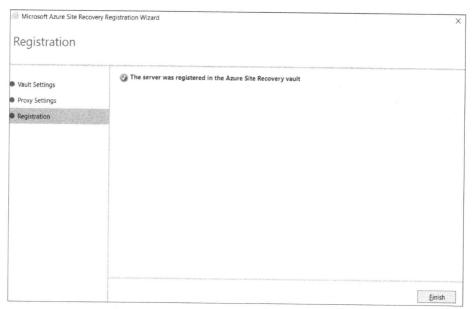

FIGURE 3-42 Successful registration.

58. Switch back to **Discover** page in the Azure Portal. (See Figure 3-43.) Under **Finalize Registration**, next to **Registered Hyper-V Hosts**, you'll see the number of Hyper-V hosts connected to your project. When all your hosts have been connected, click **Finalize Registration**.

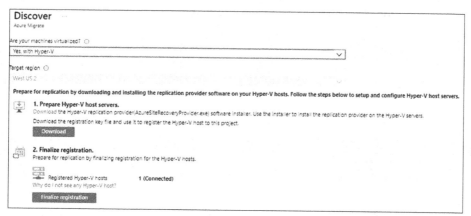

FIGURE 3-43 Finalize Registration.

59. After you have successfully registered all the necessary Hyper-V hosts, you're ready to start the replication process.

START VM REPLICATION

60. In the **Overview** tab for the Azure Migrate project you created earlier, in the **Migration Tools** section, under **Azure Migrate: Server Migration**, click **Replicate**. (See Figure 3-44.)

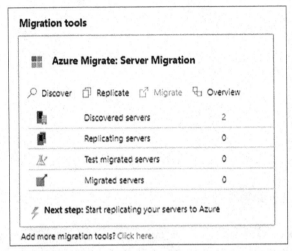

FIGURE 3-44   Migration Tools section.

61. In the **Source Settings** tab of the Replicate wizard (see Figure 3-45), open the **Are Your Machines Virtualized?** drop-down list and select **Yes, with Hyper-V**. Then click **Next**.

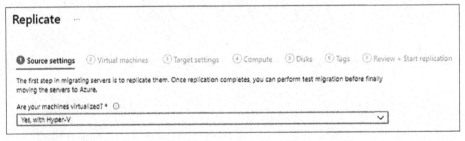

FIGURE 3-45   Source Settings tab of the Replicate wizard.

62. In the **Virtual Machines** tab (see Figure 3-46), open the **Import Migration Settings from an Assessment** drop-down list and do one of the following:

- Choose the assessment you selected earlier. If you opt for this approach, all the relevant VMs and assessment results will be applied throughout the rest of this wizard.

- Choose **No, I'll Specify the Migration Settings Manually**. This example uses this option, because it enables you to review all the configuration settings you want to implement.

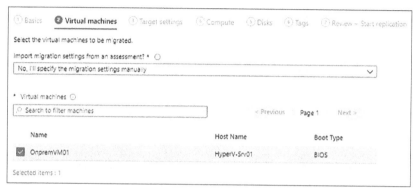

FIGURE 3-46   Virtual Machines page.

63. In the **Virtual Machines** box, enter all the VMs you want to replicate to Azure. Then click **Next**.

64. In the **Target Settings** tab (see Figure 3-47), enter the following information and click **Next**:

- **Subscription**   Select the subscription you want to use as the target environment.
- **Resource Group**   Select the resource group to use.
- **Replication Storage Account**   Select the storage account to use to store the replication logs.
- **Virtual Network**   Select the virtual network to use post-migration.
- **Subnet**   Select the subnet to use for the VM.
- **Availability Options**   Select the availability options that you would like to set for the VM.
- **Azure Hybrid Benefit**   If your Microsoft license supports this benefit, click **Yes**, and select the **I Confirm I Have an Eligible Windows Server License...** check box.

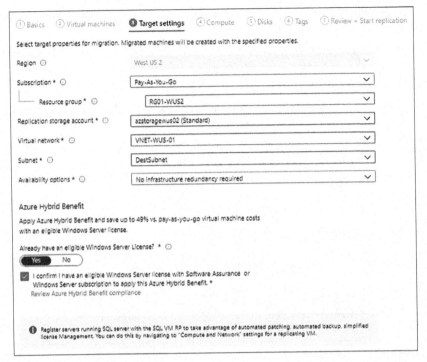

FIGURE 3-47   Target Settings tab.

65. In the **Compute** tab (see Figure 3-48), enter the following information and click **Next**:

   - **Azure VM Name**   Enter a unique name for the VM in Azure. (This can be the same name as the one the VM currently has in the on-premises environment.)

   - **Azure VM Size**   Select the VM SKU to assign post-migration or select **Automatically Select Matching Configuration** to allow Azure to choose one based on the VM assessment or current size.

   - **OS Type**   Choose **Windows** or **Linux**.

   - **OS Disk**   Select the disk that is hosting the operating system for the VM.

FIGURE 3-48   Compute tab.

66. In the **Disks** tab (see Figure 3-49), under **Disks to Replicate**, select the disks you want to replicate to Azure. Alternatively, select **All Selected** to replicate all disks associated with the VM. Then click **Next**.

FIGURE 3-49 Disks tab.

67. In the **Tags** tab (see Figure 3-50), enter any tags you would like to associate with the VMs, and click **Next**.

FIGURE 3-50 Tags tab.

68. In the **Review + Start Replication** tab (see Figure 3-51), review your settings and click **Review + Start Replication**.

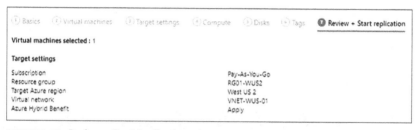

FIGURE 3-51 Review + Start Replication tab.

69. In the **Enable Replication** page (see Figure 3-52), monitor the replication jobs for each VM you set up in the earlier steps to make sure they complete successfully.

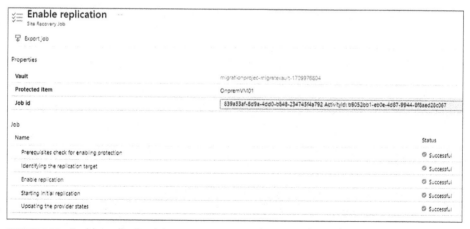

FIGURE 3-52 Enable replication job.

70. In the **Overview** tab for the Azure Migrate project you created earlier, in the **Migration Tools** section, under **Azure Migrate: Server Migration**, click **Overview**. (Refer to Figure 3-44.)

71. Select each of the replicating VMs, one at a time, to view its **Overview** tab. This shows the status of the VM. (See Figure 3-53.) When the VM has synced completely with Azure, its status is listed as **Protected**.

FIGURE 3-53   Overview page for the OnpremVM01 VM.

TEST MIGRATION

72. When a replicated VM's status has switched to Protected, you can perform a test migration for it.

> **NOTE**   You will perform the following steps on each of the Hyper-V hosts for which you want to test migration before you perform the final migration to Azure.

73. In the replicated VM's page, click the **Test Migration** button. (See Figure 3-54.)

FIGURE 3-54   Click the Test Migration button.

74. On the **Test Migration** page (see Figure 3-55), open the **Virtual Network** drop-down list and choose the virtual network in which you want to set up the test VM. Then click **OK**.

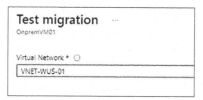

FIGURE 3-55 Test Migration page.

75. In the **Test Failover** page (see Figure 3-56), monitor the progress of the test failover job to make sure all the job steps complete successfully.

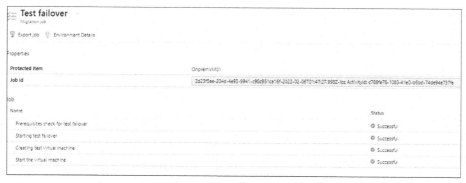

FIGURE 3-56 Test Failover page.

When the failover job is complete, the on-premises VM(s) appear in the Virtual Machines page with a **-test** suffix.

76. Select the VM and log in to it using the IP provided in the **Overview** tab. (See Figure 3-57.)

NOTE If you have not yet set up connectivity to the VM network, assign a public IP to the VM so you can access it over the internet for testing. (This is covered in Book 1 of this series, *Microsoft Azure Compute: The Definitive Guide*, in Chapter 1, "Azure Virtual Machines.")

FIGURE 3-57 Virtual Machines and the page for the page test VM.

77. Confirm that all your data and applications are available as required and perform any testing you like.

When you finish testing, you need to clean up the test VM.

CLEANUP TEST MIGRATION

78. In the **Overview** tab for the VM that is being replicated (see Figure 3-58), click **Clean Up Test Migration**.

FIGURE 3-58 OnpremVm01 page.

79. In the **Test Migrate Cleanup** dialog box (see Figure 3-59), type any notes from the test that you would like to record in the Notes box. These could include the test participants, test outcomes, issues encountered, or changes to incorporate in future tests or after testing the replication configuration.

FIGURE 3-59 Test Migrate Cleanup Notes.

80. Select the **Testing Is Complete. Delete Test Failover Virtual Machines** check box and click **OK** to initiate the cleanup job.

81. From the **Test Failover Cleanup** page (see Figure 3-60), monitor the cleanup job to ensure it completes successfully.

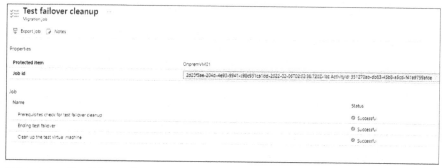

FIGURE 3-60   Test Failover Cleanup page.

When testing is complete, you are ready to migrate the VM to Azure.

PERFORM MIGRATION TO AZURE

82. In the **Overview** tab for the Azure Migrate project you created earlier (see Figure 3-61), in the **Migration Tools** section, under **Azure Migrate: Server Migration**, click **Migrate**.

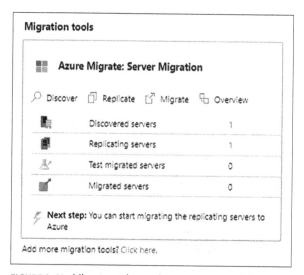

FIGURE 3-61   Migrate option under Azure Migrate: Server Migration.

83. On the **Migrate** page (see Figure 3-62), enter the following information and click **OK**.

- **Shutdown Machines Before Migration to Minimize Data Loss**   Select **Yes**.
- **Virtual Machines**   Select the VMs to migrate.

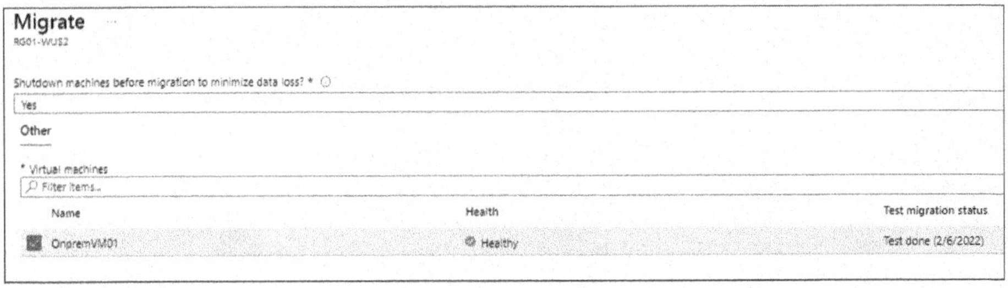

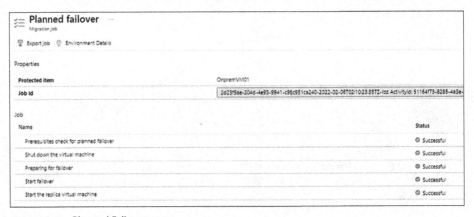

FIGURE 3-62 Migrate page.

84. In the **Planned Failover** page (see Figure 3-63), monitor the progress of the migration job to confirm it completes successfully.

> **NOTE** If any errors occur, analyze and fix any highlighted issues and rerun the failover process.

FIGURE 3-63 Planned Failover page.

When the migration is complete, the on-premises VM(s) appear in the **Virtual Machines** page with the name you set earlier. You can now turn off replication for that VM.

85. Select the VM and log in to it using the IP provided in the **Overview** tab.

> **NOTE** Again, if you have not yet set up connectivity to the VM network, assign a public IP to the VM so you can access it over the internet for testing. (Refer to Chapter 1 in Book 1 of this series.)

86. In the replicating VM's **Overview** tab (see Figure 3-64), click **Stop Replication**.

FIGURE 3-64   OnpremVM01 Overview tab.

87. In the **Stop Replication** page (see Figure 3-65), open the **Remove Replication Settings** drop-down list and choose **Stop Replication and Remove Replication Settings**. Then click **OK**.

FIGURE 3-65   Stop Replication page.

88. In the **Disable Replication** page (see Figure 3-66), monitor the progress of the job to ensure it completes successfully.

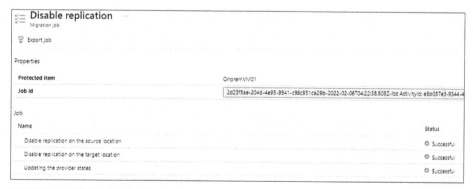

FIGURE 3-66   Disable Replication page.

89. Repeat the steps in this section for all the other VMs you want to migrate to Azure.

Best practices

Following are some general best practices regarding assessing and migrating servers to Azure VMs using the Azure Migrate service:

- **Perform discovery and assessment** Discovery and assessment are important phases in any migration. They can help IT clearly identify and plan for a migration, taking into account potential roadblocks such as lack of server readiness depending on the server OS, hypervisor version, and so on. Even the initial as-is assessment report provides a baseline understanding of the anticipated VM size and disk type to use for the migrated servers.

- **Generate performance-based assessments for servers intended for migration to Azure** This can help you to identify more accurate size and disk parameters before setting up replication for the servers.

- **Perform dependency analysis** In larger complex environments, performing dependency analysis can significantly reduce errors and downtime during migrations because it enables you to better plan and execute migrations for interconnected workloads. Dependency analysis can also help in smaller and mid-size environments if there are numerous applications and databases hosted across multiple servers.

- **Ensure confidence ratings for assessments are high** Confidence ratings are based on the number of data points that Azure Migrate is able to gather using the Azure Migrate on-premises appliance. The higher the confidence rating, the more accurate the server, disk capacity, and performance planning you can perform. Be sure to run the performance-based assessments for a period of at least a week, if not longer, to gather more data points for a better analysis.

- **Review licensing options and benefits** Different OEM licensing agreements can help you significantly reduce the cost of your server workloads post-migration. Be sure to review and understand what options are available with your existing licensing to take advantage of these benefits. Reach out to your OEM, if possible, to get deeper insights on what options are available for your organization.

- **Conduct detailed planning workshops with all business, application, and IT stakeholders** This enables you to plan and execute the migration in a collaborative manner. These workshops can help ensure internal alignment and reduce the risk of migration failure due to known but unaccounted for considerations due to a lack of collaborative planning.

- **Test migrations** Azure Migrate enables you to test migrations in an isolated Azure environment. Use this capability to ensure that interconnectivity between your servers and services is working in the Azure cloud. This can help you to plan for changes in the on-premises environment before the migration to identify, address, and possibly automate any areas of manual intervention such as IP address references in configuration files.

Chapter 4

Azure Monitor

Overview

Microsoft released Application Insights in public preview in April 2015 to provide clients deploying applications in Azure with deeper insights into each application's performance. In September 2016, Microsoft released Azure Monitor in public preview. At the start, Azure Monitor included capabilities to gather, monitor (using shared dashboards), analyze, and alert on activity logs, resource metrics, and diagnostic logs.

Over time, Microsoft has consolidated Application Insights, Log Insights, and Azure resource monitoring into Azure Monitor. Microsoft has also extended Azure Monitor's capabilities, third-party integrations, and available metrics and integrations across Azure resources.

Key benefits

Azure Monitor enables you to monitor all your Azure applications, virtual machines (VMs), and other deployed services. It offers a number of key benefits, as follows:

- Automated log collection and monitoring of Azure resources
- Deeper insights into application performance for optimization
- Automated alerts sent to resource owners for action
- DevOps integration for continuous monitoring
- Automated action to address critical issues
- Pay-as-you-go, requiring no upfront investment
- Custom dashboards to meet every requirement
- Integration with other Microsoft services, such as Power BI, for centralized dashboards across the organization
- Considerable third-party integrations to extend capabilities

Figure 4-1 provides a high-level overview of the key capabilities of Azure Monitor. As you can see, Azure Monitor supports the integration of various data sources for log, event, and metrics collection. You can gain deeper insights into different Azure resources, create visualizations using various built-in tools and integrated services, analyze data to respond with alerts and automated actions, and export data into other third-party solutions you might have in your environment.

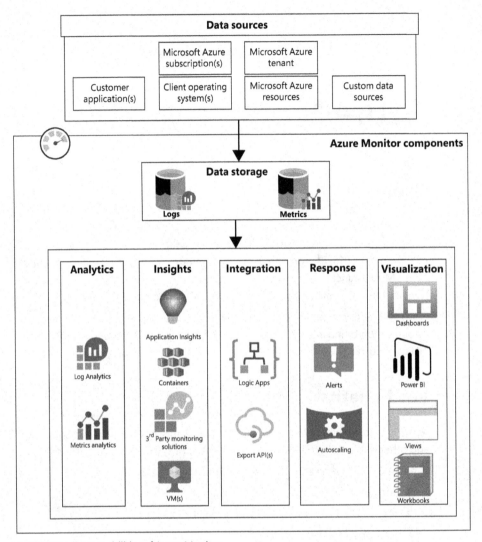

FIGURE 4-1   Key capabilities of Azure Monitor.

Concepts and considerations

Now that you have a basic overview of the features and benefits of using Azure Monitor in your environment, let's discuss the following:

- The types of data you can collect using Azure Monitor
- How to set up the data-collection process
- Available data-visualization options
- How alerts and automated actions work
- Options to integrate this service to extend its functionality

Data types

Azure Monitor supports three data types, as follows:

- Metrics
- Log data
- Distributed traces

Each data type helps Azure Monitor piece together a picture of the overall health of an Azure environment. Collecting and analyzing these data types is critical to gain deeper insights into the performance and availability of your Azure resources and to proactively take actions to avoid outages.

Metrics

Metrics are resource values collected at particular points in time, indicating system performance for monitored services or events. You define the interval at which these numerical values are captured, along with associated values that include the data and timestamp, the name of the metric, and labels that help define the metric. Metrics help reveal trends that you can analyze to identify performance bottlenecks or areas that require deeper analysis for a resource.

Azure uses a time-series database to store and optimize metrics, as this type of database is best suited to host this kind of data. Once combined with other data types, such as logs, you can better identify root causes of issues. Metrics are lightweight data points and therefore are ideal for use in Dashboards for real-time health monitoring of resources that are critical for your environment. (See Figure 4-2.)

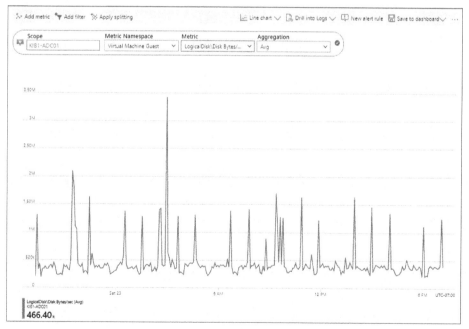

FIGURE 4-2   Real-time health monitoring with dashboards using metrics.

Log data

Every system, including VMs, storage, network infrastructure, and other Azure services, generates logs that capture changes, issues, and errors. Logs can contain numerical or text data. In the context of Azure, you can store logs in a Log Analytics workspace (see Figure 4-3) and use Azure Monitor to analyze them for specific events or errors that are of interest. You can also perform queries against log data to identify the root cause of issues or to pre-empt issues for remedial action. Finally, you can set up alerts against logged data that help you proactively respond to issues before users are affected.

> **NOTE** Logs are ideal for root cause analysis and error monitoring.

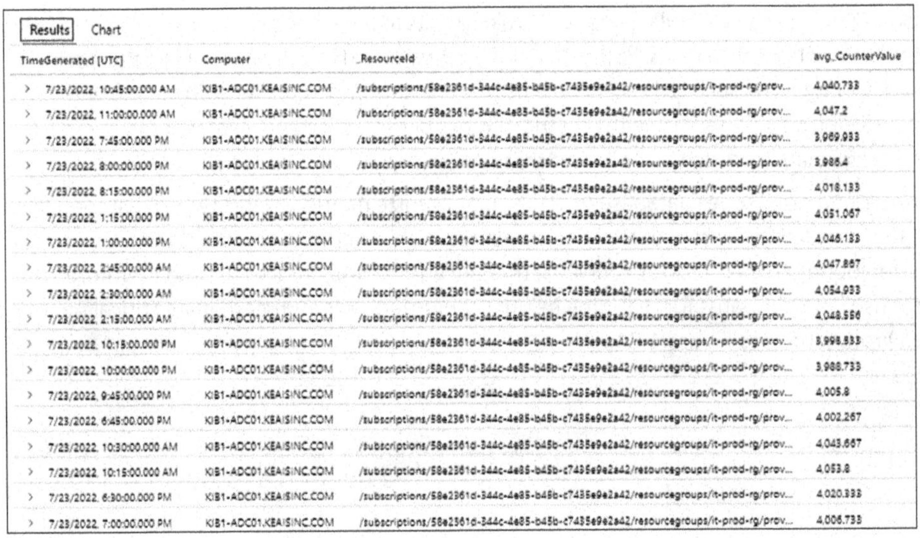

Results | Chart

TimeGenerated [UTC]	Computer	_ResourceId	avg_CounterValue
> 7/23/2022, 10:45:00.000 AM	KIB1-ADC01.KEAISINC.COM	/subscriptions/58e2361d-344c-4e85-b45b-c7435e9e2a42/resourcegroups/it-prod-rg/prov...	4,040.733
> 7/23/2022, 11:00:00.000 AM	KIB1-ADC01.KEAISINC.COM	/subscriptions/58e2361d-344c-4e85-b45b-c7435e9e2a42/resourcegroups/it-prod-rg/prov...	4,047.2
> 7/23/2022, 7:45:00.000 PM	KIB1-ADC01.KEAISINC.COM	/subscriptions/58e2361d-344c-4e85-b45b-c7435e9e2a42/resourcegroups/it-prod-rg/prov...	3,969.933
> 7/23/2022, 8:00:00.000 PM	KIB1-ADC01.KEAISINC.COM	/subscriptions/58e2361d-344c-4e85-b45b-c7435e9e2a42/resourcegroups/it-prod-rg/prov...	3,986.4
> 7/23/2022, 8:15:00.000 PM	KIB1-ADC01.KEAISINC.COM	/subscriptions/58e2361d-344c-4e85-b45b-c7435e9e2a42/resourcegroups/it-prod-rg/prov...	4,018.133
> 7/23/2022, 1:15:00.000 PM	KIB1-ADC01.KEAISINC.COM	/subscriptions/58e2361d-344c-4e85-b45b-c7435e9e2a42/resourcegroups/it-prod-rg/prov...	4,051.067
> 7/23/2022, 1:00:00.000 PM	KIB1-ADC01.KEAISINC.COM	/subscriptions/58e2361d-344c-4e85-b45b-c7435e9e2a42/resourcegroups/it-prod-rg/prov...	4,046.133
> 7/23/2022, 2:45:00.000 AM	KIB1-ADC01.KEAISINC.COM	/subscriptions/58e2361d-344c-4e85-b45b-c7435e9e2a42/resourcegroups/it-prod-rg/prov...	4,047.867
> 7/23/2022, 2:30:00.000 AM	KIB1-ADC01.KEAISINC.COM	/subscriptions/58e2361d-344c-4e85-b45b-c7435e9e2a42/resourcegroups/it-prod-rg/prov...	4,054.933
> 7/23/2022, 2:15:00.000 AM	KIB1-ADC01.KEAISINC.COM	/subscriptions/58e2361d-344c-4e85-b45b-c7435e9e2a42/resourcegroups/it-prod-rg/prov...	4,048.556
> 7/23/2022, 10:15:00.000 PM	KIB1-ADC01.KEAISINC.COM	/subscriptions/58e2361d-344c-4e85-b45b-c7435e9e2a42/resourcegroups/it-prod-rg/prov...	3,998.533
> 7/23/2022, 10:00:00.000 PM	KIB1-ADC01.KEAISINC.COM	/subscriptions/58e2361d-344c-4e85-b45b-c7435e9e2a42/resourcegroups/it-prod-rg/prov...	3,988.733
> 7/23/2022, 9:45:00.000 PM	KIB1-ADC01.KEAISINC.COM	/subscriptions/58e2361d-344c-4e85-b45b-c7435e9e2a42/resourcegroups/it-prod-rg/prov...	4,005.8
> 7/23/2022, 6:45:00.000 PM	KIB1-ADC01.KEAISINC.COM	/subscriptions/58e2361d-344c-4e85-b45b-c7435e9e2a42/resourcegroups/it-prod-rg/prov...	4,002.267
> 7/23/2022, 10:30:00.000 AM	KIB1-ADC01.KEAISINC.COM	/subscriptions/58e2361d-344c-4e85-b45b-c7435e9e2a42/resourcegroups/it-prod-rg/prov...	4,043.667
> 7/23/2022, 10:15:00.000 AM	KIB1-ADC01.KEAISINC.COM	/subscriptions/58e2361d-344c-4e85-b45b-c7435e9e2a42/resourcegroups/it-prod-rg/prov...	4,053.8
> 7/23/2022, 6:30:00.000 PM	KIB1-ADC01.KEAISINC.COM	/subscriptions/58e2361d-344c-4e85-b45b-c7435e9e2a42/resourcegroups/it-prod-rg/prov...	4,020.333
> 7/23/2022, 7:00:00.000 PM	KIB1-ADC01.KEAISINC.COM	/subscriptions/58e2361d-344c-4e85-b45b-c7435e9e2a42/resourcegroups/it-prod-rg/prov...	4,006.733

FIGURE 4-3 Log Analytics.

Distributed traces

A distributed trace is when a system traces a user request across a distributed environment and is used to identify and analyze any bottlenecks or other issues in your environment. Distributed systems contain a number of individual components; distributed traces help correlate logs generated by these individual components in the application stack. You use the Application Insights SDK to enable distributed tracing and define where to store trace data. You can then analyze trace data, along with other log data, and create dashboards, custom queries, and alerts for monitoring.

Data collection

Now that you have a better understanding of the different data types supported by Azure Monitor, let's look at the different ways Azure Monitor can collect data. Azure Monitor supports a range of data sources, including the following:

- **Subscription-level activity and monitoring logs**   Azure collects subscription-level activity logs that track the creation, modification, and deletion of resources, along with other operational and management activities that you perform on all resources.

- **Azure service-level monitoring logs**   These apply to services such as Azure Active Directory, which are built and managed by Microsoft when you create a new subscription and Azure tenant. These logs help you keep track of the health status of these services.

- **Resource-level metrics and logs**   Azure collects metrics and enables you to collect logs for all resources you create in your Azure subscription. These track the performance and health of individual resources created within your Azure subscription.

- **Azure guest VM OS performance and diagnostic logs**   You can use Azure Monitor to collect basic performance logs after you create a VM in Azure. You can even install an Azure Monitor agent on the VM to capture detailed performance metrics, logs, and events to gain deeper insights into the VM.

- **On-premises VM/server or other cloud-hosted guest VM performance and diagnostic logs**   As with Azure VMs, you can install the Azure Monitor agent on VMs or servers hosted on-premises or in other cloud environments to gather performance and diagnostic logs to monitor and manage those resources.

- **Application performance metrics and diagnostic logs**   Application Insights allows you to send extensive performance and logging data to Azure Monitor for monitoring, analysis, and alerting. This includes granular information such as page views, application requests, and application exceptions encountered during runtime.

- **Custom sources**   Azure Monitor supports data collection from any REST client using the Data Collector API. This allows you to monitor resources that do not support the use of Azure Monitor agents or integration with Application Insights.

Once collected, data from all these sources can be directly written to the Azure Monitor metrics database and/or the Log Analytics workspace database. Alternatively, you can store this data in Azure Storage accounts; Azure Monitor can then ingest it from there.

Azure Monitor supports various methods for data ingestion:

- **Application Insights**   Application Insights requires you to integrate your application with the service using the Application Insights SDK to gather rich user and application data, logs, and metrics.

- **Agents on VMs and physical servers**   You can deploy the Log Analytics or Azure Monitor agent on VMs or physical servers to gather deeper insights into performance, logs, and events.
- **Diagnostic settings on Azure Resources**   You can define diagnostic settings on Azure resources that send logs and metrics to various destinations, such as Azure Storage, a Log Analytics workspace, Azure Event Hubs, or an integrated partner solution.

Data segregation

Azure Monitor can collect many different types of data. But it has to organize all these different types of data into logical structures—not only for easy retrieval but also to maintain data separation between clients, resources, and environments.

The data segregation logic built into the Azure Monitor service ensures that all data is tagged with the associated workspace, and that all tagging is preserved for the entire data lifecycle. Every client tenant has a dedicated database instance in a storage cluster in the Azure region used by the service.

> **IMPORTANT**   Azure Monitor complies with international standards such as ISO/IEC 27001, PCI DSS, HIPAA, HITECH, and many others. For an up-to-date list of certifications, see the Microsoft Trust Center. Here, you can determine whether the service adheres to any other specific compliance measures required by your organizations.

Data retention

The Azure Monitor service retains all indexed log data and collected metrics based on the selected pricing tier:

- **Free tier**   In this tier, all collected and indexed data is retained for seven days.
- **Paid tier**   In this tier, all collected and indexed data is retained by default for 31 days. You can extend this to 730 days.

In addition, all data from the previous two weeks is stored in SSD-cache for fast retrieval.

Data redundancy

All data is replicated within the local Azure region using locally redundant storage (LRS), thereby providing some level of redundancy for your environment.

Data security

By default, Azure Monitor collects data from Azure services and resources over TLS 1.2-encrypted connections. Moreover, all data is encrypted at rest, as is all data held in SSD cache. This ensures that data is protected at every stage; there are no vulnerable areas for attack in throughout the entire data lifecycle.

> **NOTE** Data encrypted at rest uses Microsoft-managed keys, although customers have the ability to use their own keys.

In addition, once data is ingested by the service, it is stored as read-only in the database. Although you can delete data using the Azure Monitor APIs, you cannot alter it. If you don't want any data to be deleted, you can export it to an Azure Storage account that is set to prevent data deletions.

Data visualization

Azure Monitor provides two types of built-in visualizations, which allow you to monitor various Azure resources at a glance: curated visualizations and insights.

Curated visualization

Curated visualizations are limited in scope to a particular service or set of services. You can use them without having to configure them first. Examples of curated visualizations include the metrics that become visible when you click a specific Azure resource such as a VM (see Figure 4-4) or Azure Storage account (see Figure 4-5).

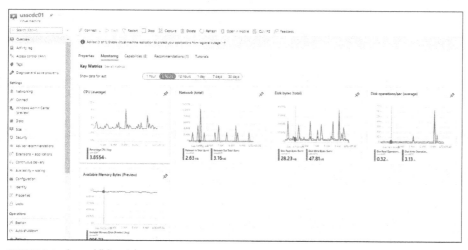

FIGURE 4-4 Azure VM metrics.

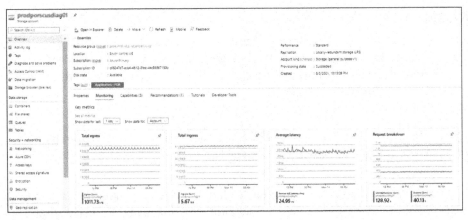

FIGURE 4-5 Azure Storage metrics.

Insights

Insights are larger scalable visualizations that focus on specific resources, such as web apps, VMs, and container services. These require integration and customization but provide deeper and richer insights. Microsoft provides several Insights tools, including Application Insights, Container Insights, VM Insights, Network Insights, Storage Insights, and many others. Four Insights that can help you monitor your environment include the following:

- **Application Insights**   Application Insights provides a deep understanding of an integrated web application's performance, availability, usage, bottlenecks, and exceptions. The web application can be hosted anywhere, including on-premises and other cloud environments. You use the Application Insights SDK to enable Application Insights configuration for your web applications and configure it to monitor and stream the required parameters to Azure Monitor for analysis. Application Insights integrates with Visual Studio to support DevOps scenarios.

- **VM Insights**   VM Insights enables you to monitor the performance and health of numerous VMs at once and to identify dependencies on external endpoints that impact the performance of a particular VM. You can use VM Insights for VMs hosted in Azure, on-premises, or in other cloud environments.

- **Network Insights**   Network Insights (see Figure 4-6) monitors the health of the various network endpoints running in your environment, including VPN gateways, VPN connections, private endpoints, virtual networks, and so on. You can also use Network Insights to monitor connection health and traffic flow logs for the different network security groups (NSGs).

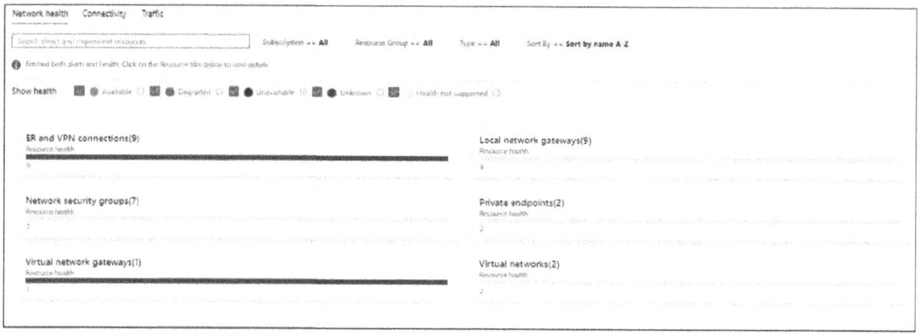

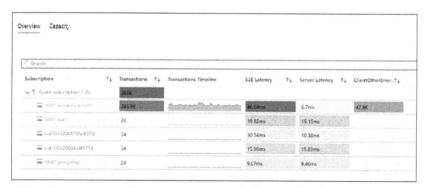

FIGURE 4-6 Network Insights.

- **Storage Insights** Storage Insights monitors the health of the various storage accounts running in your Azure subscriptions. With Storage Insights, you can easily monitor key metrics, such as the following:
  - Transactions
  - Transactions Timeline
  - E2E Latency
  - Server Latency
  - Client Errors

You can also monitor the capacity of various storage accounts to proactively identify any that are reaching their maximum thresholds. Figure 4-7 shows a Storage Accounts Insights dashboard.

FIGURE 4-7 Storage Insights.

Dashboards

Azure enables you to build customized dashboards using different data sources and data types and display them in the Azure Portal for easy viewing. You can also share your custom dashboards with other Azure users, providing a consistent view of critical resources across your IT team. Essentially, when creating a dashboard, you select tiles that contain the different data types from the different data sources for display. You can then size them and align them based on your requirements.

Figure 4-8 shows a sample dashboard that contains the following information:

- All the resources present in the tenant
- Average CPU credits consumed by some VMs
- Average memory available in bytes for those VMs
- Average CPU percentage usage for those VMs
- User sign-in graph for the past few days
- Secure Score metric
- Service Health and Marketplace shortcut tiles

FIGURE 4-8 Azure Monitor dashboards.

Workbooks

You can use Azure Workbooks to generate rich and interactive visual reports from multiple data sources. You can base these reports on publicly available templates that have been pre-configured to contain key metrics or start with a blank canvas and create your own. You can customize, save, and reuse templates as necessary. Figure 4-9 shows a list of the templates that are publicly available at the time of this writing, while Figure 4-10 shows the output of the Performance Analysis template.

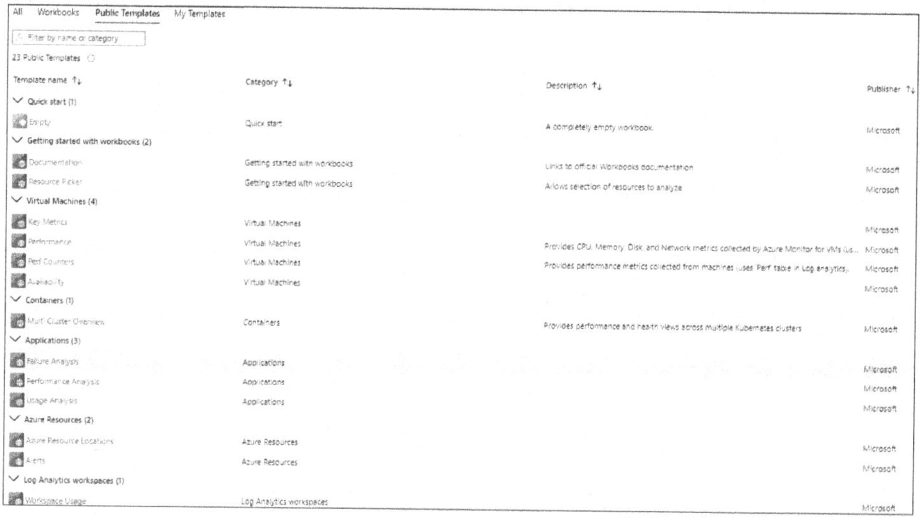

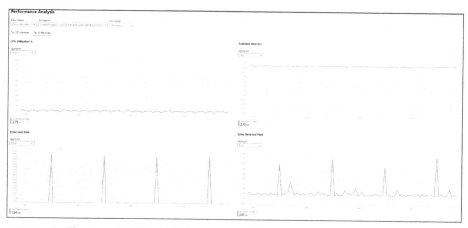

FIGURE 4-9 Azure Workbooks templates.

FIGURE 4-10 The Azure Workbooks Performance Analysis template.

Power BI

Microsoft has integrated Power BI with Azure Monitor. So, you can easily import logs from Azure Monitor into Power BI to create rich, interactive visualizations. A full-fledged business analytics service, Power BI offers extensive capabilities to create queries, custom dashboards, and reports based on your organizational needs.

Third-party integrations

Azure Monitor integrates with several types of third-party solutions. For example:

- **IT service-management (ITSM) solutions**   You can connect Azure to your ITSM tool to automatically create tickets and to manage the lifecycle of the ticket. The Microsoft site contains an extensive list of supported ITSM products, which continues to grow as more integrations come online.

- **Azure Monitor partner integrations**   Azure Monitor supports integration with partner solutions to either extend capabilities provided by Azure Monitor or export logs stored in Azure Monitor to their systems.

Data export

Azure Monitor integrates with other Azure services, such as Event Hubs and Logic Apps, to export data to other Azure services or to third-party solutions such as SIEM or monitoring tools. You can also integrate with APIs exposed by the service for direct integration and data export. Here are a few points to keep in mind:

- When using Logic Apps with Azure Monitor, you can set up automated tasks and work-flows that export data from Azure Monitor and import it into other services or solutions.

- When using Azure Event Hubs, you can transform, store, and stream Azure Monitor data to third-party SIEM and monitoring tools.

- When leveraging the APIs provided by Azure Monitor, you can read all the captured logs and metrics and alerts generated in Azure Monitor and import them into your existing monitoring solution or SIEM tool for analysis.

Alerts

Alerts are a key feature in any monitoring solution. After you have collected all the required data, identified all the events and metrics you want to monitor, and selected appropriate thresholds to accurately identify issues in your environment, you need some mechanism to inform you when events are triggered and metric thresholds are met. In Azure Monitor, this mechanism is the alert.

With Azure Monitor, you can define alert rules that identify the targeted resources, targeted metrics or events, thresholds, and frequency to determine whether to initiate some action you specify. An action is defined as part of an action group. This can include automated actions to remediate the alert, such as stopping, starting, or restarting the resource; scaling the resource in or out; triggering an automation runbook; or logging tickets in an integrated ITSM tool. Along with these automated actions, you can also define other action groups, such as one to alert responsible administrators, via email, SMS, or voice calls, of the need for manual interven-tion or monitoring to ensure automated actions have been correctly performed.

Azure Monitor walkthrough

The following sections walk you through the process of using Azure Monitor to create an alert rule to monitor the CPU usage of a VM, create a Log Analytics workspace, configure Azure VM monitoring, set up Azure VM Insights alerts, configure Azure Storage monitoring, and running queries on Azure Storage.

> **IMPORTANT** If you are following along, you'll want to select resources and unique resource names based on your environment for each of your deployments.

> **IMPORTANT** If you are following along, delete any unwanted resources after you have completed testing to reduce charges being levied by Microsoft for these resources.

> **IMPORTANT** Before you begin, create a VM and let it run for a few hours so you can gather some usage metrics. Also create an Azure Blob Storage account and upload a few test documents before and after setting up monitoring to capture usage logs.

USING THE AZURE PORTAL

To set up and use Azure Monitor using the Azure Portal, follow these steps.

CREATE METRICS ALERTS

1. Log in to the Azure Portal, and browse to the VM you created in your Azure environment for the purposes of this walkthrough.

2. In the left pane of the VM's configuration blade, under **Monitoring**, click **Metrics**. (See Figure 4-11.)

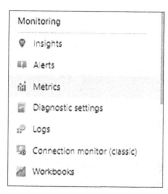

FIGURE 4-11 Select Metrics under Monitoring.

A default metrics visualization opens in the right pane. (See Figure 4-12.) This visualization contains the following options:

- **Add Metric** Click this button to add metrics to the visualization.
- **Line Chart** Click this button and choose a different view for the visualization from the drop-down list that appears. The options are **Area Chart**, **Bar Chart**, **Scatter Chart**, and **Grid**.
- **Drill Into Logs** Click this button to dig deeper into the logs captured for this resource for a better understanding of the metrics that you are viewing. (This feature is currently in preview, so we will not dive into it here, as its functionality is subject to change.)
- **New Alert Rule** Click this button to set up a new alert rule for this metric. You will learn how to do this in a moment.
- **Save to Dashboard** Click this button to pin this metric visualization to a dashboard or send it to a workbook.
- **Metrics** Click this to change the metric displayed in the visualization. The metric shown in Figure 4-12 is **Source VM CPU Credits Consumed Avg**.

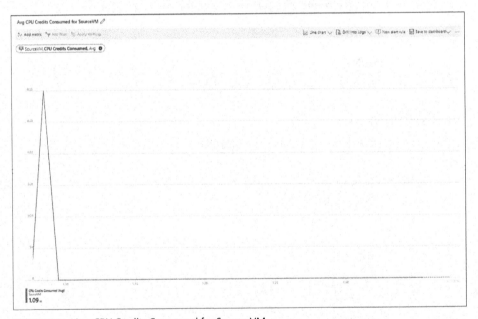

FIGURE 4-12 Avg CPU Credits Consumed for Source VM.

3. Click the **New Alert Rule** button.

   The Create an Alert Rule wizard starts with the **Condition** tab displayed. (See Figure 4-13.) Depending on your needs, you can do one of the following:

   - Leave the settings in the **Condition** tab as is.

- Click the **Add Condition** button and follow the prompts to add a new condition for the rule to assess along with the current one.

- Click the link for the condition in the **Condition Name** list to edit the condition.

> **NOTE** The **Scope** tab is automatically populated with the details of the VM you selected.

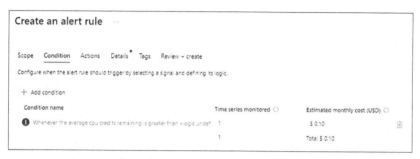

FIGURE 4-13 Create an alert rule.

For this exercise, we will edit the condition.

4. Click the link for the condition in the **Condition Name** list.

The **Alert Logic** section of the **Configure Signal Logic** dialog box offers different options depending on what you select as the **Threshold** setting. We will explore these different settings now.

5. In the **Alert Logic** section, under **Threshold**, click **Static**.

You'll see the settings shown in Figure 4-14. You don't need to change any of these settings; we are simply going to review them here:

- **Operator**   The options in this drop-down list are **Greater Than**, **Less Than**, **Greater Than or Equal To**, and **Less Than or Equal To**.

- **Aggregation Type**   The options in this drop-down list are **Average**, **Maximum**, **Minimum**, **Total**, and **Count**.

- **Threshold Value**   Here, you enter the threshold value to monitor against.

- **Unit**   This is where you select the threshold unit.

- **Aggregation Granularity (Period)**   This defines the period over which the aggregation points will be grouped for analysis.

- **Frequency of Evaluation**   This is where you specify how often the rule should be triggered.

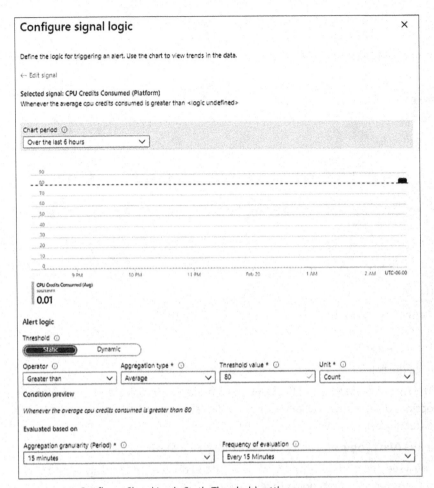

FIGURE 4-14 Configure Signal Logic Static Threshold settings.

6. In the **Alert Logic** section, under **Threshold**, click **Dynamic**.

   You'll see the settings shown in Figure 4-15. For this exercise, we will create a dynamic threshold, so you will change these settings as outlined here.

   ■ **Operator** The options in this drop-down list are the same as for the Static Threshold settings. For this example, choose **Greater or Less Than**.

   ■ **Aggregation Type** The options in this drop-down list are the same as for the Static Threshold settings. For this example, choose **Average**.

   ■ **Threshold Sensitivity** The options in this drop-down list are **High**, **Medium**, and **Low**. For this example, choose **Medium**.

   ■ **Aggregation Granularity (Period)** This option is the same as for the Static Threshold settings. For this example, choose **5 Minutes**.

   ■ **Frequency of Evaluation** This option is the same as for the Static Threshold settings. For this example, choose **Every 5 Minutes**.

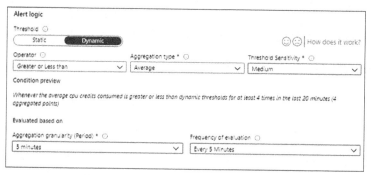

FIGURE 4-15 Configure Signal Logic Dynamic Threshold settings.

7. Click **Advanced Settings**, enter the following information, and click **OK**. (See Figure 4-16.)

   ▪ **Number of Violations** This number specifies how many violations should occur before the alert is triggered. For this exercise, choose **4**.

   ▪ **Evaluation Period** This indicates the timeframe during which the specified number of violations must occur to trigger an alert. In this case, choose **20 Minutes**.

   ▪ **Ignore Data Before** To begin monitoring for the alert conditions at some date and time in the future, select this check box and choose the desired date and time. We'll leave this unchecked in this case.

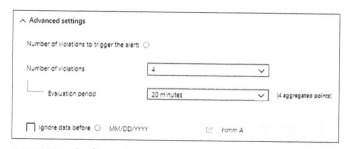

FIGURE 4-16 Configure Signal Logic Dynamic Threshold settings.

8. Back in the **Condition** tab of the Create an Alert Rule wizard (see Figure 4-17), click **Next**.

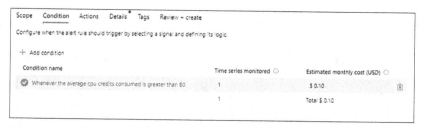

FIGURE 4-17 Back to the Condition tab of the Create an Alert Rule wizard.

In the Actions tab of the Create an Alert Rule wizard (see Figure 4-18), you can select an existing action group or create a new one. In our case, we will create a new one.

FIGURE 4-18   Actions tab.

9. Click the **Create Action Group** button.

10. In the **Basics** tab of the Create an Action Group wizard (see Figure 4-19), enter the following information. Then click **Next**.

   - **Subscription**   Select the subscription you want to use to create the action group.

   - **Resource Group**   Select the resource group you want to use to create the action group. Alternatively, click the **Create New** link and follow the prompts.

   - **Action Group Name**   Type a unique name for the action group.

   - **Display Name**   Type a unique display name for the action group. This can contain a maximum of 12 characters.

FIGURE 4-19   Basics tab in the Create an Action Group wizard.

The **Notifications** tab opens. (See Figure 4-20.) Here, you select the notification type for any alerts triggered by the role. You can choose to send the notification by email to an Azure resource manager role or to send it by email, SMS message, push, or voice to the recipient(s) of your choosing.

FIGURE 4-20 The Notifications tab of the Create an Action Group wizard.

11. In the **Notification Type** drop-down list, choose **Email/SMS Message/Push/Voice**.

12. In the **Email/SMS Message/Push/Voice** dialog box (see Figure 4-21), enter the following information. Then click **OK**.

   ■ **Email** Select this check box and enter the email address to send email notifications to when the alert rule is triggered.

> **NOTE** You can only enter one email address in this field. If you want to send the notification to multiple email addresses, use email groups or set up multiple notification types.

   ■ **SMS** Select this check box and enter a country code and phone number to send SMS notifications to when the alert is triggered.

   ■ **Azure Mobile App Notification** In this case, leave this unchecked. You would select this if you wanted to send a notification by way of an Azure mobile app.

   ■ **Voice** In this case, leave this unchecked. You would select this if you wanted to send a voice-based notification.

   ■ **Enable the Common Alert Schema** You select this option to standardize the alert schema across all the different alerting options. In this case, click **No**.

13. In the **Notifications** tab of the Create an Action Group wizard, click **Next**.

14. In the **Actions** tab, open the **Action Type** drop-down list and choose what type of action you want to perform when the alert rule is triggered. In this case, choose **Automation Runbook**. Then enter a name for the action type (here, **RestartVM**) and click Next. (See Figure 4-22.)

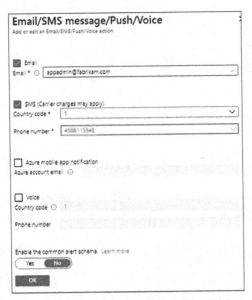

FIGURE 4-21 The Email/SMS message/Push/Voice section.

FIGURE 4-22 The Actions tab of the Create an Action Group wizard.

15. In the **Configure Runbook** dialog box (see Figure 4-23), enter the following information. Then click **OK**.

   ■ **Run Runbook**   Click **Enable** to specify that the runbook should be run.

   ■ **Runbook Source**   Select the runbook source. In this case, choose **Built-in**.

   When you choose **Built-in** as the runbook source, the dialog box displays additional settings. These are also shown in Figure 4-23.

   ■ **Runbook**   Choose the built-in runbook you want to use. In our case, we select **Restart VM**.

   ■ **Subscription**   Choose the Azure subscription that contains the Azure Automation account you want to use.

- **Automation Account** Select the automation account you want to use. Alternatively, click **New** and follow the prompts.
- **Enable the Common Alert Schema** For this example, choose **No**.

FIGURE 4-23 The Configure Runbook dialog box.

16. In the **Actions** tab of the Create an Action Group wizard, click **Next**.

17. In the **Tags** tab (see Figure 4-24), enter a name and value for any tags you want to associate with the action group, and click **Next**.

FIGURE 4-24 The Tags tab of the Create an Action Group wizard.

18. In the **Review + Create** tab (see Figure 4-25), review your settings, and click **Review + Create** to create the action group.

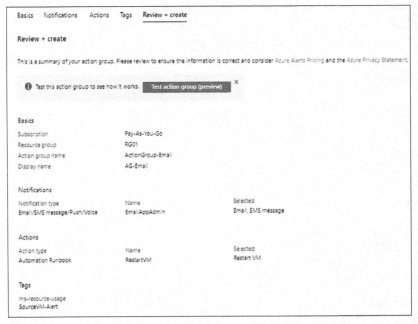

FIGURE 4-25   The Review + Create tab of the Create an Action Group wizard.

The action group you just created appears in the Actions tab of the Create a Metric Alert wizard (see Figure 4-26).

FIGURE 4-26   Back in the Actions tab of the Create a Metric Alert wizard.

19. Optionally, create additional action groups.

20. Click **Next**.

21. In the **Details** tab of the Create a Metric Alert wizard (see Figure 4-27), enter the following information. Then click **Next**:

   - **Subscription**   Select the subscription you want to use to create the metric alert.

   - **Resource Group**   Select the resource group you want to use to create the metric alert. Alternatively, click the **Create New** link and follow the prompts.

- **Severity** Choose a severity for the alert when the rule conditions are met. You can select between **Critical**, **Error**, **Warning**, **Informational**, and **Verbose** based on your requirements. Here, select **1-Error**.

- **Alert Rule Name** Type a unique name for the alert rule.

- **Alert Rule Description** Type a description of the alert rule.

- **Enable Upon Creation** Select this check box.

- **Automatically Resolve Alerts** Select this check box.

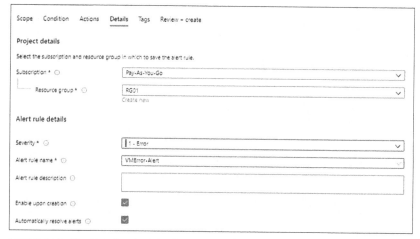

FIGURE 4-27 The Details tab of the Create a Metric Alert wizard.

22. In the **Tags** tab (see Figure 4-28), enter a name and value for any tags you want to define for the alert rule. Then click **Next**.

FIGURE 4-28 The Tags tab of the Create a Metric Alert wizard.

23. In the **Review + Create** tab (see Figure 4-29), review your settings and click **Review + Create** to create the metric alert.

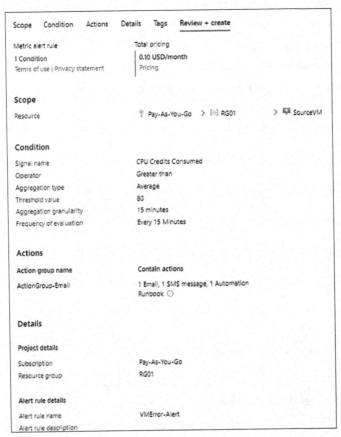

FIGURE 4-29 The Review + Create tab of the Create a Metric Alert wizard.

CREATE LOG ANALYTICS WORKSPACE

Next, you need to create a Log Analytics workspace.

24. Type **log analytics workspace** in the Azure Portal search box and select it from the list that appears. (See Figure 4-30.)

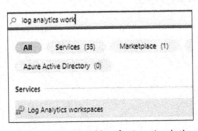

FIGURE 4-30 Searching for Log Analytics workspace.

25. Click the **Create Log Analytics Workspace** button. (See Figure 4-31.)

FIGURE 4-31   Starting the Create Log Analytics Workspace wizard in Azure Portal.

26. In the **Basic** tab of the Create Log Analytics Workspace wizard (see Figure 4-32), enter the following information. Then click **Next**:

- **Subscription**   Select the subscription you want to use to create the workspace.
- **Resource Group**   Select the resource group you want to use to create the workspace. Alternatively, click the **Create New** link and follow the prompts.
- **Name**   Enter a unique name for the workspace.
- **Region**   Select the Azure region to host the workspace.

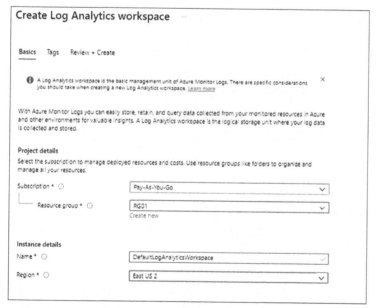

FIGURE 4-32   The Basic tab of the Create Log Analytics Workspace wizard.

27. In the **Tags** tab (see Figure 4-33), type a name and value for any tags you would like to associate with the workspace, and click **Next**.

FIGURE 4-33 The Tags tab in the Create Log Analytics Workspace wizard.

28. In the **Review + Create** tab (see Figure 4-34), review your settings, and click **Review + Create** to create the workspace.

FIGURE 4-34 Review + Create tab in the Create Log Analytics Workspace wizard.

CONFIGURE AZURE VM MONITORING

Now that you have created the Log Analytics workspace, you can set up monitoring for your Azure VM.

29. In Azure Portal, navigate to the VM for which you want to set up monitoring.

30. In the left pane of the VM's configuration blade, under **Monitoring**, click **Metrics**. (See Figure 4-35.)

Monitoring

- ♥ Insights
- ▥ Alerts
- ⋔ Metrics
- ▦ Diagnostic settings
- ⥆ Logs
- ▧ Connection monitor (classic)
- ◩ Workbooks

FIGURE 4-35 Configure monitoring for the Azure VM.

31. In the right pane, click the **Enable** button to enable Insights. (See Figure 4-36.)

FIGURE 4-36 Enable Insights.

32. Azure Monitor automatically locates an existing Log Analytics workspace and its associated subscription. If it is not the right one for your environment, select the appropriate subscription and Log Analytics workspace. (See Figure 4-37.)

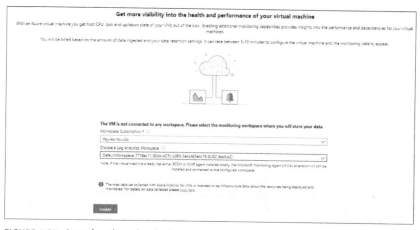

FIGURE 4-37 Locating the subscription and workspace.

33. Click the **Enable** button.

When the VM's integration with the Log Analytics workspace is complete, the VM's **Performance** tab opens with the **Logical Disk Performance** view displayed. This view includes the following metrics for VM resources by default (see Figure 4-38):

- CPU Utilization %
- Available Memory %
- Logical Disk IOPS
- Logical Disk MB/s

> **TIP** You can scroll through the list of metrics; there are many more available. You can also change the view's time range. You can also pin key metrics to a dashboard for easy viewing.

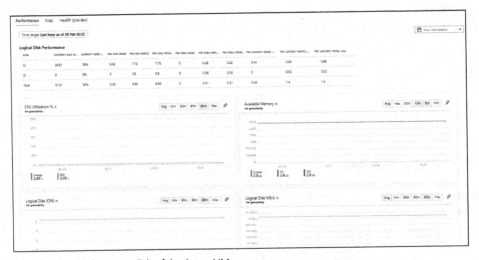

FIGURE 4-38 Performance Tab of the Azure VM.

34. Click the **Map** tab.

> **NOTE** It might take a few minutes for the map to load, depending on how much time the service has had to analyze your VM.

You will see a map similar to the one shown in Figure 4-39. This map contains all the active ports on the VM and the processes actively using each port.

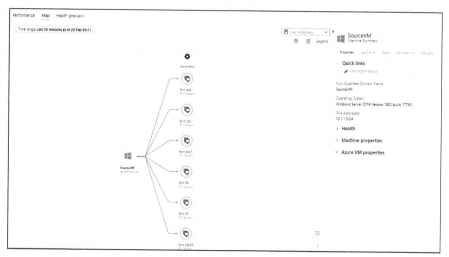

FIGURE 4-39 The Azure VM's Map tab.

35. Click a port or service to see more information about it. (See Figure 4-40.) This will give you deeper insights into the VM.

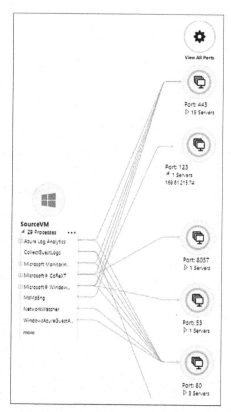

FIGURE 4-40 Viewing more information about a service or port.

SET UP AZURE VM INSIGHTS ALERTS

At this point, you're ready to set up an alert. For this example, you will create an alert for low disk space. Because your test VM likely does not have low disk space at this time, you can either set the monitoring threshold very high or add data to the VM disk to reduce the space below your monitoring threshold. In our case, we will do the former—raise an alert if the C drive goes below 90% free. (In production use, you would generally not set such a high threshold for disk space alerts.)

36. In the pane to the right of the **Map** tab, click the **Log Events** link.

37. In the **Event Type** list (see Figure 4-41), click **InsightsMetrics**.

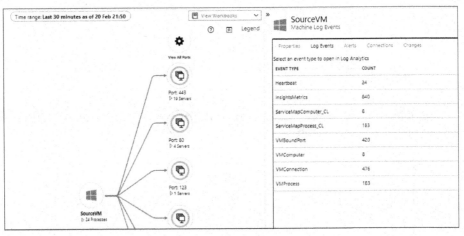

FIGURE 4-41   The Insight option in the Map tab of the Azure VM.

38. The **Log Explorer** window opens with a pre-defined query that searches for all InsightsMetrics for the VM. (See Figure 4-42.) You will see various metrics, including Network, LogicalDisk, Processor, Memory, and others.

39. Locate the metric for which you want to set up the alert—in our case, the **LogicalDisk FreeSpacePercentage** metric.

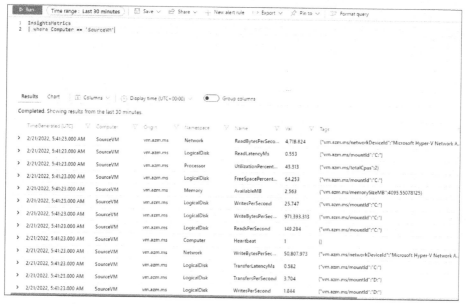

FIGURE 4-42   The InsightsMetrics for the Azure VM.

40. In the pre-populated query at the top of the Log Explorer window, enter the following code after the VM name ('SourceVM'), as shown in Figure 4-43. Then click **Run**.

```
And Namespace == 'LogicalDisk' and Name == 'FreeSpacePercentage'
```

FIGURE 4-43   The InsightsMetrics search.

41. The **Log Explorer** window returns a list of **LogicalDisk FreeSpacePercentage** metrics. (See Figure 4-44.)

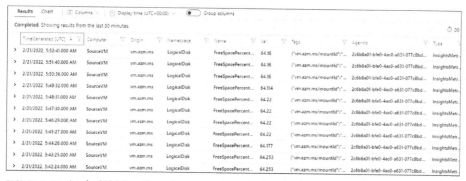

FIGURE 4-44   LogicalDisk FreeSpacePercentage metrics for the Azure VM.

42. Click the **New Alert Rule** button along the top of the **Log Explorer** window. (See Figure 4-45.)

FIGURE 4-45 The New Alert Rule button.

43. In the **Condition** tab of the **Create an Alert Rule** wizard, under **Measurement**, change the following settings (see Figure 4-46):

- **Measure** Choose **Val**.
- **Aggregation Type** Select **Average**.
- **Aggregation Granularity** Choose **5 Minutes**.

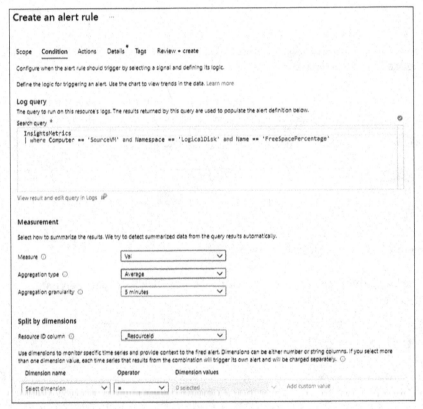

FIGURE 4-46 The Condition tab of the Create an Alert Rule wizard.

44. Leave the settings in the **Split by Dimensions** section of the **Condition** tab at their default values.

45. In the **Alert Logic** section of the **Condition** tab (see Figure 4-47), enter the following information. Then click **Next**:

- **Operator**   Select **Less Than or Equal To**.
- **Threshold Value**   Type **90**. (Remember: You want a high value here to make it easier to trigger the alert, just for the purposes of this exercise.)
- **Frequency of Evaluation**   Select **5 Minutes**.

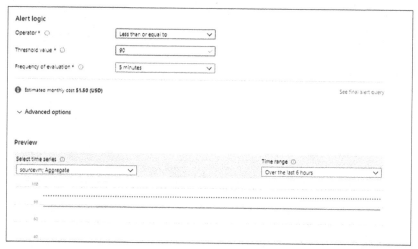

FIGURE 4-47   The Alert Logic section of the Condition tab.

46. In the **Actions** tab, click **Add Action Groups**, and select the action group you created earlier. Alternatively, you can click **Create Action Group** and follow the prompts to create a new one. (See Figure 4-48.) Then click **Next**.

FIGURE 4-48   Choose an action group.

47. In the **Details** tab (see Figure 4-49), change the following settings (leave the others at their default values). Then click **Next**:

- **Subscription**   Select the subscription you want to use to create the alert rule.
- **Resource Group**   Select the resource group you want to use to create the alert rule. Alternatively, click the **Create New** link and follow the prompts.
- **Severity**   Select **2-Warning**.

- **Alert Rule Name** Type a unique name for the alert rule.
- **Alert Rule Description** Type a description of the alert rule.
- **Region** Select the Azure region in which to create the alert rule.
- **Enable Upon Creation** Select this check box.

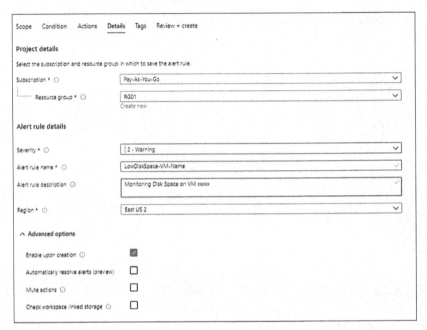

FIGURE 4-49 Enter the alert rule details.

48. In the **Tags** tab (see Figure 4-50), type a name and value for any tags you want to add for this alert rule, and click **Next**.

FIGURE 4-50 Adding tags to the alert rule.

49. In the **Review + Create** tab, review your settings, and click **Review + Create** to create the alert rule.

50. After the alert has been created, let your system run for 15 or 20 minutes.

The alert should trigger frequently, indicating low disk space on the test VM.
(See Figure 4-51.)

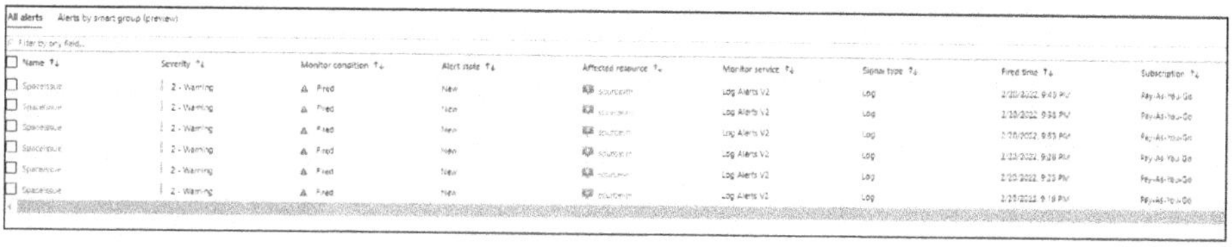

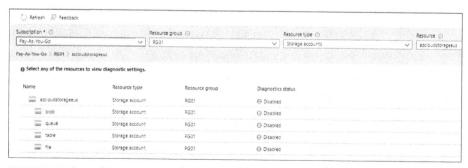

FIGURE 4-51   Test VM results.

CONFIGURE AZURE STORAGE MONITORING

Finally, you can set up monitoring for an Azure Storage account.

51. In Azure Portal, navigate to the Azure Storage account for which you would like to set up monitoring.

52. In the left pane of the Azure Storage account's configuration blade, under **Monitoring**, click **Diagnostic Settings**. (See Figure 4-52.)

FIGURE 4-52   Setting up an Azure Storage account for monitoring.

The pane on the right shows the current diagnostic status of the various storage types. (See Figure 4-53.)

FIGURE 4-53   Azure Storage account diagnostic status.

53. Click the **blob** entry in the **Name** list.

Azure displays the blob's diagnostic configuration. As shown in Figure 4-54, the blob's diagnostic settings are currently not configured.

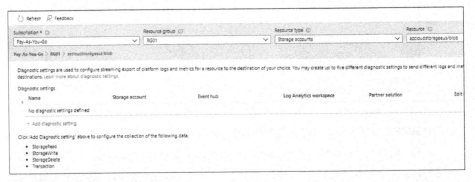

FIGURE 4-54 Blob diagnostic status.

54. Click the **Add Diagnostic Setting** link.

55. In the **Diagnostic Setting** dialog box (see Figure 4-55), change the following settings. (Leave any other settings at their default value.) Then click **Save**.

- **Diagnostic Setting Name**   Type a name for the diagnostic setting.

- **Logs/Categories**   Select the check box next to each log category you want to collect—in this case, **StorageRead**, **StorageWrite**, and **StorageDelete**.

- **Metrics**   Select the check box next to each metric you want to collect—here, **Transaction**.

- **Send Log to Analytics Workspace**   Select this check box. Then enter the details for the workspace in the settings that appear, including the workspace's subscription and name. In this case, select the workspace you created earlier.

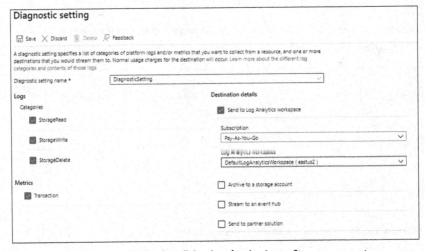

FIGURE 4-55 The Diagnostic Setting dialog box for the Azure Storage account.

You can set up the diagnostic settings for any other storage resource type by following these same steps. (See Figure 4-56.) You can apply the same settings as you did for blob or different settings based on the storage type. You can also set up diagnostic settings on the storage account level to apply the same settings across the entire account.

FIGURE 4-56 Azure Storage account diagnostic status.

RUN QUERIES ON AZURE STORAGE

Now that you've configured the diagnostic settings for log collection for your storage account, run a few queries in the Azure Portal to monitor the output and set up alerts if needed.

56. In the left pane of the configuration blade for the Azure Storage account for which you configured the diagnostic settings, under **Monitoring**, click **Logs**. (See Figure 4-57.)

FIGURE 4-57 Azure Storage account logs monitoring.

A query explorer opens, with a set of pre-defined queries for you to run. These include frequently used queries for auditing, performance monitoring, error tracking, and alerting purposes. (See Figure 4-58.)

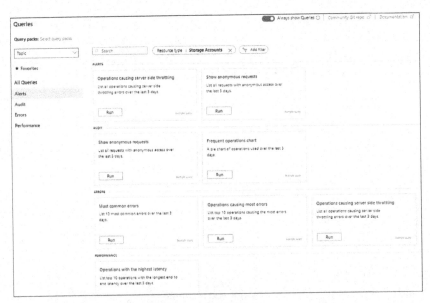

FIGURE 4-58 The Azure Storage query explorer.

Because you most likely would not have any errors or performance bottlenecks in your test storage, you need to select a query that might show some output, such as one that generates a Frequent Operations chart.

57. Click the **Run** button in the **Frequent Operations** tile of the query explorer.

The system displays a pie chart showing the frequency of all operations performed on this test storage account. (See Figure 4-59.)

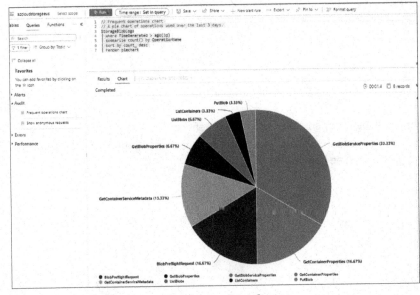

FIGURE 4-59 The frequent operations chart on Azure Storage.

Best practices

Following are some general best practices regarding using the Azure Monitor service based on real-world deployments that can help you optimize your configuration or deployment.

- **Deploy or migrate to Azure Monitor agents** Use the Azure Monitor agent on Windows and Linux VMs instead of the legacy Log Analytics agent. The Log Analytics agent will be retired in August 2024. Still, it is recommended to migrate to the newer agent as soon as possible. First, though, evaluate all the monitor solutions you are currently using. If they are compatible, you can migrate to the new agent gracefully, as Microsoft will make all new Azure Monitor functionality and capabilities available to new agent installs. The agent already supports newer functionality such as filtering, scoping, and multi-homing of data. The Azure Monitor agent also uses system-managed identities instead of the legacy workspace keys required by Log Analytics agents. This makes larger deployments of agents easier and more secure.

- **Use Application Insights for better application monitoring** Application Insights can provide you with deeper insights into user behavior, application behavior, application performance, and so on. This will help you resolve critical issues more quickly. It also provides actionable insights to optimize your product and improve responsiveness. Finally, you can use Application Insights proactively to identify and address potential issues with your application.

- **Use Private Link for private connectivity to Azure Monitor** The Private Link service allows you to connect to Azure Monitor over a private network using Azure ExpressRoute. As a result, all your logging traffic will be transmitted and accessible only over a private network. This can be advantageous in environments with compliance requirements that prohibit the transmission of such logs over public networks.

- **Use keys to encrypt Azure Storage accounts used by Log Analytics** You can use Microsoft-managed keys to encrypt this storage, or you can use your own keys integrated with Azure Key Vault to achieve this encryption. If there are compliance reasons for your environment to use your own customer-managed keys, Azure Monitor does support this, and you can use this capability if the need arises.

- **Use AutoScale when possible** Azure Monitor supports the use of monitoring rules to trigger autoscaling for various Azure workloads, such as Azure VM scale sets, Azure API Management services, Azure App Services, and Azure Cloud Services. So, you can build logic within your application to automatically scale up or down based on user load, which improves application response times and optimizes costs. This is a great feature to use, provided your application supports it.

- **Automatically enable monitoring for new Azure resources**   Azure Monitor allows you to automatically enable monitoring for new resources added into your environment to ensure they are actively observed from the start. Continuous monitoring using DevOps integration is also supported, so new application resources are automatically brought under the purview of Azure Monitor. It is a good practice to set up these capabilities so you can easily identify root causes for any issues in your environment without having to constantly intervene manually to ensure workloads are being monitored.

- **Set up actionable alerts**   Sometimes it's not enough to receive an alert. You need an alert that can perform some type of pre-defined action to mitigate whatever condition triggered the alert. These are called actionable alerts. Examples of actionable alerts include autoscaling workloads based on resource utilization, triggering Azure Automation runbooks based on resource metrics, and triggering webhooks to activate external resources based on pre-defined criteria or log events. Automatically sending email messages, SMS messages, or voice calls to relevant administrators of a resource are also classified as actionable alerts. However, when possible, it's preferable to configure automated actions that will alleviate or resolve the issue without manual intervention to minimize downtimes.

- **Use dynamic thresholds when possible**   Unlike static thresholds, dynamic thresholds enable Azure Monitor to develop monitoring baselines based on observed usage of a resource. This can in turn reduce the number of false positive alerts. Use dynamic thresholds for resources that do not have consistent usage and can have temporary fluctuations in performance that might trigger false positives.

- **Share dashboards between teams to ensure consistent monitoring**   Azure Monitor allows you to share dashboards so that different team members or inter-dependent teams monitor the same resource metrics and events. This ensures a timely response when issues arise. It is a good practice to develop these dashboards in collaboration with the different team members and interconnected teams to identify and track the correct key performance indicators (KPIs) for each application or service they are monitoring.

- **Review your monitoring thresholds and KPIs on a regular basis**   It is a good practice, especially in large organizations, to conduct regular collaborative reviews of the monitoring setup and update thresholds and KPIs based on ongoing developments, internal feedback, historical performance metrics, and other relevant criteria. This will help ensure that your monitoring solution is up to date and provides relevant alerts.

Chapter 5

Azure Network Watcher

Overview

Azure provides a suite of tools under the Azure Network Watcher service that you can use to monitor and troubleshoot network issues for IaaS resources such as virtual machines (VMs), virtual private network (VPN) gateways, ExpressRoute connections, virtual networks, application gateways, and so on. These tools can perform point-in-time checks to analyze and troubleshoot ongoing issues, or monitor, analyze, and show availability and latency trends over time to optimize performance.

The tools have evolved over time to cover different networking scenarios encountered in the Azure IaaS environment that require constant monitoring or troubleshooting on an ongoing basis. Some of these scenarios include the following:

- Analyzing and troubleshooting inbound and outbound network traffic filtering for VMs.
- Analyzing and troubleshooting network routing issues affecting IaaS workloads.
- Monitoring traffic between IaaS endpoints or IaaS and non-Azure endpoints for latency, availability, and diagnostics.
- Performing IP flow log analysis to improve network performance.
- Troubleshooting issues with VPN connectivity to Azure gateways.

To achieve each of these objectives, Network Watcher provides a toolset that includes monitoring, diagnostic, and logging tools such as the following:

- Connection Monitor
- Topology Monitor
- IP Flow Verify
- NSG Diagnostic
- Security Rules Analyzer
- VPN Troubleshooter
- Packet Capture Tool
- Connection Troubleshooter Tool
- NSG Flow Logs Capture

Enabling Azure Network Watcher

Before you can use these tools, you must enable the Azure Network Watcher service. The following steps show you how:

1. Log in to the Azure Portal, type **network watcher** in the search box, and select it from the list that appears. (See Figure 5-1.)

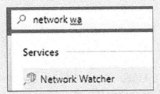

FIGURE 5-1 Search for the Network Watcher service.

2. In the **Overview** tab of the **Network Watcher** page, click the **Add** button. (See Figure 5-2.)

FIGURE 5-2 Click Add in the Overview tab.

3. On the **Add Network Watcher** page (see Figure 5-3), select the subscription and regions in which you want to enable Network Watcher, and click **Add**.

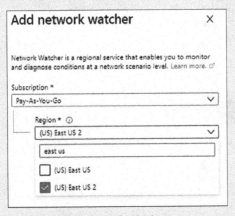

FIGURE 5-3 Add Network Watcher page.

Azure will enable support for Network Watcher in the selected regions in a matter of minutes.

Key features

This section covers each of the tools listed in the chapter overview to provide you with a better understanding of how each one can be set up and used to address networking issues in any Azure environment.

Connection Monitor

Connection Monitor enables you to regularly monitor communications between Azure IaaS VMs and other Azure IaaS workloads or endpoints and non-Azure endpoints to detect and diagnose availability, latency, and performance issues. The non-Azure workloads can include the following:

- Servers on which the Microsoft Log Analytics agent has been deployed
- Fully qualified domain names (FQDNs) such as portal.office.com
- Uniform resource locators (URLs) such as https://portal.azure.com
- IPv4 addresses such as 23.11.197.159 (resolves to www.microsoft.com)

By monitoring on a regular time interval, Connection Monitor can issue an alert when workloads or services have gone offline or are unreachable. Connection Monitor also gathers latency information from different regions to identify bottlenecks and issue alerts. This can help with future planning for workload hosting or migration.

Connection Monitor walkthrough

The following sections walk you through the process of creating a Connection Monitor instance with the Azure Portal.

> **IMPORTANT** If you are following along, you'll want to select resources and unique resource names based on your environment for each of your deployments.

> **IMPORTANT** If you are following along, delete any unwanted resources after you have completed testing to reduce charges being levied by Microsoft for these resources.

USING THE AZURE PORTAL

To create a Connection Monitor instance using the Azure Portal, follow these steps:

1. Log in to the Azure Portal, type **network watcher** in the search box, and select it from the list that appears.

2. In the left pane of the **Network Watcher** configuration blade, under **Monitoring**, click **Connection Monitor**. (See Figure 5-4.)

FIGURE 5-4 Click Connection Monitor.

3. On the **Connection Monitor** page, click the **Create** button. (See Figure 5-5.)

FIGURE 5-5 Connection Monitor – Create Connection Monitor wizard.

4. In the **Basics** tab of the Create Connection Monitor wizard (see Figure 5-6), enter the following information and click **Next**:

- **Connection Monitor Name** Enter a unique name for this Connection Monitor instance.

- **Subscription** Select the subscription you want to use.

- **Region** Select the region for the Connection Monitor instance. This should match the region hosting the workload you want to monitor.

- **Workspace Configuration** Select an existing Log Analytics workspace or let the wizard create one for you.

5. In the **Test Groups** tab (see Figure 5-7), click **Add Test Group** to define the source, destination, and testing configurations.

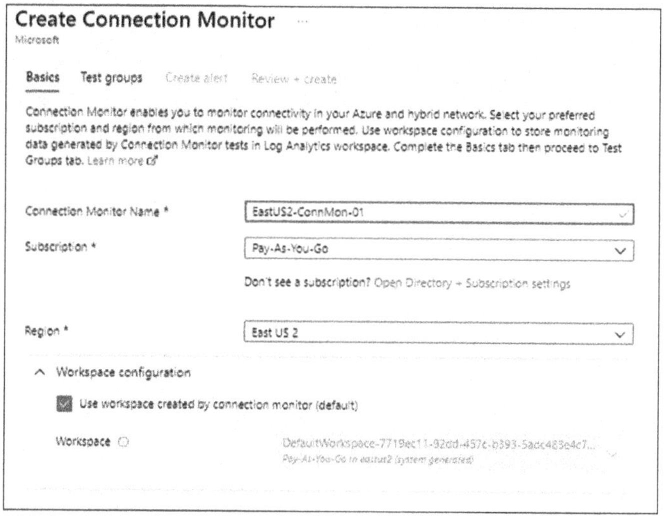

FIGURE 5-6 The Basics tab of the Create Connection Monitor wizard.

Basics   **Test groups**   Create alert   Review + create

Each test group in Connection Monitor defines a number of sources, destinations and test configurations. All sources and destinations added to a test group with te failure rate and round-trip time.

Add Test Group

Name	↑↓	Sources	↑↓	Destination
EastUS2-TestGroup-1		SrcSubnet(RG01)		DestVM(RG01) + 2more

FIGURE 5-7 The Test Groups tab of the Create Connection Monitor wizard.

6. On the **Add Test Group Details** page (see Figure 5-8), type a name for the test group in the **Test Group Name** box.

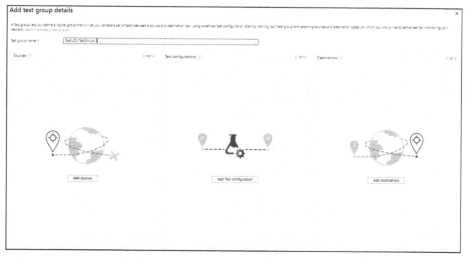

FIGURE 5-8 Add Test Group Details page.

7. Click the **Add Sources** button in the **Sources** section of the **Add Test Group Details** page.

8. Use the tabs in the **Add Sources** dialog box to add the Azure and non-Azure endpoints you want to use to monitor the connection. (See Figure 5-9.) Then click **Add Endpoints**.

NOTE You can select multiple Azure and non-Azure endpoints as sources, depending on your needs.

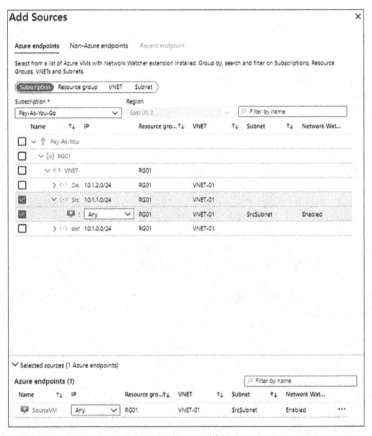

FIGURE 5-9 Create Connection Monitor – Add Sources.

9. Back in the **Add Test Group Details** page, under **Test Configurations**, click the **Add Test Configuration** button. (See Figure 5-10.)

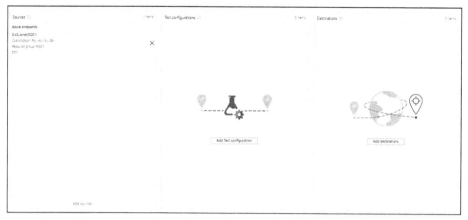

FIGURE 5-10 Create Connection Monitor – Add Test Configuration.

10. In the **New Configuration** tab of the **Add Test Configuration** page (see Figure 5-11), enter the following information. Then click the **Add Test Configuration** button:

   ■ **Test Configuration Name**   Enter a unique name for the test configuration.

   ■ **Protocol**   Select **HTTP**, **TCP**, or **ICMP**. In this case, I selected **ICMP**.

> **NOTE** Different options will appear below the Protocol setting, depending on which protocol you choose. The options shown in Figure 5-11 are what you'll see if you choose ICMP, as I did.

   ■ **Disable Traceroute**   Leave this check box checked (the default).

   ■ **Test Frequency**   Specify how often you would like to perform testing.

   ■ **Checks Failed (%)**   Specify what percentage of failure is acceptable.

   ■ **Round Trip Time (ms)**   Enter the round-trip time (in milliseconds) deemed acceptable.

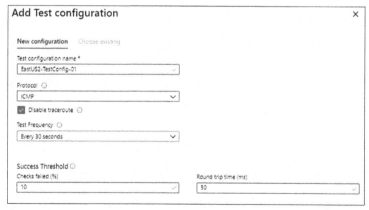

FIGURE 5-11 The Add Test Configuration page.

11. Back in the **Add Test Group Details** page, under **Destinations**, click the **Add Destinations** button. (See Figure 5-12.)

FIGURE 5-12   Click Add Destinations.

12. Use the tabs in the **Add Destinations** dialog box to add the Azure endpoints, non-Azure endpoints, and external addresses you want to use as destinations for testing. (See Figure 5-13.) Then click **Add Endpoints**.

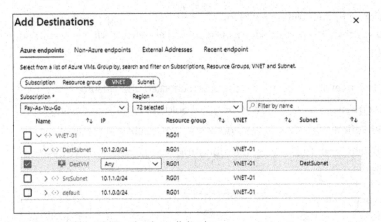

FIGURE 5-13   The Add Destinations dialog box.

> **NOTE**   You can select a combination of Azure endpoints, non-Azure endpoints, and external addresses as your destinations, depending on your needs.

13. If you click the **External Addresses** tab, you'll see that Azure provides addresses for known Microsoft Online services by default. (See Figure 5-14.) To add your own custom URLs, click **Add Endpoint** and follow the prompts.

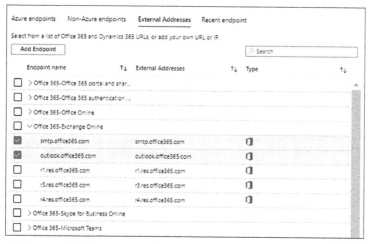

FIGURE 5-14 Add Destinations – External Addresses.

14. Back in the **Add Test Group Details** page (see Figure 5-15), verify your settings. Then click **Add Test Group**.

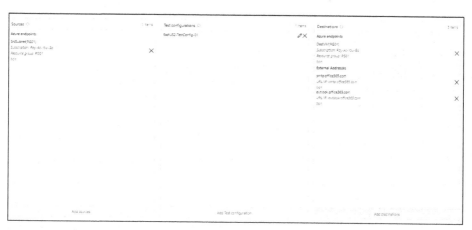

FIGURE 5-15 Check your settings and create the test group.

15. The new test group appears in the **Test Groups** tab of the Create Connection Monitor wizard. (See Figure 5-16.)

FIGURE 5-16 The Test Groups tab with the new test group listed.

16. Optionally, repeat steps 5–14 to create more test groups.

17. After you've created all the test groups you need, click the **Create Alert** tab.

18. In the **Create Alert** tab (see Figure 5-17), under **Action Group**, click the **Action Group** button to create or select an action group.

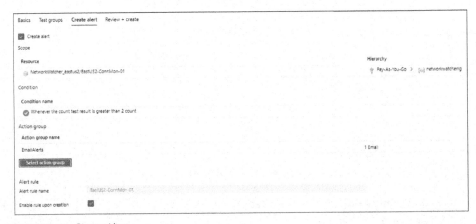

FIGURE 5-17 Create Alert.

19. Select the **Enable Rule Upon Creation** check box.

20. Click the **Review + Create** button.

21. In the **Review + Create** tab (See Figure 5-18), verify your settings. Then click the **Create** button.

FIGURE 5-18 The Review + Create tab of the Create Connection Monitor wizard.

22. Azure creates the Connection Monitor instance and displays its **Overview** tab. At first, the instance's alert status will appear as Indeterminate. (See Figure 5-19.) It will need some time to run tests and gather data to generate output.

FIGURE 5-19   The Connection Monitor Overview tab, with indeterminate status.

23. After you give Connection Monitor some time to run tests and gather data, refresh the **Overview** tab. Connection Monitor will provide an updated status that shows you that all the tests are succeeding (see Figure 5-20) or that some are failing (see Figure 5-21).

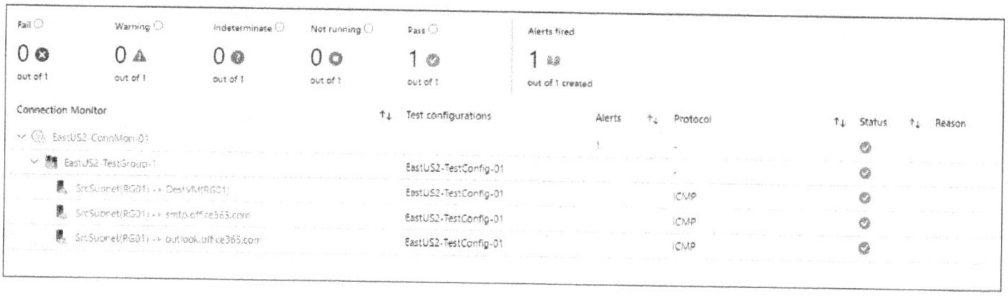

FIGURE 5-20   All tests are succeeding.

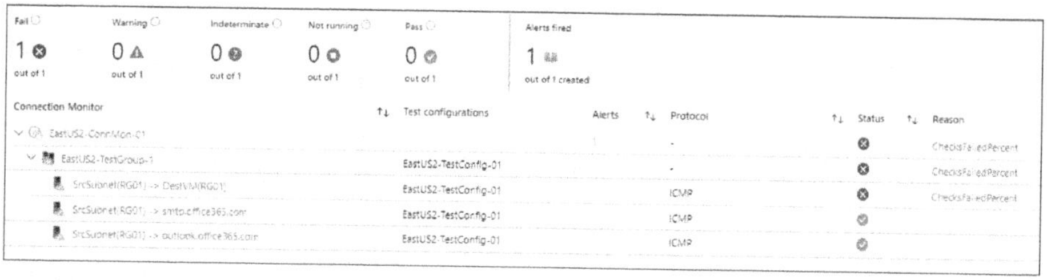

FIGURE 5-21   Some tests are failing.

Topology Monitor

Topology Monitor enables you to generate a visual representation of the interconnectivity between different network components in a virtual network. This can help you better understand how the different services are connected on the network layer. You can easily download this topology for editing and sharing purposes in SVG format.

The topology diagram in Figure 5-22, generated using Topology Monitor, shows a virtual network, VNET-01, that contains three subnets (default, SrcSubnet, and DestSubnet), each with one VM with a single network interface card (NIC), and a single network security group (NSG) attached to each.

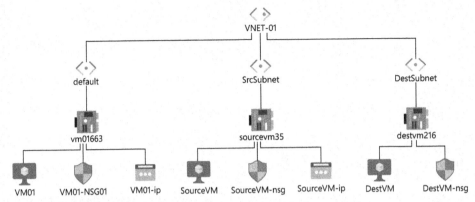

FIGURE 5-22 Topology diagram generated using Topology Monitor.

Topology Monitor walkthrough

The following sections walk you through the process of using Topology Monitor to create a topology diagram using the Azure Portal.

USING THE AZURE PORTAL

To use Topology Monitor to create a topology diagram using the Azure Portal, follow these steps:

1. Log in to the Azure Portal, type **network watcher** in the search box, and select it from the list that appears.

2. In the left pane of the **Network Watcher** configuration blade, under **Monitoring**, click **Topology**. (See Figure 5-23.)

FIGURE 5-23 Click Topology.

3. In the **Topology** page (see Figure 5-24), enter the following information:

- **Subscription** Choose the subscription that contains the network for which you want to generate a topology diagram.

- **Resource Group** Choose the resource group containing the components you want to include in the topology diagram.

- **Virtual Network** Choose any virtual networks you want to include in the topology diagram.

FIGURE 5-24 Generating a topology diagram.

Topology Monitor automatically generates the topology diagram based on your inputs in the bottom pane of the **Topology** page. (See Figure 5-25.)

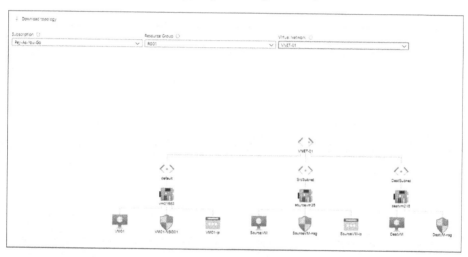

FIGURE 5-25 Topology Monitor generates a topology diagram based on your inputs.

4. To download the topology diagram, click the **Download Topology** link at the top of the page.

5. Open the downloaded file in the viewer available on your device.

IP Flow Verify

You can use IP Flow Verify to diagnose traffic restrictions to or from an Azure VM. To use this tool to analyze traffic flow and identify restrictions, you must provide six parameters:

- **Protocol** This will be TCP or UDP.

- **Direction of traffic** This will be inbound or outbound.

- **Local IP address** This will be the local IPv4 or IPv6 address to use as the source for inbound testing or destination for outbound testing.

- **Local port** This will range from 0 to 65535. A single integer value is required.
- **Remote IP address** This will be the remote IPv4 or IPv6 address to use as the destination for inbound testing or source for outbound testing.
- **Remote port** This will range between 0 and 65535. A single integer value is required.

After you provide all these parameters, IP Flow Verify tests the traffic flow, identifies any blocks, analyzes those blocks, and provides details for the security rule causing the traffic restriction.

IP Flow Verify walkthrough

The following sections walk you through the process of using IP Flow Verify to diagnose traffic flow restrictions to or from an Azure VM using the Azure Portal.

USING THE AZURE PORTAL

To use IP Flow Verify to diagnose traffic restrictions, follow these steps:

1. Log in to the Azure Portal, type **network watcher** in the search box, and select it from the list that appears.
2. In the left pane of the **Network Watcher** configuration blade, under **Network Diagnostic Tools**, click **IP Flow Verify**. (See Figure 5-26.)

FIGURE 5-26 Click IP Flow Verify.

3. Enter the following information in the right pane (see Figure 5-27). Then click the **Check** button:

- **Subscription** Select the subscription for the source VM—that is, the VM whose traffic you want to analyze.

- **Resource Group** Select the resource group containing the source VM.

- **Virtual Machine** Select the source VM.

- **Network Interface** Select the NIC on the source VM to use for the test.

- **Protocol** Select the **TCP** or **UDP** option button.

- **Direction** Select the **Inbound** or **Outbound** option button.

- **Local IP Address** Enter the local IP address to test from.

- **Local Port** Enter the local port to use.

- **Remote IP Address** Enter the remote IP address to test to.

- **Remote Port** Enter the remote port to use.

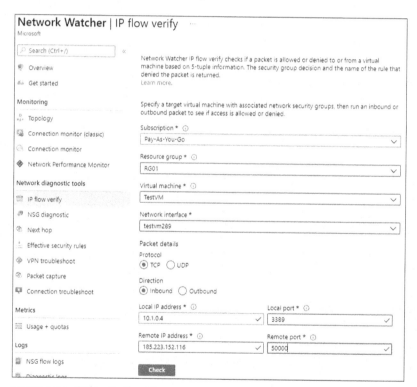

FIGURE 5-27 IP Flow Verify options.

IP Flow Verify diagnoses the flow of traffic. (This takes a few seconds.) It then returns an Access Allowed message (see Figure 5-28) or an Access Denied message (see Figure 5-29). In both cases, IP Flow Verify lists the security rule that is allowing or denying the traffic, so you can take further action if necessary.

FIGURE 5-28 IP Flow Verify – Access Allowed.

FIGURE 5-29 IP Flow Verify – Access Denied.

NSG Diagnostic

The NSG Diagnostic tool can be used to diagnose security configuration issues for VMs, VMSS, or Application gateways on your Azure network. The tool requires a set of parameters, such as the protocol, traffic direction, source and destination IP, and port details, which it uses to evaluate all the NSG rules that traffic between VMs would encounter.

It also provides a detailed analysis of these rules, including the result of each rule and whether the traffic will be allowed or denied. This can help you troubleshoot issues with traffic traversing between two endpoints and speed up resolution.

NSG Diagnostic walkthrough

The following sections walk you through the process of using NSG Diagnostic to diagnose security configuration issues in your Azure network using the Azure Portal.

USING THE AZURE PORTAL

To use the NSG Diagnostic tool to diagnose security configuration issues for a VM in your Azure network, follow these steps:

1. Log in to the Azure Portal, type **network watcher** in the search box, and select it from the list that appears.

2. In the left pane of the **Network Watcher** configuration blade, under **Network Diagnostic Tools**, click **NSG Diagnostic**. (See Figure 5-30.)

FIGURE 5-30 Click NSG Diagnostic.

3. Enter the following information in the right pane (see Figure 5-31). Then click the **Check** button:

- **Subscription** Select the subscription containing the source VM—that is, the VM whose security configuration you want to evaluate.

- **Resource Group** Select the resource group containing the source VM.

- **Supported Resource Types** Select the resource type for analysis.

- **Resource** Select the specific VM whose security configuration you want to evaluate.

- **Protocol** Select the protocol to analyze, such as **TCP**, **UDP**, or **ICMP**. Alternatively, choose **Any** to test all protocols.

- **Direction** Specify whether you want to evaluate security rules that pertain to inbound traffic or outbound traffic.

- **Source Type** Choose **IPv4 address/CIDR**.

- **IPv4 Address/CIDR** Enter the source IP address.

- **Destination IP Address** Enter the destination IP address.

- **Destination Port** Enter the destination port.

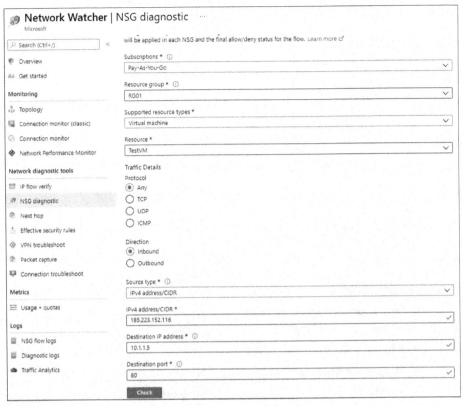

FIGURE 5-31 Configuring the NSG Diagnostic tool.

NSG Diagnostic analyzes the security configuration to confirm that traffic is allowed (see Figure 5-32) or denied (see Figure 5-33).

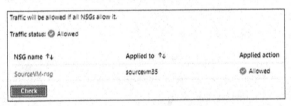

FIGURE 5-32 Traffic status: Allowed.

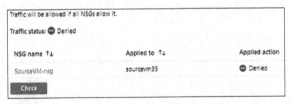

FIGURE 5-33 Traffic status: Denied.

4. Click the NSG name shown in the output to view a detailed log of the traffic flow across all the rules, and the result of each. (See Figure 5-34.)

FIGURE 5-34 Detailed log showing traffic flow across all the rules and the results of each.

Next Hop

Next Hop identifies the traffic route to a destination endpoint. This can help you pinpoint any traffic-routing issues if, for example, you want traffic to be routed via a virtual network gateway or an appliance instead of being routed incorrectly to the internet gateway.

Next Hop also identifies the route table associated with the endpoint; this route table contains route details regarding a system route or a specific user-defined route.

Next Hop walkthrough

The following sections walk you through the process of using Next Hop to identify the traffic route to a destination endpoint using the Azure Portal.

USING THE AZURE PORTAL

To use Next Hop to identify the traffic route to a destination endpoint using the Azure Portal, follow these steps:

1. Log in to the Azure Portal, type **network watcher** in the search box, and select it from the list that appears.
2. In the left pane of the **Network Watcher** configuration blade, under **Network Diagnostic Tools**, click **Next Hop**. (See Figure 5-35.)
3. Next, in the right pane (see Figure 5-36), enter the following information. Then click **Next Hop**:
    - **Subscription**   Select the subscription containing the source VM—that is, the VM that represents the beginning of the traffic route.
    - **Resource Group**   Select the resource group containing the source VM.
    - **Virtual Machine**   Select the source VM.
    - **Network Interface**   Select the network interface on the source VM.
    - **Source IP Address**   Enter the source IP address.
    - **Destination IP Address**   Enter the destination IP address.

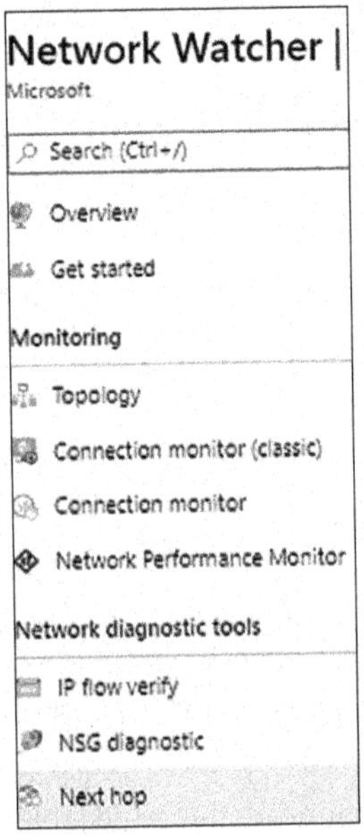

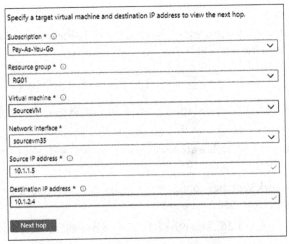

Network Watcher |
Microsoft

- Search (Ctrl+/)
- Overview
- Get started

Monitoring

- Topology
- Connection monitor (classic)
- Connection monitor
- Network Performance Monitor

Network diagnostic tools

- IP flow verify
- NSG diagnostic
- Next hop

FIGURE 5-35   Click Next Hop.

Specify a target virtual machine and destination IP address to view the next hop.

Subscription *
Pay-As-You-Go

Resource group *
RG01

Virtual machine *
SourceVM

Network Interface *
sourcevm35

Source IP address *
10.1.1.5

Destination IP address *
10.1.2.4

Next hop

FIGURE 5-36   Configuring the Next Hop tool.

Next Hop identifies the traffic route to the destination endpoint and displays the next hop type and the route table that will be applied. (See Figure 5-37.) Note that the next hop type may change, depending on the destination IP address. (See Figure 5-38.)

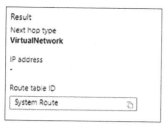

FIGURE 5-37 Next Hop output, with the next hop type displayed.

FIGURE 5-38 The next hop type may change, depending on the destination address.

Effective Security Rules

You can apply NSGs on the subnet level and the network interface card (NIC) level. When you do, however, security rules can sometimes conflict, causing unwanted traffic restrictions. The Effective Security Rules tool can help you identify all the security rules across all associated NSGs for a specific VM. This can help you identify and address conflicting rules as needed. For each traffic rule identified by Effective Security Rules, you can drill down to clearly identify affected source and destination IP ranges.

Effective Security Rules tool walkthrough

The following sections walk you through the process of using Effective Security Rules to identify conflicting rules using the Azure Portal.

USING THE AZURE PORTAL

To use Effective Security Rules to identify conflicting rules, follow these steps:

1. Log in to the Azure Portal, type **network watcher** in the search box, and select it from the list that appears.

2. In the left pane of the **Network Watcher** configuration blade, under **Network Diagnostic Tools**, click **Effective Security Rules**. (See Figure 5-39.)

FIGURE 5-39 Click Effective Security Rules.

3. In the right pane (see Figure 5-40), enter the following information. Then click **Check**:

    ■ **Subscription** Select the subscription containing the source VM—that is, the VM for which you want to check rules across associated NSGs.

    ■ **Resource Group** Select the resource group containing the source VM.

    ■ **Virtual Machine** Select the source VM.

    ■ **Network Interface** Select the NIC for the VM that you want to analyze.

FIGURE 5-40 Configuring the Effective Security Rules tool.

4. Effective Security Rules lists the security rules associated with the NIC. (See Figure 5-41.)

SourceVM-nsg								
Inbound rules								
Name ↑↓	Priority ↑↓	Source	Source Ports ↑↓	Destination	Destination Ports ↑↓	Protocol ↑↓	Access ↑↓	
RDP	300	0.0.0.0/0,0.0.0.0/0	0-65535	0.0.0.0/0,0.0.0.0/0	3389-3389	TCP	⊘ Allow	
AllowVnetInBound	65000	Virtual network (2 prefixes)	0-65535	Virtual network (2 prefixes)	0-65535	All	⊘ Allow	
AllowAzureLoadBalancerInBound	65001	Azure load balancer (2 prefixes)	0-65535	0.0.0.0/0,0.0.0.0/0	0-65535	All	⊘ Allow	
DenyAllInBound	65500	0.0.0.0/0,0.0.0.0/0	0-65535	0.0.0.0/0,0.0.0.0/0	0-65535	All	⊘ Deny	
Outbound rules								
Name ↑↓	Priority ↑↓	Source	Source Ports ↑↓	Destination	Destination Ports ↑↓	Protocol ↑↓	Access ↑↓	
AllowVnetOutBound	65000	Virtual network (2 prefixes)	0-65535	Virtual network (2 prefixes)	0-65535	All	⊘ Allow	
AllowInternetOutBound	65001	0.0.0.0/0,0.0.0.0/0	0-65535	Internet (257 prefixes)	0-65535	All	⊘ Allow	
DenyAllOutBound	65500	0.0.0.0/0,0.0.0.0/0	0-65535	0.0.0.0/0,0.0.0.0/0	0-65535	All	⊘ Deny	

FIGURE 5-41 List of NSGs associated with the NIC.

5. If there are multiple NSGs associated with the NIC, there will be multiple tabs to review. (See Figure 5-42.)

SourceVM-nsg Subnet-NSG								
Inbound rules								
Name ↑↓	Priority ↑↓	Source	Source Ports ↑↓	Destination	Destination Ports ↑↓	Protocol ↑↓	Access ↑↓	
RDP	300	0.0.0.0/0,0.0.0.0/0	0-65535	0.0.0.0/0,0.0.0.0/0	3389-3389	TCP	⊘ Allow	
AllowVnetInBound	65000	Virtual network (2 prefixes)	0-65535	Virtual network (2 prefixes)	0-65535	All	⊘ Allow	
AllowAzureLoadBalancerInBound	65001	Azure load balancer (2 prefixes)	0-65535	0.0.0.0/0,0.0.0.0/0	0-65535	All	⊘ Allow	
DenyAllInBound	65500	0.0.0.0/0,0.0.0.0/0	0-65535	0.0.0.0/0,0.0.0.0/0	0-65535	All	⊘ Deny	
Outbound rules								
Name ↑↓	Priority ↑↓	Source	Source Ports ↑↓	Destination	Destination Ports ↑↓	Protocol ↑↓	Access ↑↓	
AllowVnetOutBound	65000	Virtual network (2 prefixes)	0-65535	Virtual network (2 prefixes)	0-65535	All	⊘ Allow	
AllowInternetOutBound	65001	0.0.0.0/0,0.0.0.0/0	0-65535	Internet (257 prefixes)	0-65535	All	⊘ Allow	
DenyAllOutBound	65500	0.0.0.0/0,0.0.0.0/0	0-65535	0.0.0.0/0,0.0.0.0/0	0-65535	All	⊘ Deny	

FIGURE 5-42 Tabs for each NSG associated with the NIC.

VPN Troubleshoot

You can deploy VPN gateways to connect an Azure environment with an on-premises environment or an external environment hosted in another cloud or another Azure classic subscription. The VPN Troubleshoot enables you to test VPN connections you have established using a VPN gateway in your Azure environment to identify broken or failed connections. For VPN Troubleshoot to work, you must define a storage account in which to store logs for each connection. You can then download the logs from the storage account to analyze the entire traffic exchange and identify the root cause of communication failures.

> **NOTE** At this time, Azure limits you to running only one troubleshooting operation at a time for a single subscription.

VPN Troubleshoot walkthrough

The following sections walk you through the process of using VPN Troubleshoot using the Azure Portal.

USING THE AZURE PORTAL

To use VPN Troubleshoot to identify broken or failed VPN connections, follow these steps:

1. Log in to the Azure Portal, type **network watcher** in the search box, and select it from the list that appears.

2. In the left pane of the **Network Watcher** configuration blade, under **Network Diagnostic Tools**, click **VPN Troubleshoot**. (See Figure 5-43.)

FIGURE 5-43 Click VPN Troubleshoot.

3. In the right pane (see Figure 5-44), enter the following information. Then click **Check**:

   - **Subscription** Select the subscription containing the target VPN gateway—that is, the VPN gateway whose connections you want to analyze.

   - **Resource Group** Select the resource group containing the target VPN gateway.

   - **Location** Select the location containing the target VPN gateway.

FIGURE 5-44 Configuring VPN Troubleshoot.

VPN Troubleshoot detects any VPN gateways in the selected resource group and location shows all the connections for each VPN gateway. (See Figure 5-45.)

FIGURE 5-45 List of VPN gateways detected.

4. Select the VPN gateway whose connections you want to test and click **Start Troubleshooting**.

When testing is complete, VPN Troubleshoot lists each connection's status as Healthy or Unhealthy. (See Figure 5-46.) Depending on the connection's status, you may also see a detailed report explaining the reasons for any issues. (See Figure 5-47.)

FIGURE 5-46 Results of the VPN Troubleshoot test.

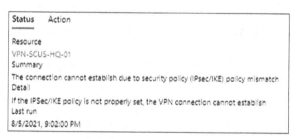

FIGURE 5-47 Explanation of status.

Packet Capture

There are times when you need to capture traffic requests, or packets—either all packets or specific ones—to and from a VM to analyze traffic patterns, gather network statistics, identify network intrusions, address network communication anomalies or problems, and so on. Packet Capture captures the packets you specify and saves them in an Azure Storage account or your local device for analysis using a SIEM or log-monitoring tool. Packet Capture requires you to define certain parameters to identify the packets that you want to log. These include the following:

- The target VM
- The log storage location
- Maximum bytes per packet
- Maximum bytes per session
- Time limit (in seconds)

> **NOTE** Packet Capture requires a VM extension, AzureNetworkWatcherExtension, on both Windows and Linux VMs. You can deploy the extension using Azure PowerShell, the Azure CLI, and JSON templates.

Packet Capture walkthrough

The following sections walk you through the process of using the Packet Capture tool to capture packets using the Azure Portal.

USING THE AZURE PORTAL

To use Packet Capture to capture packets using the Azure Portal, follow these steps:

1. Log in to the Azure Portal, type **network watcher** in the search box, and select it from the list that appears.
2. In the left pane of the **Network Watcher** configuration blade, under **Network Diagnostic Tools**, click **Packet Capture**. (See Figure 5-48.)

FIGURE 5-48 Click Packet Capture.

3. On the **Packet Capture** page, click **Add**. (See Figure 5-49.)

FIGURE 5-49 Add a Packet Capture.

4. On the **Add Packet Capture** page (see Figure 5-50), enter the following information. Then click **Create**:

   - **Subscription** Select the subscription containing the target VM—that is, the VM whose packets you want to capture.
   - **Resource Group** Select the resource group containing the target VM.
   - **Target Virtual Machine** Select the target VM.
   - **Packet Capture Name** Enter a unique name for the packet-capture operation.
   - **Capture Configuration** Select the location to store the output file.
   - **Storage Accounts** Select a storage account to store the output file.
   - **Maximum Bytes Per Packet** Enter the maximum bytes size for each packet. In this case, enter **0** to capture all packets.
   - **Maximum Bytes Per Session** Enter the maximum bytes per session that you want to capture. For now, leave this set to the default.
   - **Time Limit** Set the time limit in seconds to run the packet-capture operation.

5. After you create the Packet Capture operation, it will take a few minutes to start running. (See Figure 5-51.)

6. After the Packet Capture operation has run for some time or is complete, switch to the Azure Portal page for the Azure Storage account where the logs are saved and download them for analysis. (See Figure 5-52.)

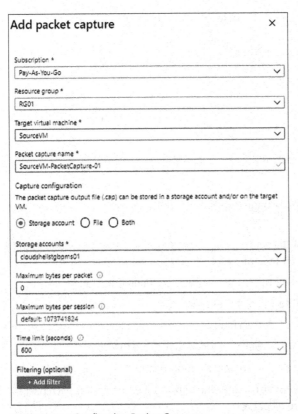

FIGURE 5-50 Configuring Packet Capture.

Name	Target	Storage	Status
SourceVM-PacketCapture-01	SourceVM	cloudshellstgbpms01	ⓘ Running

FIGURE 5-51 Packet Capture creation.

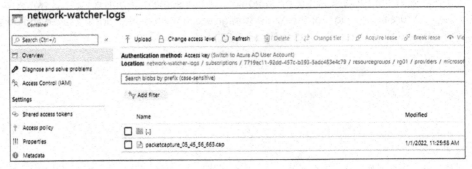

FIGURE 5-52 Packet Capture results.

7. Click the log file you want to download and click the **Download** option.

Connection Troubleshoot

You can use Connection Troubleshoot to test direct TCP or ICMP connections from an Azure VM, application gateway, or Bastion host to another Azure VM, FQDN, URI, or IPv4 endpoint. In addition to analyzing connections, Connection Troubleshoot provides specific fault information after analysis, such as the following:

- High CPU utilization
- High memory utilization
- Traffic blocked due to incorrect guest VM firewall configuration
- DNS name-resolution issues
- Traffic blocked due to an NSG rule, along with the rule name
- Traffic dropped due to system-defined (the default) or user-defined routing

By providing clarity on the root cause of connection issues, Connection Troubleshoot enables you to address issues more quickly.

Unlike Connection Monitor, Connection Troubleshoot provides point-in-time information about ongoing issues, and should be used in such scenarios rather than for historical tracking.

> **NOTE** When the source is an Azure VM, whether on Windows or Linux, you must deploy the AzureNetworkWatcherExtension Virtual Machine extension to allow Connection Troubleshoot to access the VM for testing.

Connection Troubleshoot walkthrough

The following sections walk you through the process of running Connection Troubleshoot to test connections using the Azure Portal.

USING THE AZURE PORTAL

To use Connection Troubleshoot to test connections using the Azure Portal, follow these steps:

1. Log in to the Azure Portal, type **network watcher** in the search box, and select it from the list that appears.
2. In the left pane of the **Network Watcher** configuration blade, under **Network Diagnostic Tools**, click **Connection Troubleshoot**. (See Figure 5-53.)

FIGURE 5-53 Click Connection Troubleshoot.

3. In the right pane (see Figure 5-54), enter the following information. Then click **Check**:

- **Subscription** Select the subscription containing the source resource—that is, the resource whose outgoing connections you want to analyze.
- **Resource Group** Select the resource group containing the source resource.
- **Source Type** Select the source type—in this example, **Virtual Machine**.
- **Virtual Machine** Select the VM whose outgoing connections you want to analyze.
- **Destination** Select the **Select a Virtual Machine** option button or the **Specify Manually** option button. In this case, choose **Select a Virtual Machine**.

This enables you to specify a VM (rather than an FQDN, URI, or IPv4) endpoint as the connection destination. The options change based on the destination resource type that you select.

- **Resource Group** Select the resource group containing the destination VM.
- **Virtual Machine** Select the destination VM.

- **Probe Settings: Preferred IP Version** Choose from **IPv4**, **IPv6**, or **Both**.
- **Protocol** Select **TCP** or **ICMP**.
- **Destination Port** Enter the destination port to use for testing.

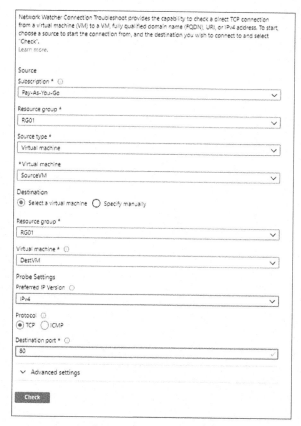

FIGURE 5-54 Configuring Connection Troubleshoot.

4. When Connection Troubleshoot finishes analyzing the connection, it displays the results, indicating whether the destination is reachable (see Figure 5-55) or unreachable (see Figure 5-56). Depending on the result, you might see the next hop address, topology view, or failure details to pinpoint the reasons for any failures.

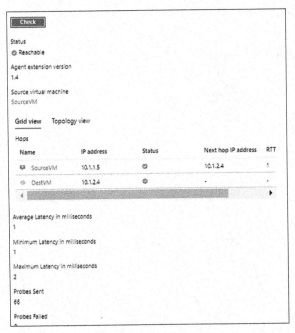

FIGURE 5-55 The destination VM is reachable.

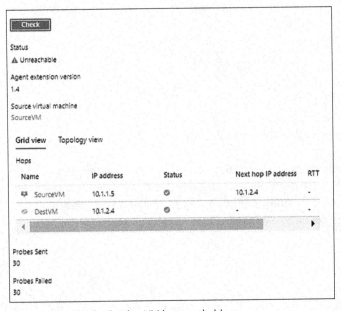

FIGURE 5-56 The destination VM is unreachable.

NSG Flow Logs

Companies must be aware of ongoing intrusions, compromised security backdoors, and network-performance bottlenecks that could seriously hamper their environment and performance. Being able to address these issues in a competent manner, whether proactively or reactively, is critical.

Azure Network Watcher includes NSG Flow Logs, which record information about network traffic flowing through a subnet or all NSGs within an environment. You can analyze this log data using visualization tools (like Power BI), SIEM tools, or IDS to identify performance bottlenecks, intrusions, and compromised systems.

> **NOTE** NSG Flow Logs are important for compliance reasons. They can help you verify that traffic within a network is isolated as needed and adheres to your enterprise's compliance policies and guidelines.

NSG Flow Logs work on the Transport layer of the OSI model to collect logs at 1-minute intervals. These logs contain detailed information about traffic passing through targeted NSGs, including the protocol, source IP, source port, destination IP, destination port, NIC details, traffic decisions to allow or deny packets, and throughput information. You can retain these logs for up to one year using Azure General Purpose v2 storage accounts.

It is highly recommended to enable NSG Flow Logs on all NSGs applied to subnets or VMs that host critical workloads. NSG Flow Logs do not affect the network performance of your workload because they gather logging information from the Azure platform without directly interacting with the traffic going to your workload.

> **NOTE** NSG Flow Logs truncate long filenames, which makes it hard to correlate events because the log information does not exactly match your environment. To prevent this, keep NSG names to fewer than 80 characters.

NSG Flow Logs walkthrough

The following sections walk you through the process of using NSG Flow Logs to record network traffic flowing through a subnet or NSG using the Azure Portal.

USING THE AZURE PORTAL

To use NSG Flow Logs to record network traffic using the Azure Portal, follow these steps:

1. Log in to the Azure Portal, type **network watcher** in the search box, and select it from the list that appears.

2. In the left pane of the **Network Watcher** configuration blade, under **Logs**, click **NSG Flow Logs**. (See Figure 5-57.)

FIGURE 5-57 Click NSG Flow Logs.

3. Click the **Create** button above the pane on the right. (See Figure 5-58.)

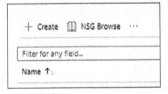

FIGURE 5-58 Create a Flow Log.

4. In the **Basics** tab of the Create a Flow Log wizard (see Figure 5-59), enter the following information and click **Next**:

- **Subscription** Select the subscription containing the NSG whose traffic you want to monitor.

- **Network Security Group** Select the NSG to whose traffic you want to monitor.

- **Flow Log Name** Enter a unique name for the Flow Log.

- **Select Storage Account Location** Select the location for the storage account where you will store the Flow Log.

- **Subscription**   Select the subscription for the storage account.
- **Storage Accounts**   Select the storage account you want to use to store the Flow Log.
- **Retention**   Specify how long the Flow Log should be retained. The maximum retention is 365 days.

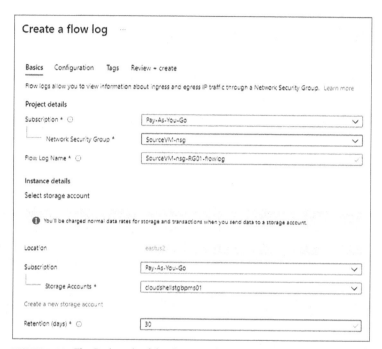

FIGURE 5-59   The Basics tab of the Create a Flow Log wizard.

5. In the **Configuration** tab (see Figure 5-60), leave the default settings as is, and click **Next**.

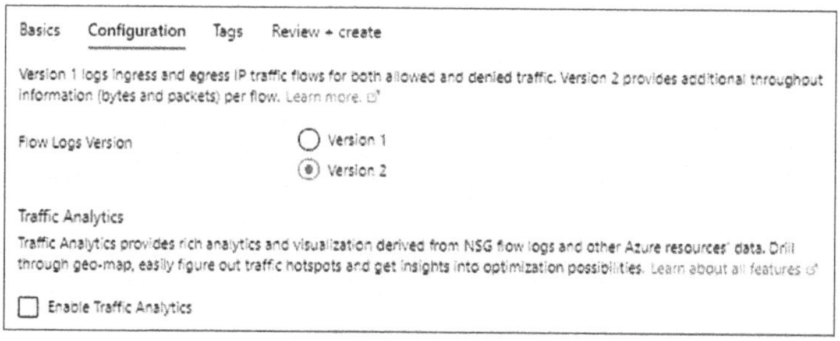

FIGURE 5-60   The Configuration tab of the Create a Flow Log wizard.

6. In the **Tags** tab (see Figure 5-61), add any tags you want to apply to the Flow Log. Then click **Next**.

Basics   Configuration   **Tags**   Review + create

Tags are name/value pairs that enable you to categorize resources and view consolidated billing by applying the same tag to multiple resources and resource groups. Learn more about tags

Note that if you create tags and then change resource settings on other tabs, your tags will be automatically updated.

Name ⓘ   Value ⓘ

[   ] : [   ]

FIGURE 5-61 The Tags tab of the Create a Flow Log wizard.

7. In the **Review + Create** tab (see Figure 5-62), check your settings. Then click **Create**.

Basics   Configuration   Tags   Review + create

Basics

Subscription   Pay-As-You-Go
Network Security Group   SourceVM-nsg
Location   eastus2
Flow Log Name   SourceVM-nsg-RG01-flowlog
Storage Accounts   cloudshellstgbpms01
Retention (days)   30

Configuration

Flow Logs Version   2
Enable Traffic Analytics   No

Tags

None

FIGURE 5-62 The Review + Create tab of the Create a Flow Log wizard.

When the Flow Log has been created, you'll see it listed, with a status of Enabled. (See Figure 5-63.)

Name ↑	Resource group ↑↓	Location ↑↓	Subscription ↑↓	Status ↑↓	Target resource ↑↓
SourceVM-nsg-RG01-flow...	NetworkWatcherRG	East US 2	Pay-As-You-Go	✓ Enabled	SourceVM-nsg

FIGURE 5-63 Flow Log status.

8. After giving the Flow Log a chance to monitor traffic for some time, open the page for the Azure Storage account where you saved the Flow Log. (See Figure 5-64.) From there, you can download the Flow Log for further analysis.

FIGURE 5-64 Download the Flow Log for analysis.

Diagnostic Logs

The Diagnostic Logs tool provides a single pane of glass for you to easily enable or disable diagnostic logging on all network resources within a subscription, including VM NICs, application gateways, NSGs, and so on. You can store the resulting logs in an Azure Storage account, stream it to an Event hub, or send it to a Log Analytics workspace for deeper analysis. You can use tools such as Power BI to analyze logs stored in an Azure storage account.

Diagnostic Logs walkthrough

The following sections walk you through the process of using the Diagnostic Logs tool, which you can use to enable or disable diagnostic logging on network resources using the Azure Portal.

USING THE AZURE PORTAL

To use the Diagnostic Logs tool to enable or disable diagnostic logging on network resources using the Azure Portal, follow these steps:

1. Log in to the Azure Portal, type **network watcher** in the search box, and select it from the list that appears.

2. In the left pane of the **Network Watcher** configuration blade, under **Logs**, click **Diagnostic Logs**. (See Figure 5-65.)

FIGURE 5-65   Diagnostic logs in Network Watcher service.

3. Using the drop-down lists in the right pane (see Figure 5-66), enter the following information to filter down to the required resources:

   - **Subscription**   Select the subscription containing the network resource for which you want to generate diagnostic logs.

   - **Resource Group**   Select the resource group containing the network resource for which you want to generate diagnostic logs.

   - **Resource Type**   Select the type of resource for which you want to generate diagnostic logs.

   - **Resource**   Select the resource for which you want to generate diagnostic logs.

FIGURE 5-66 Configuring the Diagnostic Log tool.

The page refreshes and shows a list of all the NICs, NSGs, and public IP addresses it finds. (See Figure 5-67.) In this case, diagnostics are disabled for each resource.

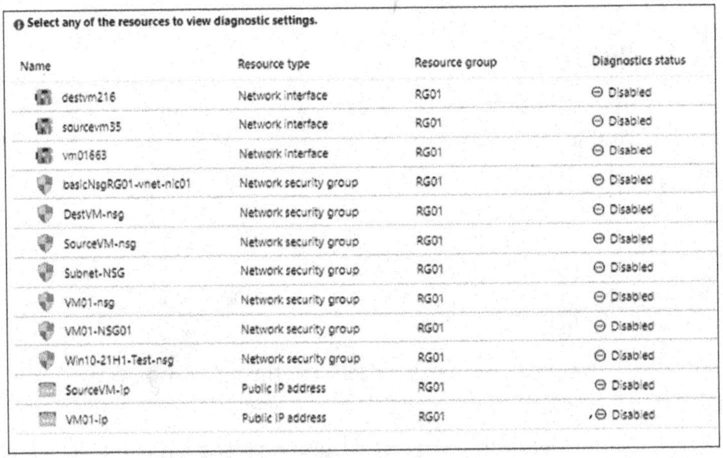

Name	Resource type	Resource group	Diagnostics status
destvm216	Network interface	RG01	⊖ Disabled
sourcevm35	Network interface	RG01	⊖ Disabled
vm01663	Network interface	RG01	⊖ Disabled
basicNsgRG01-vnet-nic01	Network security group	RG01	⊖ Disabled
DestVM-nsg	Network security group	RG01	⊖ Disabled
SourceVM-nsg	Network security group	RG01	⊖ Disabled
Subnet-NSG	Network security group	RG01	⊖ Disabled
VM01-nsg	Network security group	RG01	⊖ Disabled
VM01-NSG01	Network security group	RG01	⊖ Disabled
Win10-21H1-Test-nsg	Network security group	RG01	⊖ Disabled
SourceVM-ip	Public IP address	RG01	⊖ Disabled
VM01-ip	Public IP address	RG01	⊖ Disabled

Select any of the resources to view diagnostic settings.

FIGURE 5-67 Lists of all NICs, NSGs, and public IP addresses.

4. To enable diagnostic logging for a resource, click the resource in the list.

5. In the **Diagnostic Settings** page for the resource you selected, click the **Add Diagnostic Setting** link. (See Figure 5-68.)

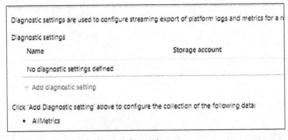

FIGURE 5-68 Add diagnostic setting.

6. In the **Diagnostic Setting** dialog box (see Figure 5-69), enter the following information. Then click **Save**:

   - **Diagnostic Setting Name**   Enter a unique name for the diagnostic setting.

   - **Metrics**   To log all metrics for the resource, select the **All Metrics** check box. Alternatively, you can choose specific metrics as needed.

   - **Retention**   Enter a retention period. For permanent retention, enter 0.

- **Destination Details** Select a destination option—in this case, **Archive to a Storage Account**. (Notice that when you choose this option, additional settings appear, enabling you to choose the storage account and subscription.)

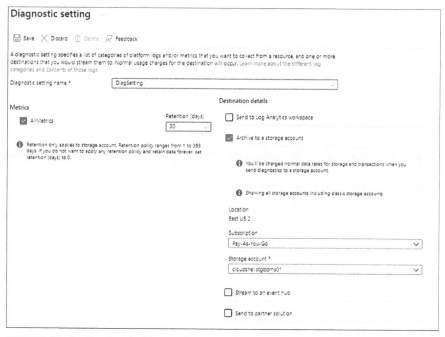

FIGURE 5-69 Configuring the Diagnostic Logs tool.

7. Switch back to the list of diagnostic settings and notice that the status for the resource you just changed is listed as **Enabled**. (See Figure 5-70.)

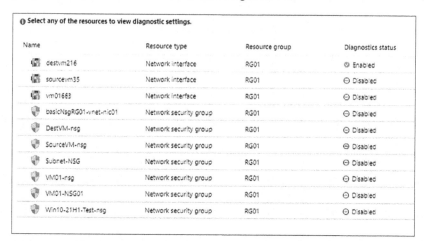

FIGURE 5-70 Diagnostics for the resource are enabled.

8. Optionally, repeat this walkthrough to enable diagnostics for other resources as required.

Chapter 6

Azure Portal

Overview

Microsoft provides various options to create and manage Azure services. Of these, one of the most widely used is the Azure Portal. A GUI-based web interface, the Azure Portal provides tools to build and manage all Azure services, ranging from simple single-service solutions to complex multi-service architectures. Each individual user can customize the Azure Portal per their unique requirements; at the same time, there are certain standardization rules that can be pushed out on an organizational level to ensure some degree of synchronicity.

Over the years, the Azure Portal has gone through a number of iterations and upgrades. The Azure Portal experience has been updated as new services have been introduced and as new features in existing services have come online.

The Azure Portal is currently accessible from https://portal.azure.com. The first time you log in to the Azure Portal using the credentials generated when you signed up or that were given to you by another admin, you will see the default version of the main Azure Portal window. (See Figure 6-1.)

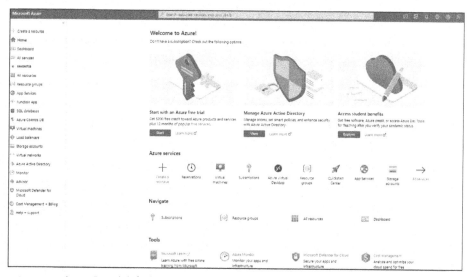

FIGURE 6-1 Azure Portal default view.

The left pane of the Azure Portal window (see Figure 6-2) contains a list of the most commonly used options. (You can customize this list to suit your needs.) They include the following:

- Create a Resource
- Home
- Dashboard
- All Services
- Favorites

FIGURE 6-2 Left pane of the Azure Portal.

In the top-right corner of the main Azure Portal screen (see Figure 6-3), you will find a second set of options. You can use these to configure the Azure Portal. These options include the following:

- Cloud Shell
- Directories + Subscriptions
- Notifications
- Settings
- Help
- Feedback

FIGURE 6-3 Portal configuration options in the Azure Portal.

Key features

The key features of the Azure Portal are as follows:

- **GUI-based experience**   The Azure Portal provides a centralized GUI web console to build and manage Azure resources.

- **Secure SSL-based web portal**   The Azure Portal works over port 443 and SSL, ensuring all communication is secure.

- **Resilient by design**   The Azure Portal is deployed across all Azure datacenters. This ensures that a regional outage will not cause the entire service to go offline. Service updates are continuous and designed to work without requiring downtimes.

- **Supported by modern browsers**   The Azure Portal is accessible using any modern browser, including the latest versions of Microsoft Edge, Google Chrome, Mozilla Firefox, and Apple Safari.

- **Supports management of all Azure services**   The Azure Portal supports the entire lifecycle management of all Azure services. It is the default method of access for most Azure architects and administrators.

- **Cloud Shell Integration**   Cloud Shell is integrated directly inside the Azure Portal interface, making it easy to initiate sessions to run scripts, bash commands, and automated activities.

- **Role-based access control (RBAC) for access management**   The Azure Portal provides RBAC to provide granular access to Azure services using Azure Active Directory.

- **Customizable dashboards**   The Azure Portal allows each user to create dashboards according to their individual needs, viewable only by them, to monitor the services most critical for them. They can also publish and share these dashboards to provide a consistent view across the environment. This flexibility maximizes productivity.

- **Global view of services and regions**   The Azure Portal provides a global view of service health across all Azure regions and services. Views can be customized on an individual basis.

- **Integration with Azure Marketplace**   The Azure Portal is deeply integrated with the Azure Marketplace, which supports the procurement and deployment of third-party solutions on Azure.

Allowlisting Azure URLs

The Azure Portal has a number of different URLs that should be allowlisted on firewalls, proxy servers, and any other intermediate devices handling traffic to these services to ensure that performance and connectivity to the service are not impacted. These URLs include the following:

*.aadcdn.microsoftonline-p.com	*.aka.ms	*.applicationinsights.io
*.azure.com	*.azure.net	*.azure-api.net
*.azuredatalakestore.net	*.azureedge.net	*.loganalytics.io
*.microsoft.com	*.microsoftonline.com	*.microsoftonline-p.com
*.msauth.net	*.msftauth.net	*.trafficmanager.net
*.visualstudio.com	*.asazure.windows.net	*.core.windows.net
*.database.windows.net	*.graph.windows.net	*.kusto.windows.net
*.search.windows.net	*.servicebus.windows.net	

Customization and usability concepts and considerations

The Azure Portal allows you to create your own personalized experience. It offers settings to set the portal's appearance and views, default dashboards, and other shared dashboards. In addition, you can use the portal to access the Azure Marketplace, which contains third-party solutions and packaged services. Finally, the Azure Portal is where you go to log support tickets and search the vast Microsoft knowledge base for information about any issues you are encountering. This section discusses all these features of the Azure Portal.

Azure Portal settings

The Azure Portal provides settings to establish a default view, select the subscriptions you want to view and manage, specify language and regional settings, enter profile information, and set your session preferences to control timeouts and notifications. With these settings, each administrator can set up their default experience when using the Azure Portal. It is a good practice to review these at least once when you begin using the Azure Portal and align them based on your needs.

Azure Portal settings walkthrough

This section walks you through the process of accessing and managing your Azure Portal settings using the Azure Portal.

USING THE AZURE PORTAL

To access and manage your Azure Portal settings using the Azure Portal, follow these steps:

1. Log in to the Azure Portal and click the **Settings** icon in the top-right bar. (See Figure 6-4.)

FIGURE 6-4   Settings icon.

2. In the **Directories + Subscriptions** tab of the **Portal Settings** page (see Figure 6-5), which opens by default, optionally click the **star** icon next to a subscription to set it as a "favorite."

FIGURE 6-5   The Directories + Subscriptions tab on the Portal Settings page.

3. Click the **Appearance + Startup Views** tab and adjust the following options according to your needs (see Figure 6-6):

   - **Menu Behavior**   Specify how the left menu bar behaves on all screens. It can be permanently docked or set as a flyout bar that opens when you scroll to it.

   - **Theme**   Select a visual theme to apply.

   - **High Contrast Theme**   Choose a high-contrast theme if desired or required due to your visual needs.

   - **Startup Page**   Choose the default startup page. This will appear when you sign in to the Azure Portal.

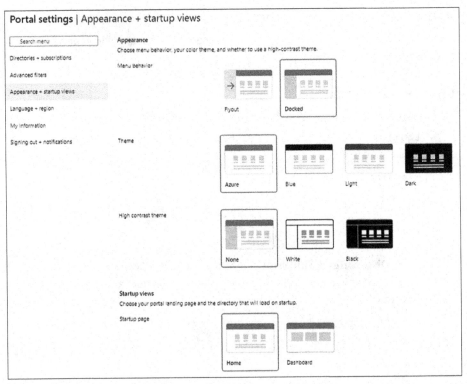

FIGURE 6-6 The Appearance + Startup Views tab on the Portal Settings page.

4. Click the **Language + Region** tab and specify your default language and regional format. (See Figure 6-7.)

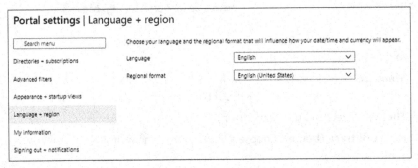

FIGURE 6-7 The Language + Region tab on the Portal Settings page.

5. Click the **My Information** tab, confirm or enter the email you want to use to receive notifications from Microsoft, and optionally select the **I Would Like to Hear from Microsoft and Its Family of Companies Via Email...** check box. (See Figure 6-8.)

FIGURE 6-8   The My Information tab on the Portal Settings page.

6. Click the **Signing Out + Notifications** tab and adjust the following options according to your needs (see Figure 6-9):

   ▪ **Enable Directory Level Idle Timeout**   Select this check box if you want sessions to time out after a certain period.

   ▪ **Sign Me Out When Inactive**   Use this drop-down list to specify how long the system should be inactive before the user is signed out.

   ▪ **Enable Pop-Up Notifications**   Select this check box if you want to receive pop-up notifications during your sessions.

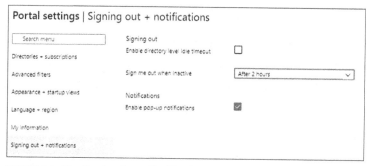

FIGURE 6-9   The Signing Out + Notifications tab on the Portal Settings page.

Custom dashboards

The Azure Portal allows you to create custom dashboards. These can be a mix of resource views, quick links, and shortcuts to day-to-day operations, critical metrics, and information about the overall health of your Azure environment.

Each administrator can create custom dashboards to view the services, resources, and information that are most critical for their day-to-day function. Custom dashboards can be shared between team members. Updates to shared dashboards are available to all admins that subscribe to that dashboard.

Custom dashboards walkthrough

This section walks you through the process of creating a custom dashboard using the Azure Portal.

USING THE AZURE PORTAL

To create a custom dashboard using the Azure Portal, follow these steps:

1. Log in to the Azure Portal and click the **Dashboard** option in the left pane. A default dashboard view opens in the right pane. (See Figure 6-10.)

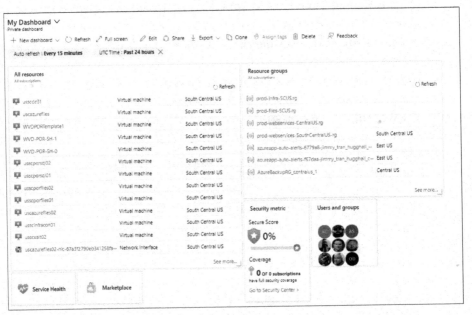

FIGURE 6-10 Default dashboard in the Azure Portal.

You can either edit this default dashboard (by clicking the Edit button) or create a new dashboard. This walkthrough shows you how to create a new one.

2. Click the down arrow to the right of the **New Dashboard** button and choose **Blank Dashboard**. (See Figure 6-11.)

FIGURE 6-11 Create a new dashboard.

The **Tile Gallery** page opens. You use this page to select predefined tiles that present different views of resources within your subscription. (See Figure 6-12.)

FIGURE 6-12 The Tile Gallery page.

3. Click a tile that represents a metric you want to include on your dashboard and drag it to the blank dashboard on the left to add it. Repeat this step for any other tiles you want to add.

> **TIP** To rearrange the tiles on the dashboard, simply click a tile and drag it to the desired location.

4. When you finish adding and arranging tiles on your new dashboard, click the **Done Customizing** button.

5. The dashboard is saved. (See Figure 6-13.)

> **TIP** You can adjust the Auto Refresh and UTC Time settings based on your personal preferences.

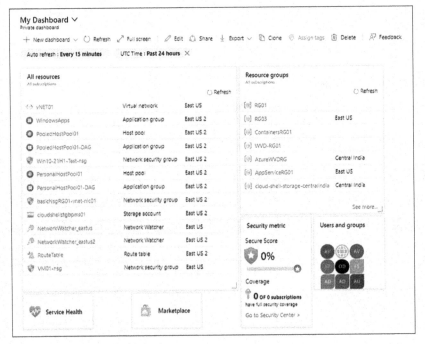

FIGURE 6-13 The new dashboard.

Azure Marketplace

Azure Marketplace is a store that contains thousands of IT applications, services, and solutions, provided by third-party vendors known as independent software vendors (ISVs). You can try and buy these solutions based on your organizational requirements. Available applications and services range from software products to back up your Azure resources to services to monitor and manage them.

Azure Marketplace walkthrough

This section walks you through the process of locating and adding solutions from Azure Marketplace to your Azure Portal.

USING THE AZURE PORTAL

To locate and add a solution from Azure Marketplace to your Azure Portal, follow these steps:

1. Log in to the Azure Portal, type **marketplace** in the search box, and select it from the list that appears. (See Figure 6-14.)

FIGURE 6-14 Search for Azure Marketplace.

The Marketplace page opens. It lists a default set of available services in the right pane. Among other options, the left pane displays a list of categories of Azure services. (See Figure 6-15.)

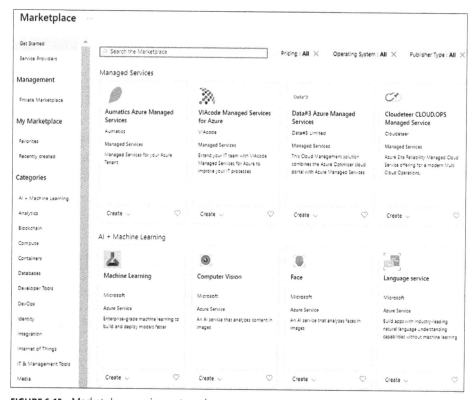

FIGURE 6-15 Marketplace services categories.

2. Click a category in the left pane—in this case, **Compute**.

   The right pane displays a list of compute solutions from Microsoft (such as Windows Server), as well as from third-party vendors (such as Red Hat Enterprise, Debian Linux, and Ubuntu), organized by subcategory. (See Figure 6-16.)

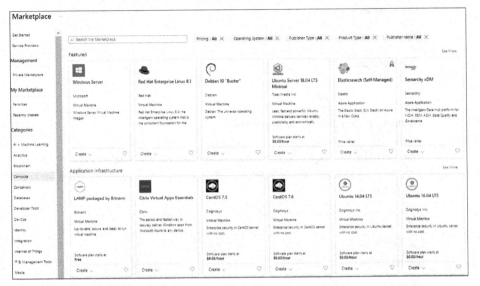

FIGURE 6-16 Marketplace services Compute category.

3. To see additional services, such as pre-built custom OS solutions (including hardened, or pre-configured versions), click the **See More** link to the right of a subcategory heading. Alternatively, use the search box above the right pane to search for a specific solution.

4. When you find the solution you're looking for, click **Create**, and follow the prompts to add it.

Help and support

The Azure Portal has a help and support section that allows you to buy support plans, raise support tickets, monitor your service health, review Azure Advisor recommendations, visit the Azure community for free guidance and support, and access many other helpful resources to improve your knowledge on Azure.

Help and support walkthrough

This section walks you through the process of finding recommended solutions from Microsoft for your issue or creating a support request in the Azure Portal.

USING THE AZURE PORTAL

To create a support request in the Azure Portal, follow these steps:

1. Log in to the Azure Portal and do one of the following:

   - Type **help + support** in the search box and select it in the list that appears.

   - Click **Help + Support** in the left pane. (See Figure 6-17.)

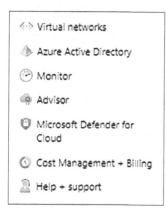

FIGURE 6-17 Click Help + Support.

2. In the **Overview** tab of the **Help + Support** page, click the **Create a Support Request** button. (See Figure 6-18.)

FIGURE 6-18 Create a support request.

3. In the **Problem Description** tab of the New Support Request wizard (see Figure 6-19), enter the following information and click **Next**:

- **What Is Your Issue Related To?** In this case, select **Azure Services**.

- **Issue Type** Select the option that matches most closely to your issue—in this case, **Technical**.

When you choose your issue type, the Problem Description tab changes to display options that relate to that issue type (in this case, Technical).

- **Subscription** Select the Azure subscription that contains the workload for which you want to log the support request.

- **Service** Select the **My Services** option button to select a specific resource or service based on your environment or the **All Services** option button if you are facing a larger issue across multiple or all services.

- **Service Type** Select the type of service for which you want to log the service request.

- **Resource** Select the exact resource from your subscription for which you want to log the support request.

- **Summary** Enter a brief description of your issue.

- **Problem Type** Choose the problem type that most closely matches the problem you are experiencing. (The options listed here will differ depending on the service type you selected previously.)

- **Problem Subtype**   Choose the problem subtype that most closely matches the problem you are experiencing. (The options listed here will differ depending on the problem type you selected previously.)

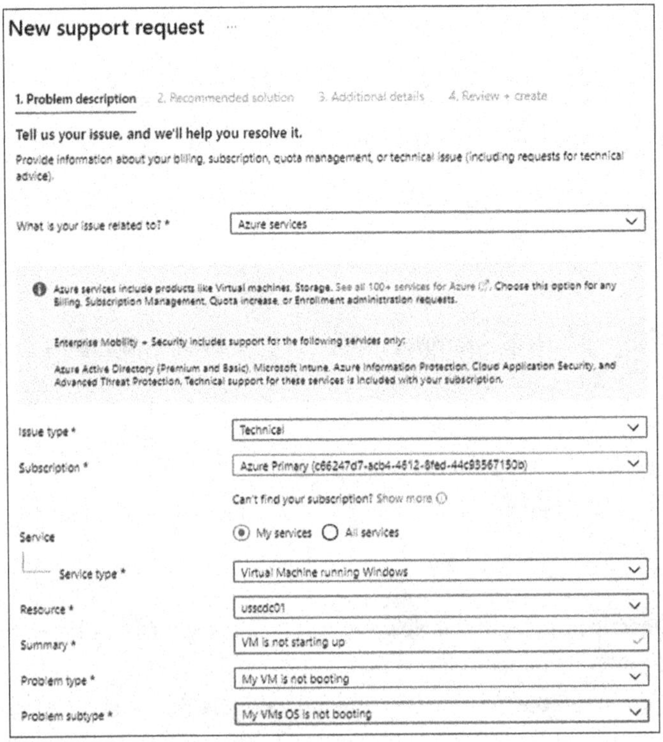

FIGURE 6-19   The Problem Description tab.

Based on the information you submitted in the **Problem Description** tab, Microsoft searches for, filters, and displays information about any ongoing issues with your workload, service type, or region already under investigation in the **Recommended Solution** tab. If none are found, Microsoft will display solutions from its knowledge base that might help you to fix your issue under **Recommended Steps and Common Issues Associated with *Your Issue Type*.** (See Figure 6-20.)

4. Review the solutions shown. If none match your needs, or if the solutions presented have already been tried unsuccessfully, click **Next**.

5. In the **Additional Details** tab, provide additional information about your issue as well as your contact information if your subscription already has a support plan. (See Figure 6-21.) If your subscription does not have a support plan, you will be asked to procure one. (See Figure 6-22.)

1. Problem description   2. Recommended solution   3. Additional details   4. Review + create

Fix this problem now using our expert solution

Expert solutions are written by Azure engineers to help you quickly resolve the problem on your own.

Diagnostics

We are running checks on your resource

4 out of 5 customers resolved their VM boot issue using the steps listed below.

Recommended steps

Note: It is recommended to follow the troubleshooting steps below to first identify the problem, then perform the remediation step(s) before opening a support ticket.

If you cannot connect to your Windows virtual machine (VM) and are unsure of the cause, the following troubleshooting steps should be performed

- Verify that your VM has been started
- If your VM fails to start and you recently applied Windows Updates please see Troubleshooting VM not booting after Windows Update ☐
- Understand how to use boot diagnostics to troubleshoot Virtual Machines ☐ in Azure

If your VM is not at the ctrl-alt-del screen, it may be experiencing a boot error

1. Restart the virtual machine to address boot issues
2. Review the common boot errors and solutions for non-bootable VMs ☐ troubleshooting guide

Common issues associated to specific boot errors:

- Updating Boot Error ☐
- Check Disk Boot Error ☐
- BitLocker Boot Error ☐
- Boot Configuration Update ☐
- Common Blue Screen Error ☐
- Critical Service Failure ☐
- Reboot loop ☐

Recommended resources

- Troubleshoot specific Remote Desktop connection errors ☐
- Detailed troubleshooting across network components ☐
- Address Remote Desktop License Server error ☐

FIGURE 6-20   The Recommended Solution tab.

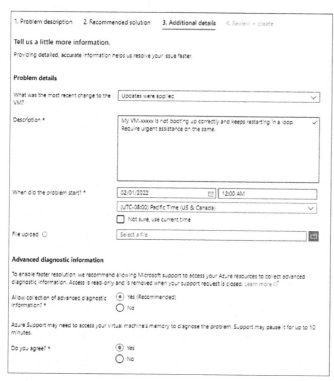

1. Problem description   2. Recommended solution   3. Additional details   4. Review + create

Tell us a little more information.

Providing detailed, accurate information helps us resolve your issue faster.

Problem details

What was the most recent change to the VM?	Updates were applied ⌄
Description *	My VM-xxxxx is not booting up correctly and keeps restarting in a loop. Require urgent assistance on the same. ✓
When did the problem start? *	02/01/2022 📅 12:00 AM
	(UTC-08:00) Pacific Time (US & Canada) ⌄
	☐ Not sure, use current time
File upload ○	Select a file 📁

Advanced diagnostic information

To enable faster resolution, we recommend allowing Microsoft support to access your Azure resources to collect advanced diagnostic information. Access is read-only and is removed when your support request is closed. Learn more ☐

Allow collection of advanced diagnostic information? *	⦿ Yes (Recommended) ○ No

Azure Support may need to access your virtual machine's memory to diagnose the problem. Support may pause it for up to 10 minutes.

Do you agree? *	⦿ Yes ○ No

FIGURE 6-21   The Additional Details tab.

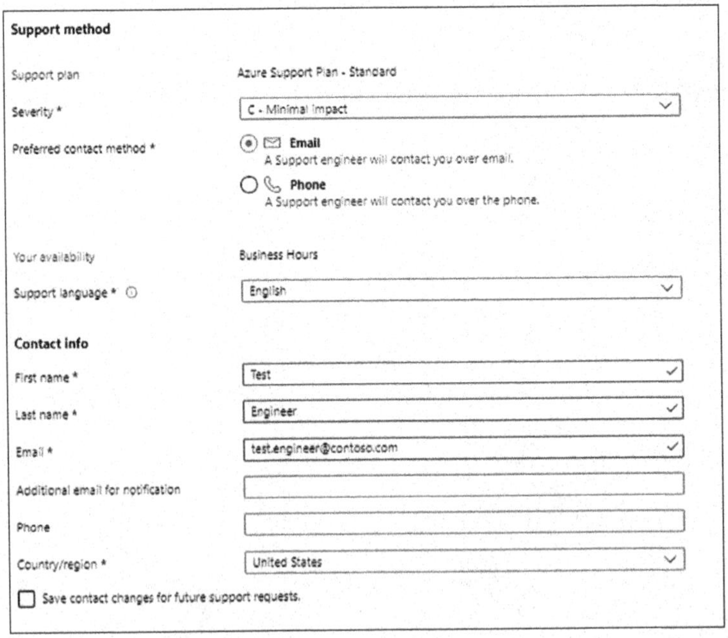

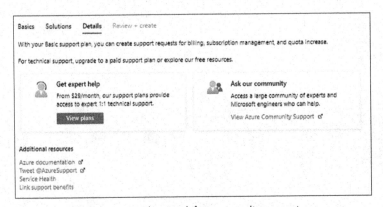

Support method

Support plan   Azure Support Plan - Standard

Severity *   C - Minimal Impact

Preferred contact method *   ● ✉ **Email**
                                      A Support engineer will contact you over email.

                                      ○ ☎ **Phone**
                                      A Support engineer will contact you over the phone.

Your availability   Business Hours

Support language * ⓘ   English

Contact info

First name *   Test ✓

Last name *   Engineer ✓

Email *   test.engineer@cortoso.com ✓

Additional email for notification

Phone

Country/region *   United States

☐ Save contact changes for future support requests.

FIGURE 6-22 The Additional Details tab (continued).

> **TIP** If you do not want to procure a plan, you can get help for free from the Microsoft Azure community by clicking the View Azure Community Support link under Ask Our Community. (See Figure 6-23.)

Basics   Solutions   **Details**   Review + create

With your Basic support plan, you can create support requests for billing, subscription management, and quota increase.

For technical support, upgrade to a paid support plan or explore our free resources.

🙂 **Get expert help**
From $29/month, our support plans provide access to expert 1:1 technical support.

[View plans]

👥 **Ask our community**
Access a large community of experts and Microsoft engineers who can help.

View Azure Community Support ☐

Additional resources

Azure documentation ☐
Tweet @AzureSupport ☐
Service Health
Link support benefits

FIGURE 6-23 Buy a support plan or ask for community support.

6. Click **Next**.

7. Review your settings in the **Review + Create** tab. Then click **Create** to create the ticket.

Best practices

Following are some general best practices for setting up and using the Azure Portal:

- **Use RBAC and MFA to protect access to the Azure Portal**   It is important to set up access to the Azure Portal using the provided RBAC options. There are a number of built-in groups that limit access to users based on their individual needs. You can also create custom groups if the standard built-in groups do not address your needs. Be sure to turn on MFA for all users accessing the Azure Portal. Azure MFA is provided free of cost. Use this service to ensure that a password breach does not open access to your Azure environment.

- **Limit access based on required geographies or known IPs**   Restrict access to the Azure Portal based on the following criteria to protect it against brute-force attacks:

    - Allow access only from known IPs. Have admins to log in centrally using only those known allowlisted IPs.

    - Block access from known botnets and malicious IPs.

    - Allow access only from geographic locations where your admins are based or accessing the environment.

    - Block access from geographic locations attempting brute-force attacks, according to the Azure Portal logs.

    You can use conditional access to accomplish this, as per your organization's requirements.

- **Limit access from managed devices**   Limit access to the Azure Portal to devices under your direct and complete management, monitoring, and control. These can be devices managed by MDM solutions such as Microsoft Intune or Microsoft SCCM. You can use conditional access to identify whether access is being attempted from unmanaged devices and block them.

- **Perform regular access audits**   Implement a regular internal audit process to track and review all administrator access assigned in the Azure Portal. Having a monthly, quarterly, or half-yearly process, based on your organization's size and complexity, can help eliminate temporary access rights that are no longer required. Automated auditing solutions for access management can make this process faster and more accurate.

- **Set up long-term log retention**   Azure Portal access and activity logs are retained for short periods of time, ranging between 90 and 180 days. To retain logs for a longer period for auditory and compliance reviews, set up long-term log retention.

- **Use a security information and event management (SIEM) tool to monitor access and activities**   Use a SIEM tool to analyze and identify patterns that indicate ongoing attacks or unwanted access to the Azure Portal. Azure Sentinel is one such tool provided in Azure. You can use other third-party services to achieve this as well.

Chapter 7

Azure Cloud Shell

Overview

In November 2017, Microsoft made Azure Cloud Shell with bash generally available, and made PowerShell modules generally available in October 2018. Azure Cloud Shell provides a browser-based shell to run bash and PowerShell cmdlets and scripts to manage Azure resources.

Azure Cloud Shell provides an interactive experience that uses role-based access control (RBAC) to provide access based on permissions. This provides users with a cloud-native command-line environment from any device, anywhere in the world. On the back end, Microsoft assigns a free VM for each user who runs Cloud Shell. This same VM is presented to the user via the tool they are using to access the service.

Key features

The key features of the Cloud Shell are as follows:

- **Authenticated and secure access**   Cloud Shell is integrated with the Azure AD service and can therefore provide secure access to authenticated users based on their permission levels.

- **Support for bash and PowerShell**   Cloud Shell provides support for both bash and PowerShell, making it easier for organizations to use their preferred language for scripting and automation.

- **Compatible with most modern browsers**   Cloud Shell is compatible with most widely used modern browsers, such as the latest versions of Microsoft Edge, Microsoft Internet Explorer, Apple Safari, Google Chrome, and Firefox.

- **Integrated editor**   Cloud Shell has an integrated graphical editor, based on the open-source Monaco Editor, that lets you easily create and edit scripts in code.

- **Multiple service connection points**   Cloud Shell is accessible using different connection access points such as portal.azure.com, shell.azure.com, Azure PowerShell connection URLs, Azure CLI connection URLs, and Visual Studio.

- **Open-source tool integrations**   Cloud Shell has deep integrations with open-source tools such as Ansible, Chef, and Terraform.

- **File persistence**   Cloud Shell supports file persistence across sessions using Azure file share. It requires a one-time setup of the file share and associated connection, and it is automatically remapped each time going forward.

- **Free to use**   Microsoft assigns a free VM in the back end to each user who runs Cloud Shell.

- **Encryption at rest**   Microsoft encrypts all Cloud Shell infrastructure with double-encryption at rest to ensure it meets the compliance needs of most organizations.

- **Support for multiple programming languages**   Cloud Shell supports the use of multiple programming languages such as .NET Core, Go, Java, Node.js, PowerShell, and Python.

Usage concepts and considerations

Azure Cloud Shell helps to automate Azure service deployment and management operations using either bash or PowerShell commands. One of the easiest ways to access the service is via the Azure Portal (assuming you are logged in to your tenant).

There are a few caveats to be aware of when using the service, as follows:

- The session times out after 20 minutes of inactivity.

- You must mount an Azure file share the first time you use it. Cloud Share will persist that configuration going forward. The same share will be used for both bash and PowerShell sessions.

- $HOME is persisted as a 5GB image mounted inside the Azure file share connected to the shell. This is the home drive where all the user's data is stored, including files and credentials stored by the user during their session.

- When using the bash shell, user permissions are set up as a regular Linux user.

Azure file share

To store their home directory—which could contain files, access tokens, and credentials—each Cloud Shell user can associate their session with a new or existing Azure file share storage account. This ensures that their data is carried forward from one session to another, making it easier for admins to continue their activities in the shell across sessions. You can use an LRS, ZRS, or GRS storage account to store this data. For redundancy purposes, it is recommended that you use a ZRS or GRS storage account, so the home directory and all files stored therein are available in case of a regional outage.

Azure file share walkthrough

The following section shows you how to create the Azure file share using the Azure Portal.

USING THE AZURE PORTAL

To create the Azure file share using the Azure Portal with the bash module, follow these steps:

1. To open Cloud Shell, do one of the following:

   - Log in to the Azure Portal and click the **Cloud Service** icon in the top-right bar. (See Figure 7-1.)

   FIGURE 7-1 Start Cloud Shell from the Azure Portal.

   - Enter https://shell.azure.com in the Address bar of any supported web browser. (See Figure 7-2.)

   FIGURE 7-2 Navigate to Cloud Shell.

   Because this is the first time you are accessing Cloud Shell, you will be prompted to create the Azure file share. (See Figure 7-3.)

FIGURE 7-3 Create cloud shell storage.

2. Click **Show Advanced Settings**.

3. On the page that opens (see Figure 7-4), enter the following information. Then click **Create Storage**:

   - **Subscription** Select the subscription to use to create the storage account and file share.

   - **Cloud Shell Region** Select the region to use to create the storage account and file share.

   - **Resource Group** Select the **Create New** option button and enter a unique name for the resource group to be created. Alternatively, select the **Use Existing** option button to select an existing resource group from the drop-down list for this deployment.

   - **Storage Account** Select the **Create New** option button and enter a unique name for the storage account to be created. Alternatively, select the **Use Existing** option button to select an existing storage account from the drop-down list for this deployment.

   - **File Share** Select the **Create New** option button and enter a unique name for the file share to be created. Alternatively, select the **Use Existing** option button to select an existing file share from the drop-down list for this deployment.

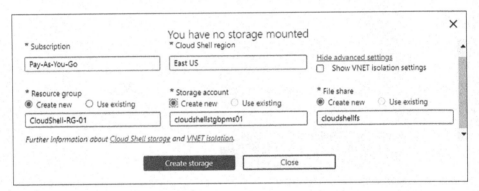

FIGURE 7-4   Create Storage.

Azure connects to or creates the resource group, storage account, and file share, and connects you to a Cloud Shell. (See Figure 7-5.)

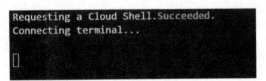

FIGURE 7-5   Cloud Shell connection.

Azure drive

When using the PowerShell module in Azure Cloud Shell, you can discover and navigate all the Azure resources provisioned in the subscription. To do so, you must use the cd Azure: command to switch the shell to the Azure drive. You can manage resources using standard PowerShell cmdlets from any of the shell drives, including the home drive (cd ~), however, to be able to browse the resource volumes, you will have to switch to the Azure drive first.

Cloud Shell Editor

The team behind the development of Azure Cloud Shell worked closely with the Visual Studio Code team as part of their open-source Monaco project to integrate the Monaco Editor into Cloud Shell. This web standards-based editor makes it easy for admins who are familiar with Visual Studio Code features—such as auto-completion, code snippets, syntax coloring, and so on—to use those same features within the Cloud Shell. Cloud Shell includes a file explorer for easy navigation and exploration of the Cloud Shell file system.

> **NOTE** You can use vi, emacs, and nano to edit files from Cloud Shell, and the "code ."
> Cmdlet to open the file explorer when accessing Cloud Shell via a web browser.

Embed Cloud Shell

You can embed the Cloud Shell URL shell.azure.com in the HTML code of your website using the standard code provided by Microsoft. This makes it easier for admins and users who need to use the service to access it easily.

To enable a JavaScript-based launch button on your web page, you can embed the following code in HTML. When this button is clicked, it launches Cloud Shell in a pop-up window:

```
<a style="cursor:pointer" onclick='javascript:window.open("https://shell.azure.com",
"_blank", "toolbar=no,scrollbars=yes,resizable=yes,menubar=no,location=no,status=no")'>
<img alt="Launch Azure Cloud Shell" src="https://shell.azure.com/images/launchcloudshell.
png"></a>
```

To force users to employ the bash or PowerShell versions of the Cloud Shell, you can change the URL in the code to one of the following based on your enforcement requirements:

- **Bash**   https://shell.azure.com/bash
- **PowerShell**   https://shell.azure.com/powershell

Cloud Shell deployment in a vNET

By default, Cloud Shell cannot access resources that are set up to be accessible only via specific private virtual networks in Azure. For example, a locked-down Kubernetes cluster cannot be accessed using kubectl unless Cloud Shell is integrated within the same virtual network. However, in some scenarios, you might want to use Cloud Shell to access such private resources.

For Cloud Shell integration, you must dedicate a subnet on the virtual network to the Azure Container Instances (ACI) service. When a user requests the creation of a Cloud Shell session, ACI deploys a container in that subnet to host the Cloud Shell.

Along with the dedicated subnet in the virtual network, as shown in Figure 7-6, an Azure Relay service is needed to control which public or private networks can be used to access the Cloud Shell service. This is not a free service, so the costs for the service should be taken into consideration when planning this deployment.

TIP To deploy these additional resources, Microsoft provides and maintains a free template online. Use this template to deploy the required resources before integrating Cloud Shell into the virtual network.

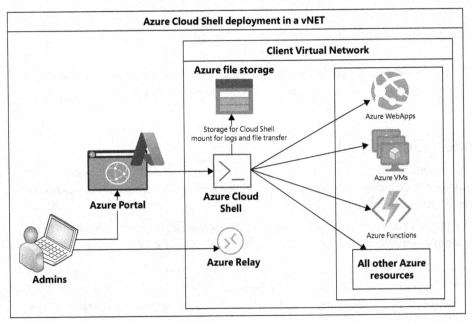

FIGURE 7-6 Cloud Shell deployment in a vNET.

Azure Cloud Shell walkthrough

This section walks you through the Cloud Shell using the Azure Portal with bash and Power-Shell modules.

USING THE AZURE PORTAL: BASH MODULE

To access and use Cloud Shell with the bash module, follow these steps:

1. To open Cloud Shell, do one of the following:
   - Log in to the Azure Portal and click the **Cloud Service** icon in the top-right bar. (See Figure 7-7.)

     FIGURE 7-7 Start Cloud Shell from the Azure Portal.

   - Enter https://shell.azure.com in the Address bar of any supported web browser. (See Figure 7-8.)

     https://shell.azure.com

     FIGURE 7-8 Navigate to Cloud Shell.

   Azure connects you to a Cloud Shell. (See Figure 7-9.) Once you are connected, you see the home directory. (See Figure 7-10.) By default, you are connected to the Bash shell. You can now run bash commands to list, get, create, modify, or delete resources as needed based on your permissions.

   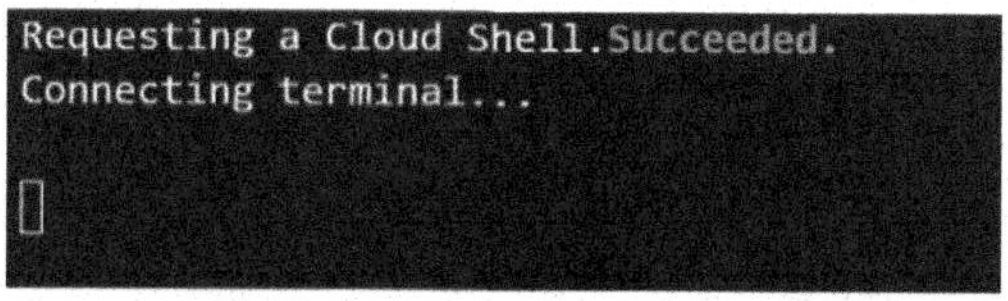
   Requesting a Cloud Shell.Succeeded.
   Connecting terminal...

   FIGURE 7-9 Cloud Shell window.

   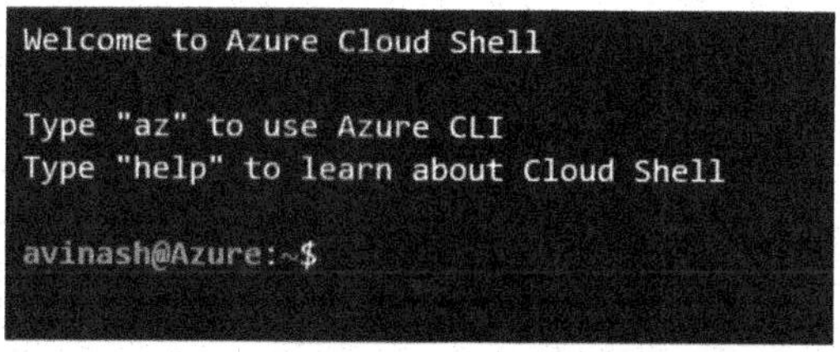
   Welcome to Azure Cloud Shell
   Type "az" to use Azure CLI
   Type "help" to learn about Cloud Shell
   avinash@Azure:~$

   FIGURE 7-10 Cloud Shell home directory.

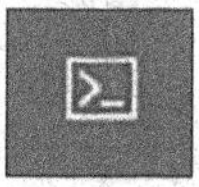

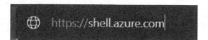

2. Run the az storage account list bash command (see Figure 7-11) to list all the storage accounts set up in your Azure subscription (see Figure 7-12).

   avinash@Azure:~$ az storage account list

   FIGURE 7-11 Cloud Shell service connection.

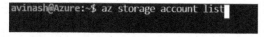

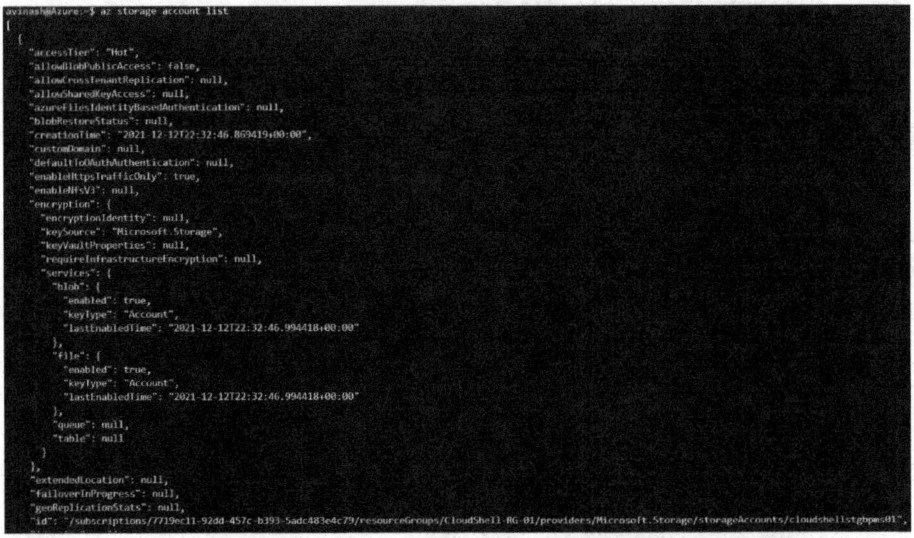

avinash@Azure:~$ az storage account list
[
  {
    "accessTier": "Hot",
    "allowBlobPublicAccess": false,
    "allowCrossTenantReplication": null,
    "allowSharedKeyAccess": null,
    "azureFilesIdentityBasedAuthentication": null,
    "blobRestoreStatus": null,
    "creationTime": "2021-12-12T22:32:46.869419+00:00",
    "customDomain": null,
    "defaultToOAuthAuthentication": null,
    "enableHttpsTrafficOnly": true,
    "enableNfsV3": null,
    "encryption": {
      "encryptionIdentity": null,
      "keySource": "Microsoft.Storage",
      "keyVaultProperties": null,
      "requireInfrastructureEncryption": null,
      "services": {
        "blob": {
          "enabled": true,
          "keyType": "Account",
          "lastEnabledTime": "2021-12-12T22:32:46.994418+00:00"
        },
        "file": {
          "enabled": true,
          "keyType": "Account",
          "lastEnabledTime": "2021-12-12T22:32:46.994418+00:00"
        },
        "queue": null,
        "table": null
      }
    },
    "extendedLocation": null,
    "failoverInProgress": null,
    "geoReplicationStats": null,
    "id": "/subscriptions/7719ec11-92dd-457c-b393-5adc483e4c79/resourceGroups/CloudShell-RG-01/providers/Microsoft.Storage/storageAccounts/cloudshellistgbpms01",

FIGURE 7-12 Account storage list in Cloud Shell.

3. To change the text size in the session window, click the **Settings** icon at the top of the Cloud Shell window, choose **Text Size**, and select **Small**, **Medium**, or **Large**. (See Figure 7-13.)

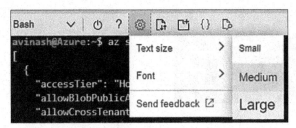

FIGURE 7-13 Change the text size.

4. To change the font in the session window, click the **Settings** icon, choose **Font**, and select the font you prefer. (See Figure 7-14.)

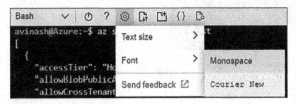

FIGURE 7-14 Change the font.

5. In case you need to restart the current Cloud Shell session—for instance, if it is not responding or has timed out—click the **Power** icon at the top of the Cloud Shell window, next to the **Bash** down arrow (see Figure 7-15), and click **Restart** in the window that appears (see Figure 7-16).

FIGURE 7-15 Click the Power button.

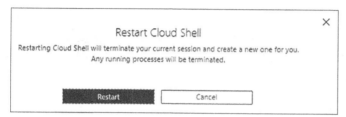

FIGURE 7-16 Click the Restart button.

6. To download a file from Cloud Shell, click the **Folder** icon at the top of the Cloud Shell window and choose **Download**. (See Figure 7-17.)

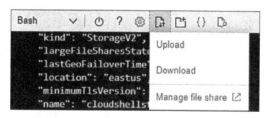

FIGURE 7-17 Choose the Download menu command.

7. Enter the path and name of the file you want to download and click the **Download** button. (See Figure 7-18.)

FIGURE 7-18 Specify the file you want to download.

8. To verify that the file was downloaded successfully, browse the **Downloads** folder in your profile. (See Figure 7-19.)

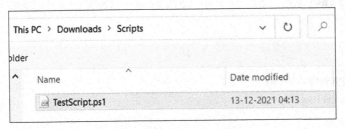

FIGURE 7-19 Verify the file was downloaded.

9. To upload a file, click the **Folder** icon and choose **Upload**. (See Figure 7-20.)

FIGURE 7-20 Choose the Upload menu command.

10. Locate and select the file you want to upload. Then click the **Upload** button. When the upload is done, it will be marked as complete. (See Figure 7-21.)

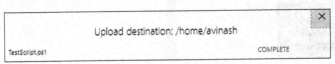

FIGURE 7-21 The upload is complete.

11. Confirm that the file has been successfully uploaded to the Cloud Shell session. (See Figure 7-22.)

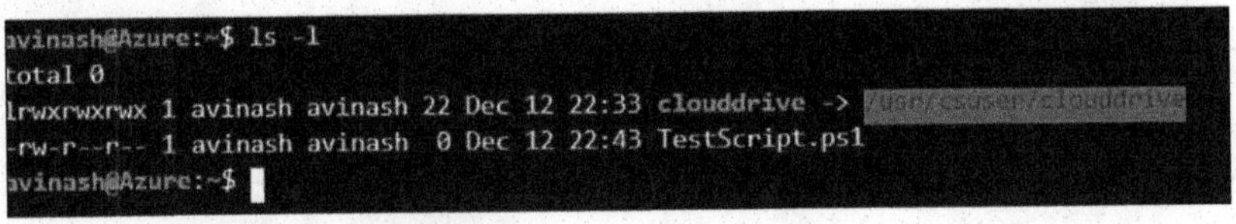

```
avinash@Azure:~$ ls -l
total 0
lrwxrwxrwx 1 avinash avinash 22 Dec 12 22:33 clouddrive -> /usr/csuser/clouddrive
-rw-r--r-- 1 avinash avinash  0 Dec 12 22:43 TestScript.ps1
avinash@Azure:~$
```

FIGURE 7-22 Confirming the file upload.

12. To open the Monaco Editor, click the **Editor** icon at the top of the Cloud Shell window. (See Figure 7-23.)

FIGURE 7-23 Open the Monaco Editor.

A new browser tab or window with the open-source Monaco Editor opens. (See Figure 7-24.) You can now edit any JSON templates stored in the home drive or create new ones as needed.

FIGURE 7-24 Monaco Editor.

USING THE AZURE PORTAL: POWERSHELL MODULE

To access and use Cloud Shell with the PowerShell module, follow these steps:

1. Open Cloud Shell and do one of the following:

   - Log in to the Azure Portal and click the **Cloud Service** icon in the top-right bar.

   - Enter https://shell.azure.com in the Address bar of any supported web browser.

2. Click the down arrow at the top of the Cloud Shell window and select **PowerShell**. (See Figure 7-25.)

FIGURE 7-25 Switch to PowerShell.

3. In the **Switch to PowerShell in Cloud Shell** pop-up, click the **Confirm** button. (See Figure 7-26.)

FIGURE 7-26 Click Confirm to switch to PowerShell.

Cloud Shell connects to the PowerShell module and switches to the home directory. You can now run standard Azure PowerShell cmdlets to access, deploy, and manage resources in your Azure environment. (See Figure 7-27.)

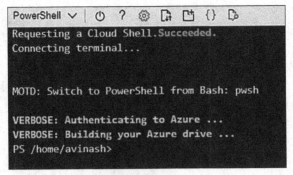

FIGURE 7-27 The PowerShell module.

4. Run the Get-AzureRMStorageAccount PowerShell cmdlet to list all the storage accounts set up in your Azure subscription. (See Figure 7-28.)

FIGURE 7-28 The Get-AzureRMStorageAccount cmdlet shows a list of storage accounts.

5. To switch to the Azure drive, run the cd Azure: cmdlet. (See Figure 7-29.)

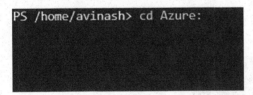

FIGURE 7-29 Switch to the Azure drive.

You'll see the **Azure:** prompt. (See Figure 7-30.) You can now run File Explorer commands to discover and manage Azure resources.

FIGURE 7-30 The Azure:\ prompt.

6. Run the dir cmdlet to view information about your subscriptions. (See Figure 7-31.) Be sure you are able to see all of your subscriptions, and that the correct subscription is currently selected. (The active subscription has a + sign next to the Mode heading.)

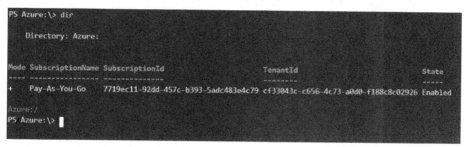

FIGURE 7-31 The cd Azure drive with a list of subscriptions.

7. To browse the subscription, run the cd subscriptioname cmdlet (see Figure 7-32).

FIGURE 7-32 Browsing to subscriptions.

You are now logged in to the subscription and can browse for resources.

8. Run the dir cmdlet again to list all the resources you can browse. (See Figure 7-33.)

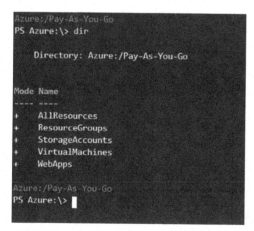

FIGURE 7-33 The list of resources in subscriptions.

9. Run the cd StorageAccounts cmdlet to browse to the storage accounts container. (See Figure 7-34.)

```
Azure:/Pay-As-You-Go
PS Azure:\> cd StorageAccounts
Azure:/Pay-As-You-Go/StorageAccounts
PS Azure:\>
```

FIGURE 7-34 The storage accounts container.

10. Run the dir cmdlet again to list all the storage accounts in the selected subscription. (See Figure 7-35.)

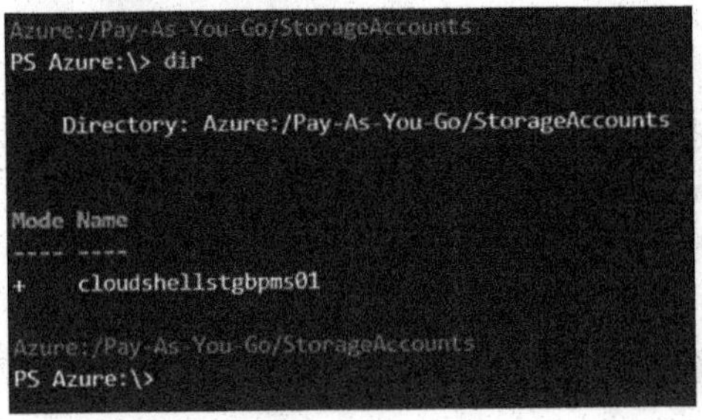

```
Azure:/Pay-As-You-Go/StorageAccounts
PS Azure:\> dir

    Directory: Azure:/Pay-As-You-Go/StorageAccounts


Mode Name
---- ----
+    cloudshellstgbpms01

Azure:/Pay-As-You-Go/StorageAccounts
PS Azure:\>
```

FIGURE 7-35 Storage accounts in the subscription.

11. Continue to run cmdlets as needed on the storage accounts and other resources. You can obtain help at any time on cmdlet options within the Cloud Shell window.

Best practices

Following are some general best practices regarding setting up and using Azure Cloud Shell:

- **Use RBAC and MFA to protect access to Cloud Shell**   Review the admins who can use Cloud Shell, and the resources and permissions they have access to, so there is a clear demarcation of roles and permissions in your environment. Take advantage of the RBAC roles provided in Azure AD or create custom roles based on your organization's needs to achieve this. Ensure that all admin accounts are set up with Azure MFA, which is provided free of cost in Azure. This can help prevent unwanted access to your environment, even in the event of a password breach.

- **Use Azure Key Vault to store secrets**   Because you can store code and credentials inside Cloud Shell or the connected file share, there is a chance of credential exposure if they are stored in plain text. You can use tools such as Credential Scanner provided by Microsoft to locate these credentials and preferably move them to Azure Key Vault or some other secure credential-storage solution.

- **Restrict access to Cloud Shell** Because Cloud Shell can be used to easily run scripts and code against your Azure services, it is a good practice to protect access to Cloud Shell from specific secured workstations using Cloud Conditional Access. You can completely restrict access to Cloud Shell from any environment using a combination of conditional access and firewall policies that target the URLs associated with the service—for example, ux.console.azure.com and ux.console.azure.us (used for Azure Government Cloud). If you need to prevent such access, you can set up policies targeting these URLs to prevent access except from specific locations, IPs, or workstations.

- **Restrict access using Azure Policy** You can prevent access to Cloud Shell by using Azure Policy and allowing only specific admins to create storage accounts. Admins who do not have such access can either select existing storage accounts accessible by them for write operations or be denied access if none exist.

Chapter 8

Azure Service Health

Overview

Azure provides a set of tools to help you monitor the health of the Azure Cloud services you are consuming. In addition to Azure Monitor, which you can use to monitor workload levels, there are tools to monitor the resources on the service layer and to alert you of service issues that could be affecting the health of your environment. These tools also relay information and alerts about ongoing maintenance activities—planned and unplanned—that could cause service-availability issues for your cloud resources. This chapter covers three of these tools:

- **Azure Status** This tool provides information about Azure service outages across all Azure regions. Because this tool provides information about outages across all regions, rather than just the regions hosting your resources, it is best to use it when there is a wider outage possibly affecting inter-region services.

- **Service Health** This tool provides a more succinct view of the health status of Azure services, focusing only on the regions and services you are using in your subscription. It monitors the services you have deployed in your subscription to provide a more personalized dashboard and alerts you to any outages, planned maintenance activities, or advisories pertaining to those services and regions alone.

- **Resource Health** This tool goes one step further: It monitors the health of individual cloud resources deployed in your subscription and alerts you to any issues affecting those resources. Resource Health works hand-in-hand with Azure Monitor to provide alerts that are critical to the health of your resources.

This chapter reviews each of these tools in more detail.

Azure Status

As mentioned, Azure Status (see Figure 8-1) monitors the overall service health across all Azure regions and provides updates on service-level issues in all regions. It is an unauthenticated service that provides status publicly for everyone at https://status.azure.com.

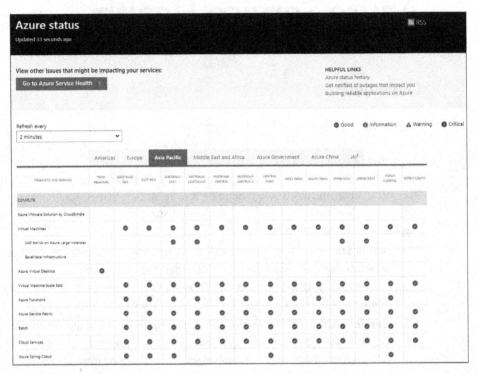

FIGURE 8-1 Azure Status page.

The only configuration options for the Azure Status page are as follows:

- **Refresh Every drop-down list**   Use this drop-down list to change the refresh interval.
- **Region tabs**   Click the tab for the region that is relevant to your environment to view region-specific details.
- **Azure Status History**   Obtain a historical view of outages.

The Azure Status History page (see Figure 8-2) keeps a record of all incidents that have occurred in the last five years, by default (starting November 20, 2019). You can filter this information by service, region, and date range to view only those incidents relevant to your needs.

Because Azure Status provides a high-level view of major outages or planned activities affecting services in all regions, it is difficult to use it to identify issues with specific resources or workloads in your environment. Service Health and Resource Health are better tools to address those scenarios.

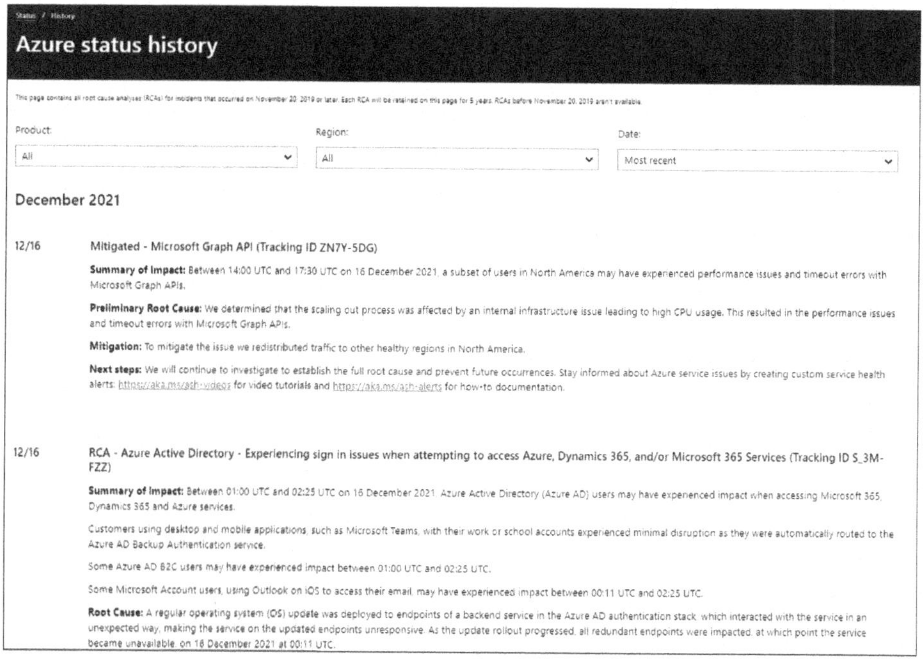

FIGURE 8-2 Azure Status History page.

Service Health

Service Health is a free dashboard provided in Azure that tracks the health status of your Azure services and the regions in which they have been deployed. This tool tracks various service events that indicate a change in the health status of your Azure services. These events include the following:

- **Planned maintenance activities** These are maintenance activities planned for the services you are using in the regions in which they are deployed.
- **Service issues** These are ongoing health issues for services that you are using in the regions in which they are deployed that could have an impact on your environment.
- **Security advisories** These are advisories related to security violations or ongoing security issues that might affect your services.
- **Health advisories** These are advisories related to the deprecation of service features or to features or services that require upgrade for continued support.

Service Health saves records of these events for 90 days. You can set up alerts to monitor issues for action from your end on an immediate basis.

Figure 8-3 and Figure 8-4 show the Service Health history for two different Azure subscriptions. As you can see, by default, Health History filters the view to only those regions in which the subscription has resources hosted. A few events that took place on a global level can be seen across both views. However, certain events that occurred in the Central US region are visible only in one image.

FIGURE 8-3 Service Health history for the Pay-As-You-Go subscription.

FIGURE 8-4 Service Health history for the Azure Primary subscription.

Service Health walkthrough

The following section walks you through the process of viewing events on the Server Health dashboard and setting up alerts for continuous monitoring using the Azure Portal.

USING THE AZURE PORTAL

1. Log in to the Azure Portal, type **service health** in the search box, and select it from the list that appears. (See Figure 8-5.)

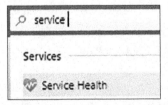

FIGURE 8-5 Search for Service Health.

The left pane of the Service Health window, under the Active Events section, contains a list of event types to choose from. By default, the Service Issues event type is selected in the left pane, and a default subscription, region, and service will be selected in the right pane, depending on your environment. (See Figure 8-6.)

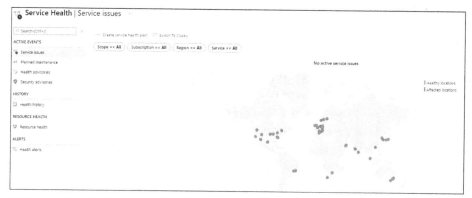

FIGURE 8-6 The Service Issues option is selected under Active Events in the left pane, and the default subscription, region, and service are selected in the right pane.

2. To view service issues in a specific subscription or region, or to choose a specific service, select the desired options from the **Subscription**, **Region**, and **Service** drop-down lists. (See Figure 8-7.)

FIGURE 8-7 Customizing the Service Health options.

Now let's set up a new Service Health alert so you can be notified of any issues with specific services in specific Azure regions. This involves creating an alert rule.

3. Click the **Create Service Health Alert** button.

4. In the **Create an Alert Rule** dialog box (see Figure 8-8), enter the following information:

   - **Subscription** Select the subscription that hosts the services for which you want to create an alert.

   - **Service(s)** Choose the service(s) for which you want to create an alert.

   - **Region(s)** Choose the region(s) for which you want to create an alert.

   - **Event Type** Select the event type(s) for which you want to create an alert.

   - **Actions** Select the **Add Action Groups** option. This will allow you to define an action, such as sending notifications via email, SMS, or voice call; the associated recipients; or triggering automated actions.

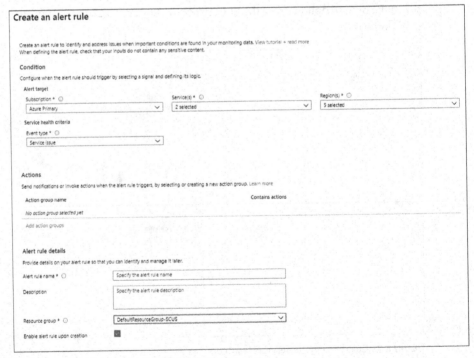

FIGURE 8-8 The Create an Alert Rule dialog box.

5. In the **Basics** tab of the Create an Action Group wizard (see Figure 8-9), enter the following information. Then click **Next**:

- **Subscription**   Select the subscription in which you want to create the action group.
- **Resource Group**   Select the resource group in which you want to create the action group. Alternatively, click the **Create New** link and follow the prompts to create a new resource group.
- **Action Group Name**   Enter a unique name for the action group.
- **Display Name**   Enter a unique display name for the action group. This name is limited to 12 characters.

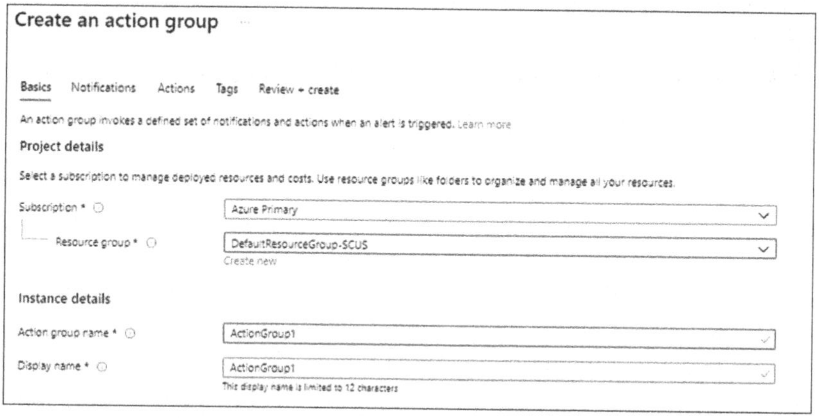

FIGURE 8-9   The Basics tab of the Create an Action Group wizard.

6. In the **Notifications** tab (see Figure 8-10), enter the following information:

- **Notification Type**   Select **Email/SMS Message/Push/Voice**.
- **Name**   Enter a unique name for the notification.

FIGURE 8-10   The Notifications tab of the Create an Action Group wizard.

7. In the **Email/SMS Message/Push/Voice** pop-up box that opens on the right (see Figure 8-11), enter the following information (if applicable to your environment). Then click **OK**:

- **Email** Select this check box and enter the address to which Service Health alerts should be sent via email.

- **SMS** Select this check box and enter the country code and phone number to which Service Health alerts should be sent via SMS message.

- **Azure App Push Notifications** Select this check box and enter the Azure account email address to which Service Health alerts should be sent via the Azure app.

- **Voice** Select this check box and enter the country code and phone number to which Service Health alerts should be sent via voice call.

- **Enable the Common Alert Schema** Leave this option set to **No**.

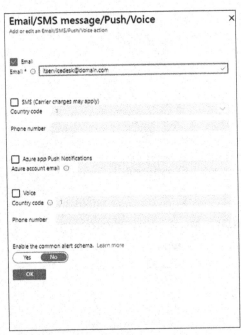

FIGURE 8-11 Configure the action.

8. Back in the **Notifications** tab, check your settings. Then click **Next**.

9. In the **Actions** tab, optionally open the **Action Type** drop-down list (see Figure 8-12) and choose any additional actions you want to take (in addition to notifications). Then type a name for the action in the **Name** box and click **Next**. (In this example, I have not set additional actions.)

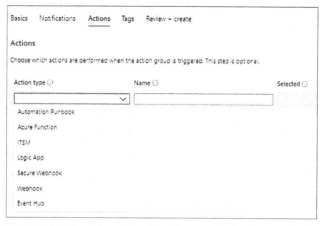

FIGURE 8-12 The Actions tab of the Create an Action Group wizard.

10. In the **Tags** tab (see Figure 8-13), enter any tags you want to associate with the action group and click **Review + Create**.

FIGURE 8-13 The Tags tab of the Create an Action Group wizard.

11. In the **Review + Create** tab (see Figure 8-14), check your settings. Then click **Review + Create** to create the action group.

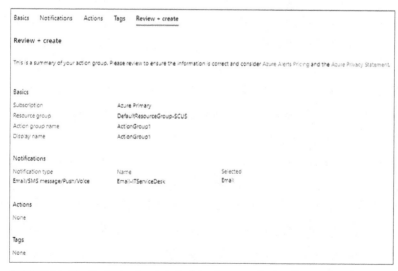

FIGURE 8-14 The Review + Create tab of the Create an Action Group wizard.

12. Back in the **Create an Alert Rule** dialog box (see Figure 8-15), enter the following information. Then click **Create Rule**:

- **Alert Rule Name**   Enter a unique name for the alert rule.
- **Description**   Enter a description of the alert rule for easy reference for other admins.
- **Resource Group**   Select the resource group in which to create the alert rule.
- **Enable Alert Rule Upon Creation**   Leave this check box selected.

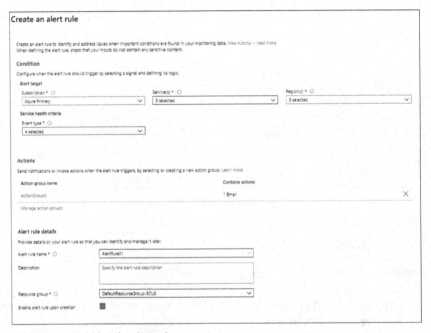

FIGURE 8-15   Finishing the alert rule.

13. To view the rule, click the **Health Alerts** option in the left pane of the **Service Health** window, under **Alerts**. (See Figure 8-16.)

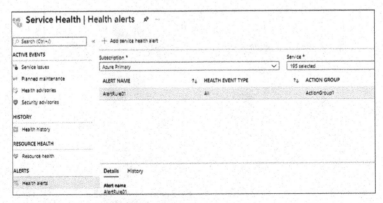

FIGURE 8-16   The Health Alerts page.

14. Click **Service Issues**, **Planned Maintenance**, **Health Advisories**, or **Service Advisories** (depending on what type of alert it is) in the left pane to view more details about health alerts that are ongoing in the right pane. Figure 8-17 shows the Service Issues page.

> **TIP** You can view closed health alerts by clicking Health History in the left pane.

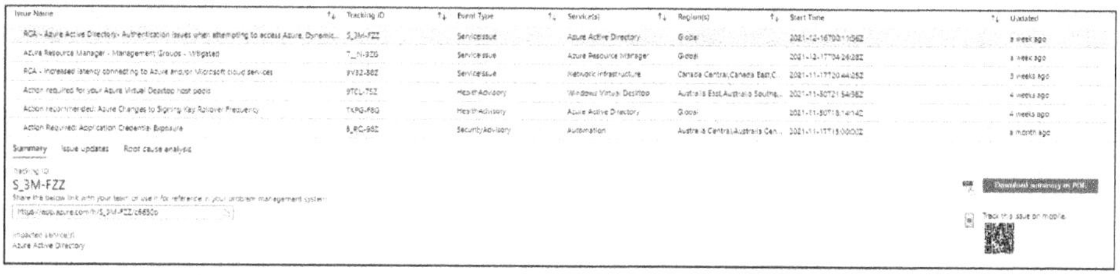

FIGURE 8-17 See more details about a specific alert.

15. Optionally, click the **Download Summary as PDF** button to download event details, including root cause explanations published by Microsoft.

Resource Health

Resource Health enables you to closely monitor the health of resources deployed in your Azure environment. You can set up alerts in Resource Health to allow you to take action when issues arise. This can also help you diagnose the root cause of the issue. Resource Health is available free of charge for all Azure customers.

Resource Health interprets various signals from different Azure services to determine if a resource is healthy or not. If a resource is deemed unhealthy, the service collects additional information to determine the source of the problem. For example, if a virtual machine (VM) is deemed to be unhealthy, the service performs the following checks are performed:

- Is the server hosting this VM up and running?
- Has the host OS completed booting?
- Is the VM container provisioned and powered up?
- Is there network connectivity between the host and the storage account?
- Has the guest OS completed booting?
- Is there ongoing planned maintenance?
- Is the host hardware degraded and predicted to fail soon?

If, on the other hand, a website is deemed as unhealthy, the following checks are performed:

- Is the host server up and running?
- Is the Internet Information Server running?

- Is the load balancer running?
- Can the web app be reached from within the datacenter?
- Is the storage account hosting the site content available?

As you can see, the checks are very different in each case, and depend on the service features and capabilities. Resource Health performs these checks on the individual resource instance that is deemed to be unhealthy, so it is critical to monitor Resource Health alerts and actions, as they will reveal issues in your environment.

You can set up personalized dashboards that show the health of your resources. The health data captured by Resource Health is maintained for historical reference and comparison for a period of 30 days. Additionally, in the case of VM workloads, as and when a health issue is resolved, root cause analysis information is published regarding the VM resource within 72 hours.

Health status indicators

Resource Health displays various health status indicators. Possible status values are as follows:

- **Available**   The resource is working as expected, and there have been no ongoing issues in the last 24 hours. If an issue was resolved in the last 24 hours, the service will indicate this, too.

- **Unavailable**   An issue has been detected that is affecting the health of the resource. This could be a platform issue or a non-platform issue. A platform issue is an issue with the Azure infrastructure, such as a service outage, planned maintenance, or unplanned resource restarts or host restarts. Non-platform issues include issues triggered by user actions, such as a resource restart or shutdown.

- **Unknown**   The health of the resource could not be determined for the last 10 minutes. This might be because the resource did not broadcast any health information because it is offline, or it could be due to an underlying service issue.

- **Degraded**   The service is detecting some ongoing issue that is affecting the performance of the resource. Depending on the type of resource, the reasons behind a degraded status are different. For example, a storage account might indicate a degraded status if the underlying hardware is detecting corruption, whereas a traffic manager service might indicate a degraded status if some of the regions that provide the service are offline.

Based on the health status indicator, Resource Health will provide you with a set of recommendations and next steps to help you troubleshoot the issue as quickly as possible to reduce downtime. These recommendations are based on a historical analysis of common solutions for similar events across all Azure customers.

Create a Resource Health alert walkthrough

The following section walks you through the process of setting up a Resource Health alert rule using the Azure Portal.

USING THE AZURE PORTAL

To use Resource Health to monitor the health of your system and to set up an alert in the Azure Portal, follow these steps:

1. Log in to the Azure Portal, type **service health** in the search box, and select it from the list that appears. (See Figure 8-18.)

FIGURE 8-18   Service Health service search.

2. In the left pane of the Service Health window, under **Resource Health**, click the **Resource Health** option. (See Figure 8-19.)

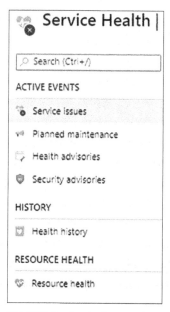

FIGURE 8-19   Service issues.

3. On the Resource Health page, click the **Add Resource Health Alert** button. (See Figure 8-20.)

FIGURE 8-20 Click the Add Resource Health Alert button.

4. In the Create Resource Health Alert Rule dialog box (see Figure 8-21), enter the following information:

- **Subscription** Select the subscription that hosts the services for which you want to create an alert.

- **Resource Type** Select the specific resource type(s) for which you want to create an alert or choose **Select All**.

- **Resource Group** Select the resource group(s) that contain the resource(s) for which you want to create an alert or choose **Select All**.

- **Include All Future Resource Groups** Leave this check box selected to automatically apply the new alert rule to all resource groups created in the future.

- **Resource** Select the resource(s) (such as the specific VMs) for which you want to create an alert or choose **Select All**.

- **Include All Future Resources** Leave this check box selected to automatically apply the new alert rule to all resources created in the future.

- **Event Status** Select the event status you want to monitor or choose **Select All**.

- **Current Resource Status** Select the Resource Health status indicators for which you want to receive alerts based on their current status in Azure or choose **Select All**.

- **Previous Resource Status** Select the Resource Health status indicators for which you want to receive alerts based on their previous status or choose **Select All**.

- **Reason Type** Select the reasons to generate the alert or choose **Select All**.

- **Actions** Click the **Add Action Groups** link.

5. In the Add Action Groups pop-up window, do one of the following:

- Click **Create Action Group** and follow steps 9–15 in the "Service Health walkthrough" section earlier in the chapter.

- Select the existing action group(s) with which you want to associate the rule. (See Figure 8-22.)

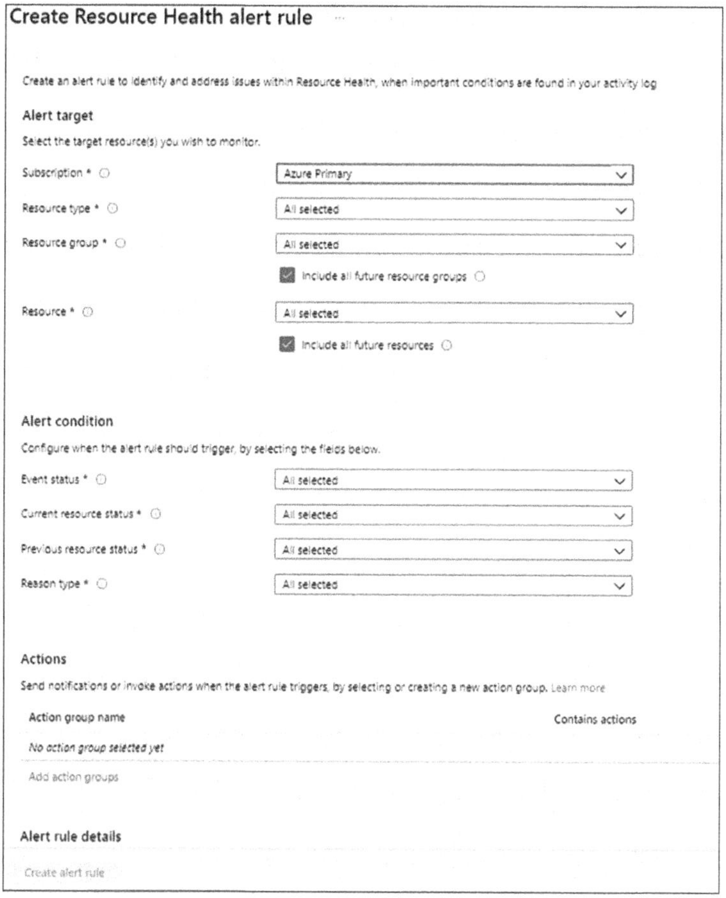

Create Resource Health alert rule ...

Create an alert rule to identify and address issues within Resource Health, when important conditions are found in your activity log

Alert target

Select the target resource(s) you wish to monitor.

Subscription * ◯ | Azure Primary   ▽ |

Resource type * ◯ | All selected   ▽ |

Resource group * ◯ | All selected   ▽ |

                          ☑ Include all future resource groups ◯

Resource * ◯ | All selected   ▽ |

                          ☑ Include all future resources ◯

Alert condition

Configure when the alert rule should trigger, by selecting the fields below.

Event status * ◯ | All selected   ▽ |

Current resource status * ◯ | All selected   ▽ |

Previous resource status * ◯ | All selected   ▽ |

Reason type * ◯ | All selected   ▽ |

Actions

Send notifications or invoke actions when the alert rule triggers, by selecting or creating a new action group. Learn more

Action group name	Contains actions
No action group selected yet	

Add action groups

Alert rule details

Create alert rule

FIGURE 8-21 The Create a Resource Health Alert Rule dialog box.

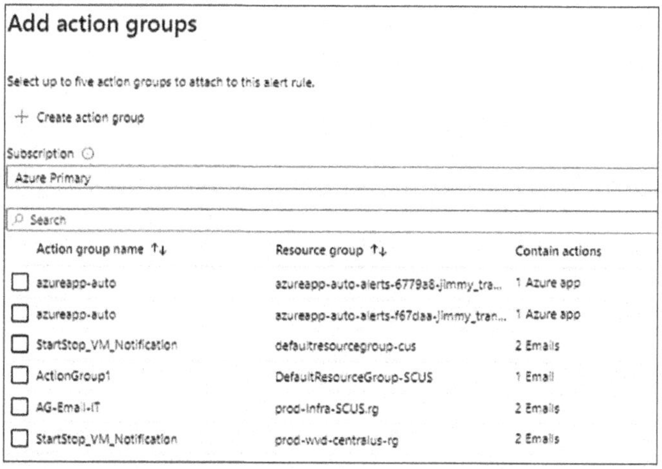

Add action groups

Select up to five action groups to attach to this alert rule.

+ Create action group

Subscription ◯

| Azure Primary |

| 🔎 Search |

Action group name ↑↓	Resource group ↑↓	Contain actions
☐ azureapp-auto	azureapp-auto-alerts-6779a8-jimmy_tra...	1 Azure app
☐ azureapp-auto	azureapp-auto-alerts-f67daa-jimmy_tran...	1 Azure app
☐ StartStop_VM_Notification	defaultresourcegroup-cus	2 Emails
☐ ActionGroup1	DefaultResourceGroup-SCUS	1 Email
☐ AG-Email-IT	prod-Infra-SCUS.rg	2 Emails
☐ StartStop_VM_Notification	prod-wvd-centralus-rg	2 Emails

FIGURE 8-22 Add action group.

6. Back in the **Create Resource Health Alert Rule** dialog box, under **Alert Rule Details** (see Figure 8-23), enter the following information. Then click the **Create Alert Rule** button:

- **Alert Rule Name** Enter a unique name for the alert rule.

- **Description** Enter a description of the alert rule for easy reference for other admins.

- **Resource Group** Select the resource group in which to create the alert rule.

- **Enable Alert Rule Upon Creation** Leave this check box selected.

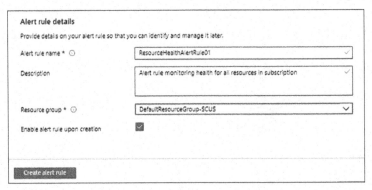

FIGURE 8-23 Finishing the Resource Health alert rule.

7. To view all the alerts set up for your subscription, type **monitor service** in the search box and select it from the list that appears.

8. In the left pane of the **Monitor** page, click **Alerts**. (See Figure 8-24.)

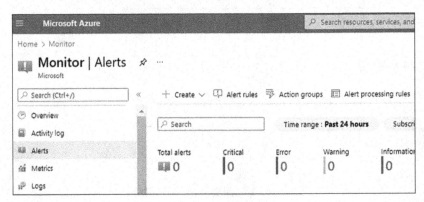

FIGURE 8-24 Select Alerts in Azure Monitor.

9. Click the **Alert Rules** button.

10. On the **Alert Rules** page, view all rules that have been set up, or type a rule name in the search bar on the left to locate a particular rule. Figure 8-25 shows a search for the **Resource Health** alert rule.

FIGURE 8-25 Search for the Resource Health alert rule.

Check a resource's health walkthrough

The following section walks you through the process of viewing the health of a particular resource using the Azure Portal.

USING THE AZURE PORTAL

To check the health of a particular resource using the Azure Portal, follow these steps:

1. In the Azure Portal, browse to the resource whose health status you want to check.

2. In the left pane of the resource's page in the Azure Portal, under **Support + Troubleshooting**, click the **Resource Health** option. (See Figure 8-26.)

FIGURE 8-26 Check the health of a particular resource.

The right pane displays current and past health status details for the resource in question, such as whether it's available, and if not, why not. (See Figures 8-27 and 8-28.)

Resource health watches your resource and tells you if it's running as expected. Learn more

✓ Available
There aren't any known Azure platform problems affecting this virtual machine.

What actions can you take?

1. If you're having problems, use the Troubleshoot tool to get recommended solutions.

Health history

Date	Description
12/25/2021	✓ Available
12/24/2021	✓ Available
12/23/2021	✓ Available
12/22/2021	✓ Available
12/21/2021	✓ Available
12/20/2021	✓ Available
12/19/2021	✓ Available
12/18/2021	✓ Available
12/17/2021	✓ Available
12/16/2021	✓ Available
12/15/2021	✓ Available
12/14/2021	✓ Available
12/13/2021	✓ Available
12/12/2021	✓ Available
12/11/2021	✓ Available

FIGURE 8-27 Detailed Resource Health status information for an available resource.

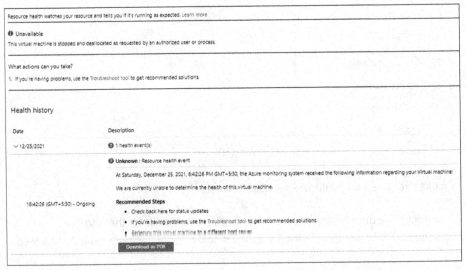

Resource health watches your resource and tells you if it's running as expected. Learn more

ⓘ Unavailable
This virtual machine is stopped and deallocated as requested by an authorized user or process.

What actions can you take?

1. If you're having problems, use the Troubleshoot tool to get recommended solutions.

Health history

Date	Description
⌄ 12/25/2021	❓ 1 health event(s)
	❓ Unknown : Resource health event
	At Saturday, December 25, 2021, 6:42:26 PM GMT+5:30, the Azure monitoring system received the following information regarding your Virtual machine:
	We are currently unable to determine the health of this virtual machine.
18:42:26 (GMT+5:30) - Ongoing	**Recommended Steps**
	• Check back here for status updates
	• If you're having problems, use the Troubleshoot tool to get recommended solutions.
	• Redeploy this virtual machine to a different host server

Download as PDF

FIGURE 8-28 Resource Health status information for a resource that is unavailable.

Best practices

Following are some general best practices for the Service Health and Resource Health tools:

- **Set up Service Health alerts for regular monitoring**   It is highly recommended that you set up Service Health alerts for all services you use in all active Azure regions to proactively identify any ongoing service issues and address them if possible. Some Service Health issues might not be addressable; still, being aware of them can help with internal user communications, planning future service redundancy options, or failing over the service if such options are already in place.

- **Set up Resource Health alerts for critical resources**   It is highly recommended that you set up Resource Health alerts for all resources—or at the very least, those resources that are most critical to your organization—to proactively identify and address any ongoing issues. These alerts should be sent to a mailbox that is monitored 24/7.

- **Set up custom dashboards**   Set up dashboards to monitor the health of the various services and resources on a continuous basis to ensure they are online as per your SLA requirements.

- **Setup automated actions if possible**   Setup automated actions to trigger workflows or runbooks to fix health issues or to enlist resources in the same or other regions to take over the load of any resources experiencing issues.

Chapter 9

Azure Cost Management

Overview

When deciding whether to use Microsoft Azure Cloud, one of the key determining factors for any organization is the anticipated cost of migrating and running their resources in a cloud environment over time. Every organization is cost conscious and must ensure their Azure spends are in line with their needs and provide the maximum return on investment (ROI).

The Azure Cost Management service helps organizations better understand their Azure spends by providing detailed cost breakdowns of all resources for which they are billed on a monthly basis. You can set up alerts to monitor your spends or budgets to curtail spending. You can also optimize your spends by getting a better understanding of how the costs are being incurred for each resource. Finally, Cost Management helps you set up billing information to ensure that internal resources in charge of ongoing payments are automatically sent bills on a monthly basis.

> **NOTE** Your Cost Management and billing configurations will depend on your subscription type. This chapter assumes you have a Pay-As-You-Go subscription. If you have a different type of subscription, you will need to work with your Microsoft representative or partner to obtain a better understanding of how to manage this for your environment.

Key features

Some of the key features of Cost Management are as follows:

- **Detailed analysis and breakdown of costs per resource** You can use Cost Management to obtain a detailed breakdown of all resource- and subscription-level costs incurred during the previous month, previous quarter, or a custom time period. This helps you analyze spends and identify areas for optimization.

- **Budgeting and planning for spends** You can use Cost Management to better understand your monthly, quarterly, and yearly spends based on resources and services. This can help you budget and plan spends for upcoming expansions or resource scaling activities.

- **Setting up alerts to track and monitor spends** You can set up alerts in Cost Management to receive notifications when budgets are being reached or exceeded. This can help you plan, manage costs, and take proactive action to address issues that arise from unplanned spends.

- **Integration with third-party solutions for automated analysis and actions** You can integrate Cost Management with third-party solutions to obtain an automated breakdown and analysis of workload spends that deviate from planned spends and areas for optimization to reduce spends.

Design and deployment concepts and considerations

Cost Management requires a concerted effort from various internal resources responsible for building and managing your Azure environment. In most environments, there is a tendency to look for ways over time to optimize or cut down cloud spends. Sometimes, however, there is pressure to take immediate action, which can result in unintended consequences, such as performance issues on critical workloads due to a drastic reduction in workload sizing. It is therefore a good practice to follow practical steps to regularly monitor and analyze costs so that workloads are optimized on a regular basis; this results in reduced pressure for urgent optimizations due to changing business environments.

Cost planning

Using a structured approach to plan your Azure spends can help prevent the arrival of a large unplanned bill at the end of the month. Planning involves identifying all the workloads you want to set up in the Azure environment and estimating the spends on these resources based on various factors, such as the following:

- Region to host the resource
- Redundancy level required for each resource
- OS and features required for each resource
- Resource uptime anticipated
- Downtime acceptable in outages
- Acceptable data loss limits

This is not an exhaustive list of factors; every environment is unique, and different organizations have various compliance and budgetary pressures. However, it provides a good starting point for planning.

> **TIP** Identify other factors that are relevant to your organization and include those inputs in your planning decisions.

After you have identified all the factors that can affect your Azure design, you can use the Azure calculator at https://azure.microsoft.com/en-us/pricing/calculator to generate an estimate of monthly spends. Use this as a starting point to plan for design changes, budgeting, and future correlation against actual spends.

Budgets

Budgeting can help provide clarity for internal resources regarding approved spends and can influence the design choices they may need to make at the outset to align with the budgets.

Cost Management enables you to put budgets in place, to assign budgets to various users to spend on Azure resources based on approve spends, and to set thresholds to alert various resources, subscriptions, and business owners of charges that exceed budgetary limits. This enables you and your Azure admin to remain informed of any deviations and provides visibility into which workloads might be causing unplanned spends.

> **TIP** You should implement manual or automatic processes to track and monitor spends on a regular basis to ensure they are in line with approved budgets. You should also implement manual or automatic processes to alert you to deviations and to identify the source of those as quickly as possible. This can reduce the impact of incorrect deployment decisions that might cause spending to exceed your targets.

Budgets walkthrough

The following section walks you through the process of setting up a budget and cost alerts using the Budgets tool in the Azure Portal.

USING THE AZURE PORTAL

To set up a budget and cost alerts using the Budgets tool in the Azure Portal, follow these steps:

1. Log in to the Azure Portal, type **cost management + billing** in the search box, and select it from the list that appears. (See Figure 9-1.)

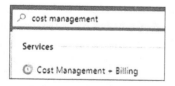

FIGURE 9-1 Search for Cost Management + Billing.

2. In the left pane, click the **Cost Management** option. Then click the **Budgets** option that appears underneath the **Cost Management** option. (See Figure 9-2.)

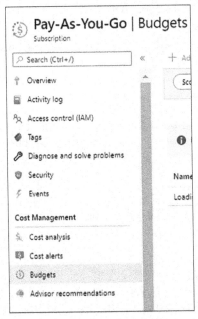

FIGURE 9-2 Click the Budgets option.

3. In the right pane of the **Budgets** page, click the **Add** button. (See Figure 9-3.)

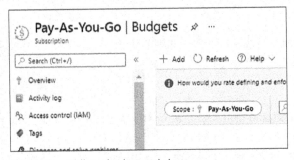

FIGURE 9-3 Adding a budget and alert.

4. In the **Create Budget** dialog box (see Figure 9-4), enter the following information. Then click **Next**:

- **Scope** This setting lists the subscription you are currently using. To set up a budget for a different subscription, click the **Change Scope** link, and choose the desired subscription when prompted.

- **Filters** Click **Add Filter** to apply any filters scope the budget view—for example, to apply the budget to specific resource groups or regions.

- **Name** Enter a unique name for the budget.

- **Reset Period** Specify how frequently the budget should be reset.
- **Creation Date** Specify the budget's creation date.
- **Expiration Date** Set an expiration date for the budget.
- **Amount** Enter the threshold at which an alert should be triggered.

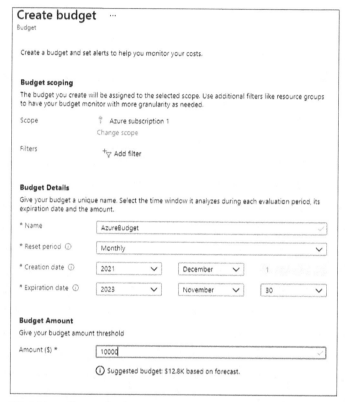

FIGURE 9-4 Create a budget.

5. In the **Set Alerts** tab (see Figure 9-5), enter the following information. Then click **Create**:

- **Type** Choose the type of alert condition—either **Actual** or **Forecasted**.
- **% of Budget** Enter the minimum percent threshold to trigger alerts.
- **Action Group** Select an existing action group. Alternatively, to create a new action group, click the **Manage Action Group** link and follow the prompts in the Create an Action Group wizard, as detailed in the section "Service Health walkthrough" in Chapter 8, "Azure service health."
- **Alert Recipients** Enter the email address of each person you want to receive the alert.
- **Languages** Select the language in which to issue the alerts.

FIGURE 9-5 The Set Alerts tab of the Create Budget dialog box.

Cost Analysis

The Cost Analysis tool (see Figure 9-6) provides a detailed breakdown of your billing across resources and subscriptions. It provides you with various filters and views to review spending patterns across the subscription and to obtain similar breakdowns across resource types, resource groups, timelines, and so on. Charges for resources from the Azure Marketplace are shown separately, making it easier to identify those costs.

> **NOTE** At this time, Cost Analysis does not show charges for reservations, support, and applicable taxes.

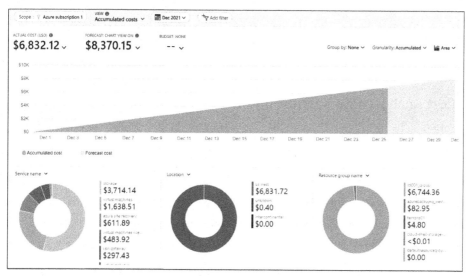

FIGURE 9-6 Cost Analysis graphs.

You can export and analyze this data in various ways:

- **Export to Azure Storage account**   You can schedule the automated export of usage data to an Azure Storage account for further analysis. Collecting this data over time can help you use analysis tools such as Microsoft Excel and Power BI for cost comparison and analysis purposes.

- **Microsoft Excel**   You can analyze exported data within Microsoft Excel and filter and sort the data as needed. You can also drill down to specific resources, resource groups, and resource categories to obtain a better understanding of your spends.

- **Power BI**   With Power BI, you can drill down to individual resources for a better under-standing of budgets versus actual spends. Power BI is a great tool to analyze exported usage data for a deeper understanding and more thorough comparison of spends across various time periods.

- **Power BI Data Connector**   You can set up Power BI Data Connector to automatically transfer data directly into Power BI on a daily basis. This allows for a more up-to-date spend analysis in an automated manner, which facilitates more accurate forecasting.

- **Usage APIs**   Microsoft provides various APIs to automate the export and integration of data from Cost Analysis to third-party solutions for analysis.

> **TIP**   You can also set up Cost Analysis to automatically send data and reports to various individuals within your organization. For example, you might have them sent to person-nel who have write access to the subscription and resource groups so they can identify areas of deviation that could explain unplanned charges.

View Cost Analysis data walkthrough

The following section walks you through the process of viewing Cost Analysis data in the Azure Portal.

USING THE AZURE PORTAL

To view Cost Analysis data in the Azure Portal, follow these steps:

1. Log in to the Azure Portal, type **cost management + billing** in the search box, and select it from the list that appears. (See Figure 9-7.)

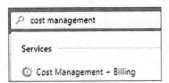

FIGURE 9-7 Search for Cost Management + Billing.

2. In the left pane, click the **Cost Management** option. Then click the **Cost Analysis** option that appears underneath the **Cost Management** option. (See Figure 9-8.)

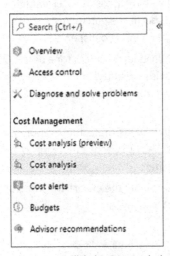

FIGURE 9-8 Click the Cost Analysis option.

The right pane shows a summary of the accumulated costs for the current month. (See Figure 9-9.)

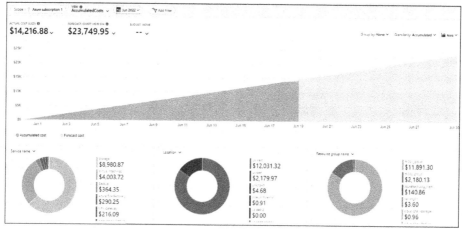

FIGURE 9-9 Cost Analysis graphs.

3. To see a view from a different date range, click the **Date Range** drop-down list at the top of the page and choose the desired date range. (See Figure 9-10.)

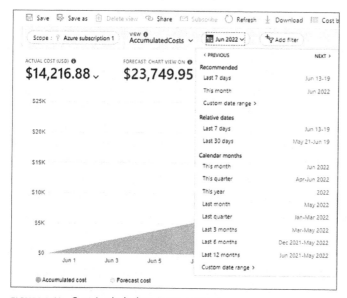

FIGURE 9-10 Cost Analysis date range options.

4. To add a filter to the view, click **Add Filter**. Then use the left drop-down list that appears to choose a filter type. (See Figure 9-11.)

FIGURE 9-11 Cost Analysis filters.

5. Click the right drop-down list to choose a subfilter. The subfilters in this drop-down list will differ depending on which filter type you choose. (See Figure 9-12.)

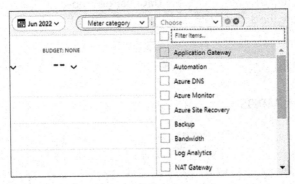

FIGURE 9-12 Cost Analysis subfilters.

6. Verify that the view conveys the information you need. (See Figure 9-13.)

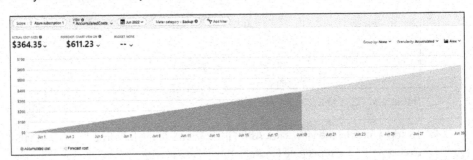

FIGURE 9-13 Filtered Cost Analysis view.

7. To save this view, click the **Save As** button along the top of the **Cost Analysis** page.

8. In the **Save As** dialog box, type a name for the view in the **Name** box, select the **Make This View Private** check box if you want to create the view only for your own use, and click the **Save** button. (See Figure 9-14.)

FIGURE 9-14 Saving your Cost Analysis view.

In addition to Save As, which you use to save a view for the first time or to save the current view as a new view, the bar along the top of the Cost Analysis page features the following buttons (see Figure 9-15):

- **Save** Save changes made to the current view.
- **Delete View** Delete the current view.
- **Share** Share the current view with other users.
- **Subscribe** Obtain daily, weekly, or monthly updates to the view via email.
- **Refresh** Refresh the current view with the up-to-date data.
- **Download** Download the data in the current view in CSV format.
- **Cost by Resource** Change the view with various filters.
- **Configure Subscription** Configure scheduled export of the view and AWS integration.

FIGURE 9-15 Cost Analysis button options.

Schedule data exports walkthrough

The following section walks you through the process of scheduling the export of Cost Analysis data in the Azure Portal.

USING THE AZURE PORTAL

To schedule the export of Cost Analysis data in the Azure Portal, follow these steps:

1. Log in to the Azure Portal, type **cost management + billing** in the search box, and select it from the list that appears. (See Figure 9-16.)

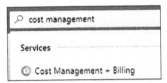

FIGURE 9-16 Search for Cost Management + Billing.

2. In the left pane, click the **Cost Management** option. Then click the **Cost Analysis** option that appears underneath the **Cost Management** option. (See Figure 9-17.)

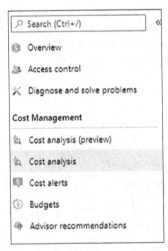

FIGURE 9-17 Click the Cost Analysis option.

3. Click the **Configure Subscription** button along the top of the Cost Analysis page.

4. On the **Configuration** page, under **Manage Your Cost**, click **Exports**. (See Figure 9-18.)

5. Click the **Schedule Export** button. (See Figure 9-19.)

FIGURE 9-18 The Configuration page.

FIGURE 9-19 Schedule the export.

6. In the **New Export** dialog box (see Figure 9-20), enter the following information. Then click the **Create Alert** button:

■ **Name** Enter a unique name for the export operation, or rule.

■ **Metric** Choose the desired metric—**Actual** or **Amortized Cost**.

■ **Export Type** Choose the export type, based on the desired time frame.

■ **Start Date** Select or enter the start date for the automatic export operation.

■ **File Partitioning** Enable this if you are exporting a large dataset that might be better managed across multiple Excel files rather than a single large file.

■ **Storage** Select the **Use Existing** or **Create New** option button.

If you choose **Create New**, you'll see settings to specify the storage resource you want to use, including **Subscription**, **Resource Group**, **Account Name**, **Location**, **Container**, and **Directory**.

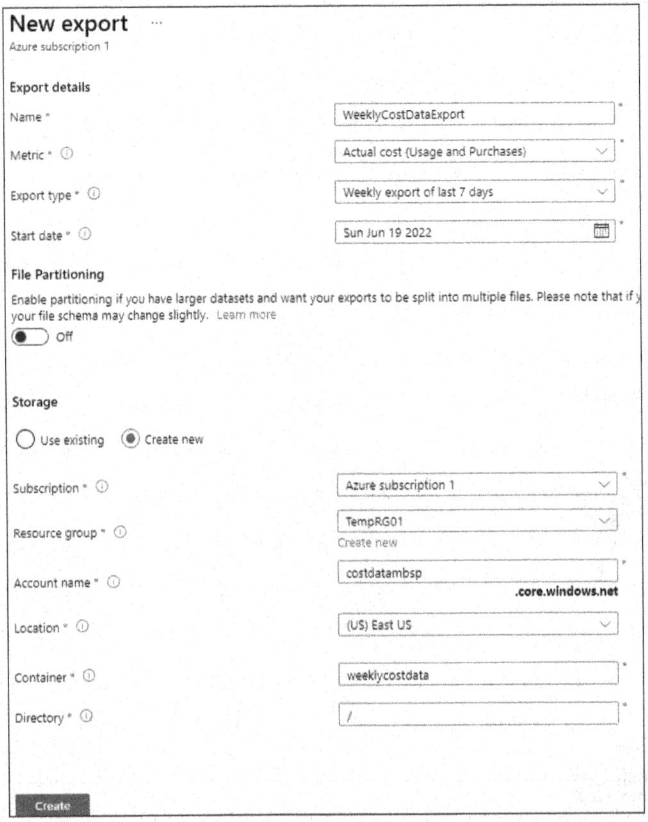

FIGURE 9-20 New Export wizard.

Advisor recommendations

Cost Management has a recommendation engine that uses pre-programmed cost-optimization best practices to identify workloads that can be resized or reserved to save on charges, potentially saving your organization hundreds or thousands of dollars each year. It does this by taking into account the idle time and usage information captured for each resource. (See Figure 9-21.) When you receive a recommendation, Cost Management indicates the impact level of the recommendation. It also guides you to manually resize, redeploy, or reconfigure your resources to achieve the stated cost benefits in the future.

You can download the recommendations in CSV format for analysis, internal discussions, and approvals. You can also set up alerting to be made aware of new recommendations as they are identified and set up a recommendation digest to obtain a consolidated set of recommendations on a predetermined schedule. These can be sent to relevant stakeholders for their review and actions. Finally, you can use an API to export recommendations to third-party solutions for a consolidated view.

FIGURE 9-21 Advisor recommendations.

Respond to a recommendation walkthrough

The following section walks you through the process of responding to a recommendation using the Azure Portal.

USING THE AZURE PORTAL

To respond to a recommendation using the Azure Portal, follow these steps:

1. Log in to the Azure Portal, type **cost management + billing** in the search box, and select it from the list that appears. (See Figure 9-22.)

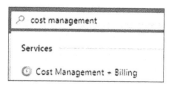

FIGURE 9-22 Search for Cost Management + Billing.

2. In the left pane, click the **Cost Management** option. Then click the **Cost Analysis** option that appears underneath the **Advisor Recommendations** option. (See Figure 9-23.)

FIGURE 9-23 Click the Advisor Recommendations option.

3. Click a recommendation in the list that appears. (See Figure 9-24.)

FIGURE 9-24 Click a recommendation.

The **Recommendation Details** page lists manual actions you can take to respond to the recommendation. (See Figure 9-25.)

FIGURE 9-25 Actions to take to respond to the recommendation.

4. Click a link in the **Recommended Action** column to see more details about the recommendation for a particular resource. (See Figure 9-26.)

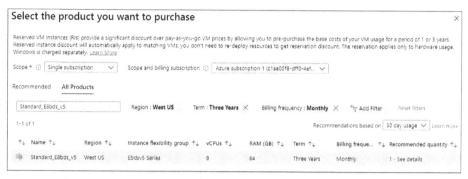

FIGURE 9-26 See more details about a recommendation.

5. Back on the **Recommendation Details** page, do one of the following:

   ■ Manually perform the recommended action.

   ■ Select the check box next to a resource listed on the page and click the **Postpone** button to indicate your intention to perform the recommended action at a later date.

   ■ Select the check box next to a resource listed on the page; click the **Dismiss** button to dismiss the alert if it is not suitable for your environment or if you have recently performed manual changes in response to the recommendation, but the system has not yet updated the status of that recommendation. When you dismiss an alert, the recommendation engine will no longer display that recommendation.

Manage Advisor recommendations and create recommendation alerts walkthrough

The following section walks you through the process of managing Advisor recommendations and creating a recommendation alert using the Azure Portal.

USING THE AZURE PORTAL

To manage Advisor recommendations and create a recommendation alert using the Azure Portal, follow these steps:

1. Log in to the Azure Portal, type **cost management + billing** in the search box, and select it from the list that appears. (See Figure 9-27.)

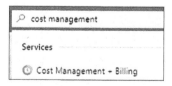

FIGURE 9-27 Search for Cost Management + Billing.

2. In the left pane, click the **Cost Management** option. Then click the **Cost Analysis** option that appears underneath the **Advisor Recommendations** option. (See Figure 9-28.)

FIGURE 9-28 Click the Advisor Recommendations option.

3. In the **Advisor Recommendations** page (see Figure 9-29), click the **Download as CSV** button to download the recommendations in a CSV file, or click **Download as PDF** to download the recommendations in a PDF file.

FIGURE 9-29 Managing Advisor recommendations.

4. To create an alert, click the **Create Alert** button. (Refer to Figure 9-29.)

5. In the **Create Advisor Alerts** dialog box (see Figure 9-30), enter the following information. Then click the **Create Alert** button:

  ▪ **Subscription** Select the subscription for which you want to set up the alert.

  ▪ **Resource Group** Select the resource group for which you want to set up the alert.

- **Configured By** For this example, select the **Category and Impact Level** option button.

- **Category** Choose **Cost**.

- **Impact Level** Select the impact level to use to filter the recommendation alert.

- **Action Group Name** Click **Select Existing** and follow the prompts to select an existing action group. Alternatively, to create a new action group, click **Create New** and follow the prompts in the Create an Action Group wizard, as detailed in the section "Service Health walkthrough" in Chapter 8, "Azure Service Health."

- **Alert Rule Name** Enter a unique name for the alert rule.

- **Description** Enter a detailed description of the alert rule.

- **Enable Rule Upon Creation** Click **Yes**.

- **Save Alert to Resource Group** Select the resource group in which to save the alert.

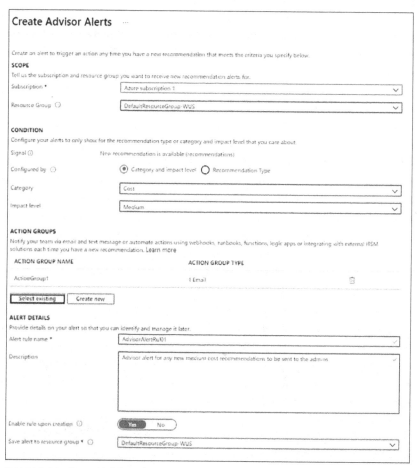

FIGURE 9-30 Create Advisor alerts.

Create a recommendation digest walkthrough

The following section walks you through the process of creating a recommendation digest using the Azure Portal.

USING THE AZURE PORTAL

To create a recommendation digest using the Azure Portal, follow these steps:

1. Log in to the Azure Portal, type **cost management + billing** in the search box, and select it from the list that appears. (See Figure 9-31.)

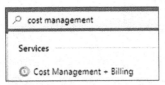

FIGURE 9-31 Search for Cost Management + Billing.

2. In the left pane, click the **Cost Management** option. Then click the **Cost Analysis** option that appears underneath the **Advisor Recommendations** option. (See Figure 9-32.)

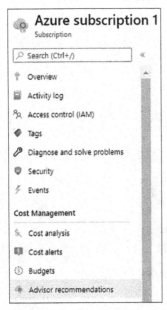

FIGURE 9-32 Click the Advisor Recommendations option.

3. In the **Advisor Recommendations** page (see Figure 9-33), click the **Create Recommendation Digest** button.

FIGURE 9-33 Create a recommendation digest.

4. In the **Add an Advisor Recommendation Digest** dialog box (see Figure 9-34), enter the following information. Then click **Create**:

- **Subscription**   Select the subscription for which you want to create a recommendation digest.

- **Frequency**   Choose how often you want to receive the recommendation digest.

- **Recommendation Category**   For this example, leave this set to **Cost**.

- **Language**   Choose the language you want the recommendation digest to use.

- **Action Group Name**   Click **Select Existing** and follow the prompts to select an existing action group. Alternatively, to create a new action group, click **Create New** and follow the prompts in the Create an Action Group wizard, as detailed in the section "Service Health walkthrough" in Chapter 8, "Azure Service Health."

- **Recommendation Digest Name**   Enter a unique name for the recommendation digest.

- **Enable Recommendation Digest**   Click **Yes**.

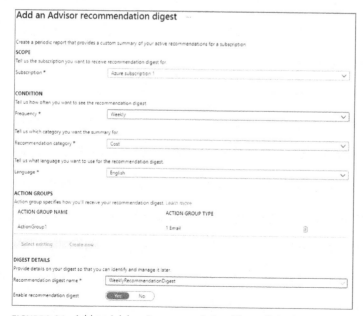

FIGURE 9-34 Add an Advisor Recommendation Digest dialog box.

Index

A

Advisor recommendations.
See recommendations, Cost
Management
agent-based dependency
analysis, 74
agentless dependency analysis,
74
alerts, 150
  Advisor recommendation,
261–263
  Azure Backup, 9
  Azure Monitor, 122
  metric, creating, 123–134
  Resource Health, creating,
237–241
  VM Insight, setting up,
140–145
APIs, 251
Application Insights, 118, 149
ASR (Azure Site Recovery), 23
  Azure-to-Azure disaster
recovery, 24–25
  Azure-to-Azure VM
replication, setup, 28–32
  cleanup test failover, 36–37
  customize replica
configurations, 33–34
  monitor replication, 33
  perform failover, 37–40
  test failover, 35–36
  best practices, 67–68
  data security, 26
  failover, 27

planned, 28
test, 27–28
Hyper-V-to-Azure disaster
recovery, 40
  cleanup test failover, 60–61
  create Recovery Services
vault, 46–47
  data security, 44
  failover and failback, 44
  integrate Hyper-V
environment for
replication, 47–56
  network requirements, 45
  planned failover, 45
  replication components, 41
  replication policy, 41–44
  setup replication, 56–60
  test failover, 44–45, 60
  unplanned failover, 45
key features, 23–24
multi-VM replication groups,
24, 26
network security, 28
pricing, 24
recovery plans, 61–67
replication, 23–24
target environment
configuration, 26–27
assessment
  Azure Migrate setup, 90–92
  tools, Azure Migrate, 70–71,
72–73
automation, ASR (Azure Site
Recovery), 24

az backup protection enable-
for-vm command, 19–21
az backup vault create
command, 19–21
Azure AD, 5
Azure Automation, 24
Azure Backup
  alerts, 9
  archive tier, 22
  backup agents and solutions,
7
  Backup Center, 5
  backup compression, 8
  backup policy
    retention, 8
    scheduling, 8
  best practices, 21–22
  data encryption, 9
  data plane, 6
  design and deployment
concepts and
considerations, 4
  DPM (Microsoft System
Center Data Protection), 4
  key features, 3–4
  management plane, 6
  MARS (Microsoft Azure
Recovery Services), 7
  RBAC (role-based access
control), 9–10
  Recovery Services vault, 4–5
  security, data in transit, 9
  service backup support, 2
  service charges, 3
  supported backup types, 7

Azure calculator, 247
Azure CLI, commands
    az backup protection enable-
        for-vm, 19–21
    az backup vault create, 19–21
    cd Azure:, 213
Azure Cloud Shell, 209-
    Azure drive, 213
    Azure file share, walkthrough,
        210–212
    bash module, 214–219
    best practices, 222–223
    Editor, 213
    key features, 209–210
    PowerShell module, 219–222
    URL, embedding, 213
    vNET deployment, 213–214
Azure Cost Management, 245
    Budgets tool, 247–250
    Cost Analysis tool, 250–252
        scheduling data exports,
            255–258
        viewing cost analysis data,
            252–255
    Cost Planning tool, 246–247
    key features, 245–246
    recommendations, 258–259
        digest, creating, 264–265
        managing and creating
            alerts, 261–263
        responding to, 259–261
Azure Data Box, 71
Azure Database Migration
    Service, 71
Azure Marketplace,
    walkthrough, 200–202
Azure Migrate
    assessment tools, 70–71
    best practices, 110
    Discovery and Assessment
        tool, 72–73
    features, 69
    key features, 70
    networking, 76–77

discovery and assessment,
    77
replication and migration,
    77–78
scaling, 77
Server Migration Tool, 74–76
setting up using Azure Portal,
    78
    cleanup test migration,
        106–107
    configure Azure Migrate
        appliance, 85–90
    create Azure Migration
        appliance, 79–84
    perform migration to
        Azure, 107–109
    setup assessment, 90–92
    setup replication
        appliance, 94–100
    start VM replication,
        100–104
    test migration, 104–106
    view assessment results,
        92–94
Azure Migrate Discovery and
    Assessment, 72–73
Azure Monitor, 111
    agents, 149
    alerts, 122
    best practices, 149–150
    dashboards, 119–120
    data collection, 115–116
    data export, 122
    data ingestion, 115–116
    data retention, 116
    data security, 117
    data segregation, 116
    key benefits, 111–112
    Power BI, 121
    setting up using Azure Portal
        configure Azure Storage
            monitoring, 145–147
        configure Azure VM
            monitoring, 136–139

create Log Analytics
    workspace, 134–136
create metric alerts,
    123–134
run queries on Azure
    Storage, 147–149
set up Azure VM Insights
    alerts, 140–145
supported data types, 113
    distributed traces, 114
    log data, 114
    metrics, 113
third-party integrations, 122
visualizations
    curated, 117–118
    Insights, 118–119
    Workbooks, 120–121
Azure Network Watcher
    Connection Monitor, 153–161
    Connection Troubleshoot,
        179–182
    Diagnostic Logs, 187–189
    Effective Security Rules,
        identifying conflicting
        rules, 171–173
    enabling, 152
    IP Flow Verify, 163–166
    Next Hop, identifying
        the traffic route to a
        destination, 169–171
    NSG Diagnostic, 166–169
    NSG Flow Logs, 183–186
    Packet Capture
        parameters, 176
        walkthrough, 176–179
    tools, 151
    Topology Monitor, 161–163
    use cases, 151
    VPN Troubleshoot, 173–175
Azure Policy, 22
Azure Portal
    Azure Cloud Shell
        bash module,
            walkthrough, 214–219

PowerShell module, walkthrough, 219–222

Azure file share, walkthrough, 210–212

Azure Marketplace, walkthrough, 200–202

Azure Migrate, setup, 78
cleanup test migration, 106–107
configure Azure Migrate appliance, 85–90
create Azure Migration appliance, 79–84
perform migration to Azure, 107–109
setup assessment, 90–92
setup replication appliance, 94–100
start VM replication, 100–104
test migration, 104–106
view assessment results, 92–94

Azure Monitor, setup
configure Azure Storage monitoring, 145–147
configure Azure VM monitoring, 136–139
create Log Analytics workspace, 134–136
create metric alerts, 123–134
run queries on Azure Storage, 147–149
set up Azure VM Insights alerts, 140–145

Azure-to-Azure VM replication, setup, 28–32
cleanup test failover, 36–37
customize replica configurations, 33–34
monitor replication, 33
perform failover, 37–40
test failover, 35–36

backing up Azure VMs, 10–19

best practices, 207

Budgets tool, walkthrough, 247–250

checking a resources health, walkthrough, 241–242

conflicting rules, identifying using Effective Security Rules, 171–173

Connection Monitor instance, creating, 153–161

Connection Troubleshoot walkthrough, 179–182

creating a Recovery Services vault, 10–19

creating a Resource Health alert, walkthrough, 237–241

custom dashboards, creating, 197–200

default view, 191–193

diagnosing traffic restriction using IP Flow Verify, 163–166

Diagnostic Logs walkthrough, 187–189

help and support walkthrough, 202–206

Hyper-V-to-Azure replication
cleanup test failover, 60
create Recovery Services vault, 46–47
integrate Hyper-V environment for replication, 47–56
perform failover, 60–61
setup replication, 56–60
test failover, 60

identifying the traffic route to a destination using Next Hop, 169–171

key features, 193

NSG Flow Logs walkthrough, 183–186

Packet Capture walkthrough, 176–179

recommendations
creating a digest, walkthrough, 264–265
managing and creating alerts, 261–263
responding to, 259–261

recovery plan walkthrough, 62–67

scheduling data exports, walkthrough, 255–258

security configuration issues, diagnosing with NSG Diagnostic, 166–169

Service Health, walkthrough, 228–235

settings, walkthrough, 194–197

URLs, allowlisting, 194

using VPN Troubleshoot, 173–175

viewing cost analysis data, walkthrough, 252–255

Azure PowerShell
backing up Azure VMs, 19–21
commands
Enable-AzRecoveryServicesBackupProtection, 19–20
New-AzRecoveryServicesBackupProtectionPolicy, 19–20
New-AzRecoveryServicesVault, 19–20
creating a Recovery Services vault, 19–21

Azure Status, 226

Azure Storage
monitoring, 145–147
querying, 147–149

Azure VMs. See also VM(s)
backing up
using Azure Portal, 10–19
using Azure PowerShell, 19–21

failover, 27
Insights alerts, setting up,
    140–145
monitoring, 136–139
Azure Workbooks, 120–121
Azure-to-Azure VM replication,
    setup, 28–32
    cleanup test failover, 36–37
    customize replica
        configurations, 33–34
    monitor replication, 33
    perform failover, 37–40
    test failover, 35–36

B

backing up VMs
    using Azure Portal, 10–19
    using Azure PowerShell,
        19–21
Backup Center, 5, 21
Backup Explorer, 9
backup(s). *See also* BCDR
    (business continuity and
    disaster recovery)
    Azure Backup-supported, 7
    compression, 8
    monitoring, 9
    policy
        retention, 8
        scheduling, 8
    snapshot, 6, 24
bash module, Azure Cloud Shell,
    214–219
BCDR (business continuity and
    disaster
    recovery), 23
best practices
    ASR (Azure Site Recovery),
        67–68
    Azure Backup, 21–22
    Azure Cloud Shell, 222–223
    Azure Migrate, 110
    Azure Monitor, 149–150

Azure Portal, 207
Resource Health, 243
Service Health, 243
Budgets tool, walkthrough,
    247–250

C

commands
    Azure CLI
        az backup protection
            enable-for-vm, 19–21
        az backup vault create,
            19–21
        cd Azure:, 213
    Azure PowerShell
        Enable-AzRecoveryServ
            icesBackupProtection,
            19–20
        New-AzRecoveryServices
            BackupProtectionPolicy,
            19–20
        New-
            AzRecoveryServicesVault,
            19–20
compression, backup, 8
Connection Monitor, 153–161
Connection Troubleshoot,
    179–182
Cost Analysis tool, 250–252
    scheduling data exports,
        255–258
    viewing cost analysis data,
        252–255
Cost Planning tool, 246–247
creating
    alerts
        metric, 123–134
        Resource Health, 237–241
    Azure Migration appliance,
        79–84
    custom dashboards in Azure
        Portal, 197–200

Log Analytics workspace,
    134–136
Recovery Services vault
    using Azure Portal, 10–19
    using Azure PowerShell,
        19–21
    support request, 202–206
    topology diagram, 162–163
curated visualization, 117–118

D

dashboards, 150
    Azure Monitor, 119–120
    Azure Portal, creating,
        197–200
data collection, Azure Monitor,
    115–116
data plane, Azure Backup, 6
data retention, Azure Monitor,
    116
data security, Azure Monitor, 117
data segregation, Azure
    Monitor, 116
data types, Azure Monitor-
    supported, 113
    distributed traces, 114
    log data, 114
    metrics, 113
dependency analysis, 73–74
Diagnostic Logs, 187–189
diagrams, topology, creating,
    162–163
differential backups, 7
disaster recovery. *See* DR
    (disaster recovery)
discovery and assessment,
    72–73, 77
distributed traces, 114
DPM (Microsoft System Center
    Data Protection), 1, 4
DR (disaster recovery). *See also*
    recovery plans; recovery
    points

Azure-to-Azure VM
replication, setup, 28–32
cleanup test failover,
36–37
customize replica
configurations, 33–34
monitor replication, 33
perform failover, 37–40
test failover, 35–36
Hyper-V-to-Azure, 40
cleanup test failover, 60–61
create Recovery Services
vault, 46–47
data security, 44
failover and failback, 44
integrate Hyper-V
environment for
replication, 47–56
network requirements, 45
planned failover, 45
replication components, 41
replication policy, 41–44
setup replication, 56–60
test failover, 44–45, 60
unplanned failover, 45
recovery plans, 61–67
recovery points, 25
dynamic thresholds, 150

E

Effective Security Rules,
identifying conflicting rules,
171–173
Enable-AzRecoveryServicesB
ackupProtection command,
19–20
enabling, Azure Network
Watcher, 152
encryption, Azure Backup, 9
events, Service Health, 227
exports, scheduling, 255–258
extensions, Azure VM, 7

F

failover, 37–40
Azure VMs, 27
planned, 28
target VM, 44
test, 27–28, 35–37
features
ASR (Azure Site Recovery),
23–24
Azure Backup, 3–4
Azure Cloud Shell, 209–210
Azure Cost Management,
245–246
Azure Migrate, 69, 70
Azure Portal, 193
Recovery Services vault, 4–5
full backups, 7

H

health monitoring tools
Azure Status, 226
Resource Health, 235–236
alerts, creating, 237–241
checking a resources
health, 241–242
health status indicators,
236
Service Health
events, 227
history, 227–228
walkthrough, 228–235
history, Service Health, 227–228
HTML code, embedding Cloud
Shell in, 213
Hyper-V
disaster recovery, 40
cleanup test failover, 60–61
create Recovery Services
vault, 46–47
data security, 44
failover and failback, 44

integrate Hyper-V
environment for
replication, 47–56
network requirements, 45
planned failover, 45
replication components, 41
replication policy, 41
setup replication, 56–60
test failover, 44–45, 60
unplanned failover, 45
replication, 77–78

I

incremental backups, 7
Insights, 118–119
Application, 149
Azure VM, setting up alerts,
140–145
IP Flow Verify, 163–166. *See also*
networking
ISVs (independent software
vendors), 70, 200
J-K-L
KPIs, 150
launch button, Cloud Shell, 213
Log Analytics, 6, 9, 22, 134–136
logs and log data, 114
audit, 252
data collection, 115–116
Diagnostic Logs, 183–186
NSG Flow Logs, 183–186
LRS (locally redundant storage),
116

M

MABS (Microsoft Azure Backup
Server), 1
management plane, Azure
Backup, 6
MARS (Microsoft Azure
Recovery Services), 1, 7

metrics, 113, 123–134
migration. *See also* Azure
  Migrate
  agent-based, 76
  agentless, 76
  assessment tools, 70–71
  Azure Migrate Discovery and
    Assessment tool, 72–73
  Azure Migrate Server
    Migration Tool, 74–76
  dependency analysis, 73–74
  third-party solutions, 69
  tools, 71
  VM
    cleanup test migration,
      106–109
    configure Azure Migrate
      appliance, 85–90
    create Azure Migration
      appliance, 79–84
    setup assessment, 90–92
    setup replication
      appliance, 94–100
    start VM replication,
      100–106
    view assessment results,
      92–94
monitoring
  Azure Storage, 145–147
  Azure VMs, 136–139
  backup, 9
multi-VM replication groups,
  24, 26

N

Network Insights, 118–119
networking
  Azure Migrate, 76–77
    discovery and assessment,
      77
    replication and migration,
      77–78
    scaling, 77

Cloud Shell deployment in a
  vNET, 213–214
configuration issues,
  diagnosing, 166–169
traffic restrictions,
  diagnosing, 163–166
New-AzRecoveryServicesBacku
  pProtectionPolicy command,
  19–20
New-AzRecoveryServicesVault
  command, 19–20
Next Hop, identifying the traffic
  route to a destination, 169–171
NSG Diagnostic, 166–169
NSG Flow Logs, 183–186
NSGs (network security groups),
  28

O-P

OVA (Open Virtualization
  Appliance) template, 72
Packet Capture
  parameters, 176
  walkthrough, 176–179
physical server migration, 78
planned failover, 28, 45
policy(ies)
  Azure Backup, 8
  backup retention, 8
  backup scheduling, 8
  replication, 25, 41–44
Power BI, 121, 251
PowerShell module, Azure Cloud
  Shell, 219–222
pricing, ASR (Azure Site
  Recovery), 24
Private Link, 149

Q-R

querying, Azure Storage,
  147–149

RBAC (role-based access
  control), 6, 209
  accessing Azure Portal, 207
  Recovery Services vault, 5
  security roles, 9–10
recommendations, Cost
  Management, 258–259
  digest, creating, 264–265
  managing and creating
    alerts, 261–263
  responding to, 259–261
recovery plans, 61–67
recovery points, 25. *See also* DR
  (disaster recovery)
Recovery Services vault,
  4–5
  creating
    using Azure Portal, 10–19,
      46–47
    using Azure PowerShell,
      19–21
  monitoring, 9
redundancy, Azure Monitor,
  116
regulatory compliance, Azure
  Monitor, 116
replication, 23–24, 77–78. *See
  also* DR (disaster recovery)
  groups, 24, 26
  policy, 25, 41–44
  VM, 24–25, 28–40, 94–104
Resource Health, 235–236
  alerts, creating, 237–241
  best practices, 243
  checking a resources health,
    241–242
  health status indicators, 236
responding to
  recommendations, 259–261
rules
  alert, 122
  conflicts, identifying,
    171–173
  NSG, 28

S

scalability
  Azure Migrate, 77
  Recovery Services vault, 5
scheduling
  backups, 8
  data exports, 255–258
security
  ASR (Azure Site Recovery), 26
  Azure Backup, 3, 9
  configuration issues,
    diagnosing,
    166–169
  network, 28
  Recovery Services vault, 4
service charges
  ASR (Azure Site Recovery), 24
  Azure Backup, 3
Service Health
  best practices, 243
  events, 227
  history, 227–228
  walkthrough, 228–235
SIEM (security information and
  event management) tools, 207
snapshots, 6, 24
SQL Server AlwaysOn, 24
storage. See also Azure Storage
  Azure file share, 210–211
  locally redundant, 116
support request, creating,
  202–206

T

target environment
  configuration, ASR (Azure Site
  Recovery), 26–27
test failover, 27–28, 35–37,
  44–45
third-party solutions, Azure
  Monitor, 122
tool(s)

Azure Cost Management
  Budgets, 247–250
  Cost Analysis, 250–258
  Cost Planning, 246–247
Azure Network Watcher, 151
  Connection Monitor,
    setting up with Azure
    Portal, 153–161
  Connection Troubleshoot,
    179–182
  Diagnostic Logs, 183–186
  Effective Security Rules,
    171–173
  IP Flow Verify, 163–166
  Next Hop, 169–171
  NSG Diagnostic, 166–169
  NSG Flow Logs, 183–186
  Packet Capture, 176–179
  Topology Monitor, 161–163
  VPN Troubleshoot, 173–175
backup, 1–2, 3
health monitoring
  Azure Status, 226
  Resource Health, 235–242
  Service Health, 227–235
migration, 71
  assessment, 70–71
  Azure Migrate Discovery
    and Assessment, 72–73
  Azure Migrate Server
    Migration, 74–76
  SIEM (security information
    and event management),
    207
Topology Monitor, 161–163
transaction log backups, 7
troubleshooting. See also
  Connection Troubleshoot;
  VPN Troubleshoot

U

unplanned failover, 45
URLs

allowlisting, 194
  Cloud Shell, embedding in
    HTML code, 213
use cases, Azure Network
  Watcher, 151

V

visualizations, Azure Monitor
  curated, 117–118
  Insights, 118–119
VM(s). See also Hyper-V
  backing up
    using Azure Portal, 10–19
    using Azure PowerShell,
      19–21
  discovery and assessment,
    72–73, 77
  failover, 27
    planned, 28, 45
    test, 27–28, 44–45
    unplanned, 45
  Insights, 118
  international standards
    compliance, 116
  recovery plans, 61–67
  replication, 24–25, 28–40,
    77–78,
    94–104
  replication groups, 24, 26
VMs
  monitoring, 136–139
  setting up Insights alerts,
    140–145
VMware, 71, 78
vNET, Cloud Shell deployment,
  213–214
VPN Troubleshoot, 173–175

W-X-Y-Z

Web App Migration Assistant, 71
zones, 5

Plug into learning at

MicrosoftPressStore.com

The Microsoft Press Store by Pearson offers:

- Free U.S. shipping

- Buy an eBook, get three formats – Includes PDF, EPUB, and MOBI to use with your computer, tablet, and mobile devices

- Print & eBook Best Value Packs

- eBook Deal of the Week – Save up to 50% on featured title

- Newsletter – Be the first to hear about new releases, announcements, special offers, and more

- Register your book – Find companion files, errata, and product updates, plus receive a special coupon* to save on your next purchase

 Pearson

Microsoft Press

Find more Definitive Guides to Azure success at MicrosoftPressStore.com

Microsoft
Azure Compute
The Definitive Guide

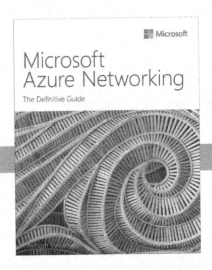

Microsoft
Azure Networking
The Definitive Guide

Microsoft Azure
Monitoring & Management
The Definitive Guide

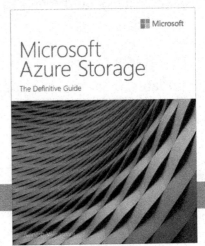

Microsoft
Azure Storage
The Definitive Guide